QUALITATIVE RESEARCH METHODS FOR BUSINESS STUDENTS

T0323107

QUALITATIVE RESEARCH METHODS FOR BUSINESS STUDENTS

A GLOBAL APPROACH

KINGSLEY O. OMEIHE

CHRISTIAN HARRISON

1 Oliver's Yard
55 City Road
London EC1Y 1SP

2455 Teller Road
Thousand Oaks
California 91320

Unit No 323-333, Third Floor, F-Block
International Trade Tower
Nehru Place, New Delhi – 110 019

8 Marina View Suite 43-053
Asia Square Tower 1
Singapore 018960

© Kingsley O. Omeihe and Christian Harrison 2024

Apart from any fair dealing for the purposes of research, private study, or criticism or review, as permitted under the Copyright, Designs and Patents Act, 1988, this publication may not be reproduced, stored or transmitted in any form, or by any means, without the prior permission in writing of the publisher, or in the case of reprographic reproduction, in accordance with the terms of licences issued by the Copyright Licensing Agency. Enquiries concerning reproduction outside those terms should be sent to the publisher.

Editor: Amy Minshull
Assistant editor: Charlotte Hegley
Production editor: Rabia Barkatulla
Copyeditor: Mary Dalton
Proofreader: Mary Dalton
Indexer: Silvia Benvenuto
Marketing manager: Lucia Sweet
Cover design: Shaun Mercier
Typeset by: C&M Digitals (P) Ltd, Chennai, India
Printed in the UK

Library of Congress Control Number: 2023942902

British Library Cataloguing in Publication data

A catalogue record for this book is available from the British Library

ISBN 978-1-5296-0173-2
ISBN 978-1-5296-0172-5 (pbk)

Table of Contents

Online Resources

This textbook is accompanied by online resources to aid teaching and support learning. To access these resources, visit: https://study.sagepub.com/omeihe

For lecturers

- **PowerPoint Slides** that can be downloaded and adapted to suit individual teaching needs
- A **Teaching Guide** providing practical guidance and support and additional materials for each chapter
- A **Testbank** that can be used for both formative and summative student assessment

How to Use this Book

For educators

Dear educators,

Welcome to 'Qualitative Research for Business Students: A Global Approach.' Our aim is to equip you with the necessary tools and resources to effectively teach qualitative research to your business students. This book has been meticulously crafted to provide a holistic approach to qualitative research, tailored specifically to the needs and interests of future business professionals.

The book follows a student-centric and pedagogically sound approach to teaching qualitative research. Concepts are introduced gradually, starting from the basics, and are complemented by real-world examples and case studies. This approach encourages active student engagement and fosters a deeper understanding of the subject matter.

Our primary objective is to present complex qualitative research concepts in an accessible manner. And as such, the book is structured to provide clear explanations, step-by-step methodologies, and practical tips for conducting qualitative research in the business context. This ensures that both instructors and students can grasp the material effectively.

Each chapter begins with clear learning objectives that outline the specific knowledge and skills students will acquire. This helps you align your teaching goals with the content and enables students to track their progress as they work through the material.

To capture students' interest and demonstrate the real-world applications of qualitative research, the book incorporates a plethora of examples. These case studies showcase how qualitative research has been instrumental in shaping business decisions and strategies, making the subject matter more engaging and relatable for students.

As an instructor, you will appreciate the varied exercises and activities provided at the end of each chapter. These thought-provoking exercises encourage students to apply what they have learned and develop their research skills. They can be used for individual work, group discussions, or class presentations.

The book is designed to stimulate class discussions and critical thinking. We urge you to encourage students to share their thoughts on the case studies, exercises and research scenarios presented in the book. And we believe that by facilitating discussions, students can develop a deeper exploration of qualitative research methodologies and their implications.

As part of your teaching strategy, we suggest that you consider assigning research projects that require students to apply qualitative research techniques in a business context. The book's content and examples can serve as a foundation for students to build their research projects and demonstrate their comprehension of the material.

To aid in the assessment process, we have included quizzes and assessments that can be used to gauge students' understanding of key concepts and their ability to apply qualitative research methods.

In addition to the book's content, we have compiled supplemental resources that will support your teaching efforts and offer further opportunities for student engagement.

As you teach with this book, we encourage you to seek feedback from your students regularly. Their insights and experiences can help you adapt your teaching approach and identify areas where additional support may be needed.

In closing, teaching qualitative research to business students is a rewarding endeavour. We believe that 'Qualitative Research for Business Students: A Global Approach' will not only empower your students to become adept researchers but also foster a deeper appreciation for the value of qualitative inquiry in the business world.

Thank you for choosing this book as your teaching companion, and we wish you a successful and enriching teaching experience!

Kingsley and Christian

For students

Dear students,

Welcome to 'Qualitative Research for Business Students: A Global Approach.' This book is designed to provide business students with a practical and in-depth understanding of qualitative research methods and how they can be effectively applied to various business contexts. In this section, we will explain how to use this book to maximise your learning experience and develop your qualitative research skills.

Understanding the Structure: The book is organised into logical sections, starting with an introduction to qualitative research and its relevance to the business world. As you progress, you will explore essential topics such as **research design**, data collection, **data analysis**, and interpretation of findings. Each chapter builds upon the previous one, creating a cohesive learning journey.

Learning Objectives: At the beginning of each chapter, you will find clear and concise learning objectives. These objectives outline what you should expect to grasp after completing the chapter. Always refer to these objectives as you read, as they will help you stay focused on the key takeaways.

Case Studies: Throughout the book, you will encounter detailed case studies that provide in-depth analyses of real qualitative research projects. These case studies will challenge you to apply your knowledge to practical scenarios and think critically about the research process.

Exercises and Activities: Learning by doing is crucial in qualitative research. We have included thought-provoking exercises and activities at the end of each chapter to reinforce your understanding. These activities may involve designing research plans, analysing sample data or brainstorming potential research questions.

Key Terms and Definitions: New terms and concepts are highlighted and defined within the text. Additionally, a glossary is provided at the end of the book, serving as a quick reference for any unfamiliar terms encountered throughout your reading.

Further Reading and Resources: For students interested in diving deeper into specific topics, we offer a curated list of additional resources and **references**. These will help you expand your knowledge and explore more specialised aspects of **qualitative research**.

Engage in Discussions: To make the most of this book, consider forming or joining a study group or online discussion forum with fellow students. Engaging in conversations about the material can offer valuable insights and foster a collaborative learning environment.

Seek Feedback: If you are using this book as part of a course, take advantage of any opportunities for feedback from your instructor or peers. Constructive feedback can help you refine your research ideas and improve your research skills.

Apply Your Learning: As you progress through the book, begin thinking about potential research projects you could undertake. Applying what you learn in real-world scenarios will deepen your understanding and provide practical experience.

Remember that qualitative research is a dynamic field, and there is always room to grow as a researcher. Embrace the challenges and enjoy the process of exploring the human side of business through qualitative research. Happy learning and researching!

About the Authors

Dr Kingsley O. Omeihe is known for his contributions to the fields of trust, African studies, and the emergence of alternative institutions in response to dysfunctional formal systems. Currently, he holds positions at the University of the West of Scotland (Paisley), where he serves as co-head of Postgraduate Research, Managing Editor of African Development Policy and Insights, and Associate Professor of Marketing and Small Business.

Previously, Omeihe held the position of Head of the Business Management Department at the University of Aberdeen Business School. During his tenure, he achieved notable improvements in league table rankings and the NSS Survey, while nurturing student enterprise. He played a key role as the founding director of the MSc Entrepreneurship Programme and director of the Global MBA Online at the University of Aberdeen. Prior to this, he held significant appointments at Edinburgh Napier University, where he led the Apprenticeship Programme, as well as roles at the University of Glasgow and the University of Wales Trinity Saint David.

Dr Omeihe holds selected fellowship positions at the West African Transitional Justice Centre and the Centre for Research on African Digital Policy and Innovation. He actively contributes to advisory boards of various businesses, mentors start-ups, and chairs the Ethnic Minority Groups at the Institute of Small Business and Entrepreneurship. Dr Omeihe currently serves as the President of the Academy for African Studies and co-founding Chair of African Studies at the British Academy of Management.

Dr Omeihe's academic journey includes studies in development studies, economics, and business at institutions such as the University of Cambridge (United Kingdom), Lagos State University (Nigeria), and the University of Aberdeen (United Kingdom). He obtained his PhD in Development Studies from the University of the West of Scotland. Dr Omeihe brings valuable experience from the private sector, having worked at financial institutions such as Zenith Bank, Standard Chartered Bank, Access Bank, and Standard Bank. Presently, he holds the role of senior economic advisor at Marcel.

Professor Christian Harrison is a scholar in the field of Leadership and Enterprise, currently holding the position of Professor of Leadership and Enterprise at the University of Bolton. Prior to his tenure at the University of Bolton, he served as a Reader in Leadership at the University of the West of Scotland, United Kingdom. His academic journey began with a First-class degree in Pharmacy, and he practised as a pharmacist, assuming managerial roles before transitioning to the field of Management. Professor Harrison further expanded his academic qualifications, earning an MBA with Distinction from the University of Aberdeen Business School, where he was the valedictorian of his class. He also holds a PhD in Leadership and possesses various postgraduate research and teaching qualifications.

As a recognised scholar, Professor Harrison is actively engaged in research projects both nationally and internationally. He is a member of several learned organisations, playing a prominent role within the British Academy of Management as the Chair of the Leadership and Leadership Development Special Interest Group, co-founding Chair of African Studies, and a council member. Additionally, he serves as the Chair of the Academy for African Studies and holds a fellowship as a member of the Institute of Business Administration and Knowledge Management (FIBAKM). Professor Harrison also serves as an external examiner for reputable UK universities, including Heriot-Watt University, De Montfort University and the University of Aberdeen.

Professor Harrison's contributions to academic publications and editorial roles are noteworthy. He serves as the editor of *New Frontiers in African Business and Society* published by Emerald Publishing and the editor of *Routledge Studies in Leadership and Leadership Development*. He holds the position of associate editor-in-chief for the *International Journal of Business Research and Management (IJBRM)* and associate editor for *Humanities and Social Sciences Communications (HSS)*. Moreover, he is a review editor for *Organisational Psychology* and is associated with several other esteemed journal editorial boards.

Beyond academia, Professor Harrison actively engages with organisations as a consultant, speaker and trainer, imparting valuable leadership skills development. He is also the visionary founder of the NGO, 'The Leadership Mould Initiative International,' dedicated to supporting students and moulding the leaders of tomorrow.

Professor Harrison's scholarly pursuits extend to the publication of the bestselling book entitled *Leadership Theory and Research: A Critical Approach to New and Existing Paradigms,* published by Palgrave Macmillan.

Preface

Dear readers,

It is with great pleasure that we present this comprehensive guide, which has been carefully crafted to empower business students with the knowledge and skills needed to navigate the dynamic landscape of qualitative research. In today's interconnected world, businesses face an ever-expanding array of challenges and opportunities. Understanding the human dimensions of business has become imperative for success, as qualitative research offers a powerful lens through which we can explore and comprehend these dimensions.

For us as authors, our journey in creating this book began with a vision to bridge the gap between theoretical concepts and practical application. In doing so, we sought to provide business students with not just theoretical knowledge but a toolkit they could confidently wield to explore key aspects of real-world business phenomena.

We understand that the business world knows no boundaries, and neither should our approach to qualitative research. As a result, this book embraces a global perspective, recognising the richness of diverse cultures, industries, and organisational contexts. On our part, we believe that qualitative research can transcend borders, offering insights that resonate with students and practitioners across the globe.

We do not neglect the importance of understanding today's fast-paced business environment. That is why we have filled this book with a plethora of quizzes, case studies and real-world examples. These vivid illustrations showcase how qualitative research has influenced decisions across the board.

We are deeply committed to the success of our readers. With a student-centric pedagogy, each chapter unfolds progressively, building upon the previous one to develop a strong foundation. We have included learning objectives to guide your journey, interactive exercises to stimulate critical thinking and thought-provoking discussions that inspire deeper exploration of qualitative research.

It is very essential to recognise the ethical responsibilities that come with conducting qualitative research. We have devoted a significant portion of this book to the principles of research ethics and integrity. It is our hope that you will carry these values with you as you embark on your own research endeavours.

This book is not just our creation; it is the product of collaboration and shared knowledge. We extend our gratitude to the countless researchers, educators and students whose contributions have enriched this work. We hope that this book will inspire a culture of collaboration, where ideas are shared, and knowledge is nurtured collectively.

As you know, learning is an endless journey, and qualitative research is an ever-evolving field. We encourage you to view this book as a springboard for further exploration and growth. As you dive into the pages of this exciting text, let your curiosity guide you, and may it spark a lifelong passion for learning and discovery.

To our fellow educators, we hope this book serves as a valuable companion in your mission to enlighten and empower your students. And to our dear readers, we invite you to embark on this exciting journey of qualitative research with us.

Kingsley and Christian

Authors of *Qualitative Research for Business Students: A Global Approach*

Acknowledgements

Writing a book of this magnitude has been an enriching journey, and we, the authors, wish to take this opportunity to express our deep gratitude to all those whose unwavering support and contributions have made the development of *Qualitative Research for Business Students: A Global Approach* possible.

First and foremost, our heartfelt thanks go to our families, whose love, understanding and encouragement sustained us throughout the long hours of research and writing. Your unwavering belief in us and the grace with which you embraced our writing routines have been instrumental in bringing this project to fruition.

We are indebted to our colleagues and friends who generously offered their insights, feedback and expertise during the development of this book. Your constructive criticism and valuable suggestions have significantly shaped the content and enhanced the quality of our work.

To the reviewers and editors, we extend our sincere appreciation for your meticulous scrutiny and thoughtful comments, which have contributed to the refinement and clarity of the book. Your dedication to improving the research methods discourse has been invaluable.

We would also like to acknowledge the academic institutions and libraries that provided access to valuable resources, enriching our research, and making it more comprehensive. Additionally, our gratitude extends to the authors and/or publishers whose articles we have included in key sections of the book.

To the publishing team, we extend our thanks for your unwavering professionalism, support and commitment to excellence. Your efforts have been instrumental in bringing this book to fruition.

We are proud to be associated with the institutions we have worked with, where dedicated research and professional teaching practices inspire us. Your support for this incredible adventure has been immensely valuable.

Lastly, we want to express our sincerest thanks to everyone who played a part in the creation of this book. Your invaluable contributions have made *Qualitative Research for Business Students: A Global Approach* possible, and we hope it serves as a valuable resource for students, educators, and researchers in the field of business studies.

With heartfelt appreciation,

Kingsley O. Omeihe and Christian Harrison

1

The Nature of Qualitative Research

Learning outcomes

By the end of this chapter, you should be able to:

- define research and its importance
- conceptualise the nature of qualitative research
- explain the stages of a research process via our research wheel
- have a rich understanding of the book's design and features.

1.1 Introduction

In this first edition of *Qualitative Research Methods for Business Students*, we aim to respond to the many tensions and hesitations faced by non-quantitative students. This has strengthened our resolve to interpret, solidify and organise the field of qualitative research in the face of methodological barriers and differences. We acknowledge that a quiet methodological revolution is taking place, with more scholars operating within the boundaries of interpretation, **ethnography**, unstructured and semi-structured interviewing and phenomenological studies. This has led us to research and develop this new book, one that provides significant implications for business students and academics alike.

We do not neglect that a host of methodological textbooks have been published over the years. In the field of qualitative research, qualitative research in business and management texts already exists. Yet, to date, we believe that there has been no attempt to capture the field fully, especially in taking stock of the major paradigms, strategies and techniques through a global lens. *Qualitative Research for Business Students* is our attempt to address this gap. This book represents a distillation of knowledge that locates the field shaping the qualitative discipline.

We have taken a predominantly student-specific approach in our writing. By doing this, we have been able to take stock of our reflexivity, the perspectives of current and past students, as well as those of scholars and tutors in assessing and presenting the major techniques for qualitative studies. Ultimately, we share the belief that the broader relevance and applicability of the book will be dedicated to shaping the present and future of the qualitative revolution.

However, by recognising the many challenges students face, our experience of teaching, mentoring and supervising students suggests novel approaches to qualitative research and the need to provide new contemporary learning materials. Consequently, we have taken the opportunity to capture up-to-date examples that reflect varied national and cultural differences. For the readers, we want them to locate qualitative studies within their own spaces.

We have also taken the opportunity to capture the real world of business; we isolate the major world issues using major strategies for inquiry by examining methods of collecting and analysing empirical data. In this book, we explore some of the philosophical traditions that exert an influence on how qualitative research can be approached and how businesses can be better understood. These issues are all captured in this book.

Qualitative Research for Business Students aims to open a new chapter as it seeks to advance discussions which consolidate conventional knowledge. The purpose of this initiative is to cover the research territory and navigate our way through areas fraught with high debates. For example, we introduce the research wheel that describes the stages a researcher must pass when developing an effective qualitative methodology.

To date, there have been many distinguished books on aspects of qualitative studies and large general, impressionist assessments have been made. However, between specialised research and the general methodological studies, we demonstrate that our book is socially constructed, resonating with generations of graduate students and scholars, providing valuable insights that they can apply in their scholarly work. Thus, when examined with adequate care, our approach forces you to rethink the very nature of qualitative research. Hence our focus is on a book that serves as a catalyst for new thought, one that is fresh and amplifies our understanding of the social world.

It is these issues that form the central thrust of this book. We recognise the need to better equip students with a clearer and easily understood appreciation of how qualitative research is conducted and what the process involves. This includes convincing students that qualitative methods constitute a rich empirical field on their own, thus allowing the reader to position their studies firmly rooted in the qualitative convention.

Inevitably, the body of knowledge to be developed would contribute to the quiet revolution and gentle influence of qualitative research in business studies. This book is written to help you embark on your research project, whether you are an undergraduate or postgraduate student of business and management or across any discipline. It is also valuable for researchers, managers and practitioners for gaining insights into conducting research needed to yield the best results. This book will provide a clear guide as you enter the magical realm of empirical research.

Within empirical research, there are two acknowledged research methods: qualitative and quantitative. Specifically, we provide a broad and comprehensive discourse of qualitative research. The careful scholarship presented throughout the chapters provides important answers to some of the problems within research methodology, capturing the real-world challenges and issues.

We recognise that there are many challenges encountered while conducting research and the methodological choices made could influence the outcome of your study. After reading this book, you will have been introduced to the multi-method stance of qualitative research, approaches, strategies, philosophies and techniques which will be valuable in conducting your research. The research wheel proposed in the book describes the stages you should go through when developing an effective research project. The wheel provides more insights on the decisions you should make while considering ostensibly different options.

1.2 The book's outlook for qualitative research: an essential text

The emphasis in this book is to provide a basis for a timely essential text which provides rich contributions to the field of qualitative research. *Qualitative Research for Business Students* provides a broad, reasonably comprehensive discourse of various qualitative research methods and their philosophical underpinnings. The careful scholarship presented throughout the chapters makes the book an important answer to some of the problems within research methodology. We project the multi-method stance of qualitative research, involving interpretations of natural settings and a range of phenomena. We attempt to locate effectively approaches for collecting empirical data: case studies, observations, introspections, and documentary analysis, that capture the real world of the local actors. The book has much to offer, and we have been able to examine the qualitative field through contemporary examples and case studies.

We do not ignore the fact that there may be differences and scholars may have to cope with our vastly different styles in thinking about a variety of topics, such as our epagogic approach to reasoning which builds on the inductive and deductive research approach, stage model of the systematic literature review, or depiction of the research strategies, the research wheel, and our codebook analysis. Nonetheless, we believe that future studies may build on our strengths and flaws to advance our contributions.

On our part, we are intrigued by the possibility that the business world continues to present a fertile ground for qualitative studies. Although much progress has been made by this book, the evidence across the chapters indicates that on its own, qualitative research is a field of inquiry that cuts across disciplines and subject matters. It is our hope that readers are keen to use this text to evaluate the extent to which they can be applied to produce a reliable knowledge stock.

Pedagogical features

This text includes features such as:

- chapter objectives and learning outcomes
- introduction
- short vignette examples
- boxed conclusion/summaries
- review and discussion test questions
- self-check questions/answers
- key terms/glossary
- annotated further reading
- case studies with questions. The case studies are short, frequent, and embedded within the text. The cases include a broad range of narratives that embraces our global reach.

1.3 Rationale for research

There are several reasons why research has become so important for everyone and not just students, academics and researchers. In fact, it has become necessary and valuable in our daily lives. We will provide four hypothetical examples across different spheres of life.

- A pandemic is plaguing the world at the moment, yet there is no cure for the lethal disease. Many people across the world are dying in their thousands. Imagine that you are the head of research and development in a well-recognised pharmaceutical company. What will you do to end the widescale deaths across the globe?
- Second, imagine that you have been appointed the new sales manager of an information communications technology firm. The firm's sales have been in decline for five years and you have been recruited to change the trajectory of the company. What will you do?

- Third, imagine that you are a football manager who has just been recruited by a football club who are currently at the bottom of the league and almost certain of being relegated to the second division next season. The players are not motivated and are currently not playing well. Their rival team in the city are top of the league and will be playing your team in a month's time. Many people have acknowledged the work ethic and style of this team. How will you go about the match?
- Finally, imagine that you are the president of the country, and the inflation rate is at a record high. There is an impending recession. How will you go about solving the problem?

The answer to all these scenarios is to conduct research. The four examples across health, business, sports and politics show that research is necessary and plays a fundamental part in our lives. As a result, it is pertinent that we study and acquire the appropriate skills to conduct research.

Research builds knowledge. Knowledge is a highly valued state in which a person is in cognitive contact with reality (Zagzebski, 2017). Knowledge is the awareness or understanding of a particular phenomenon. It essentially refers to facts and information obtained through cognition and study. Knowledge may be new as in cases where this is a new territory, and nothing is known about the phenomenon or context. It could also be already existing where there is need to expand the existing information about that subject or concept. Research contributes to forming new knowledge and expanding the existing knowledge base.

Another rationale for doing research is to provide solutions to problems. Organisations are plagued with a lot of uncertainties and today's global environment is faced with a lot turmoil and uncertainty. As a result, it is pertinent that you are able to solve problems. These problems and issues can be investigated in the form of a research project where high quality information is obtained and used to provide solutions to the issue. Such solutions can contribute to our understanding of the issue investigated and provide novel approaches to organisational challenges.

Research helps us to understand a phenomenon, situation or behaviour under study. For example, entrepreneurs are often keen to share their experiences and enjoy telling their stories hence being able to understand better their lived experience; you may take time to interview them. You might also consider working within their establishment or observing them to have a more holistic view of their behaviour.

As a researcher, you will need to know how to conduct high quality research. This competence is more important today than before whether you are a student, academic researcher or manager. That is why in this book, we have examined with adequate care the research process and specifically the very nature of qualitative research.

1.4 What is research?

Having looked at and examined the need to conduct research, it is important to know what research really means. Research is a buzzword, and its use has become commonplace in today's world. Many people view research as just a means of collecting data. A classic example is a sales company that states that they have conducted research because they distributed questionnaires to determine their customers' preferences. Though it is not wrong to relate research with data collection, taking such a singular perspective to research represents a narrow view of such a wide concept.

Research has been defined by scholars in different ways. Saunders et al. (2012) define research as something that people undertake to find out things in a systematic way, thereby increasing their knowledge. It is a systematic inquiry aimed at providing information to solve managerial problems (Blumberg et al., 2011). Most of these definitions highlight the need for taking a systematic approach, building knowledge and solving problems. This draws on what we had discussed earlier about the rationale for conducting research.

We can therefore define research as a form of systematic enquiry undertaken to contribute to new knowledge or expand the existing knowledge base. It involves the systematic collection and analysis of information to increase understanding of a topic and provide solutions to an existing issue.

Business and management research which is integral to this book covers a wide range of phenomena. Drawing from our earlier definition of research, it is reasonable to define business and management research as a systematic enquiry undertaken to contribute to knowledge within the field of business and management and to know more about the phenomena. This process involves a wide range of activities and is more than just conducting surveys. It includes idea and theory development, purpose and problem definition, a thorough literature review, planned research design, data collection, data analysis, adhering to ethical standards, ensuring the findings are credible, communicating these findings and their implications unambiguously and reflecting on your experiences and limitations.

One useful way to conceptualise business and management research is based on its purpose. Research could be viewed as either basic or applied based on its purpose. Basic research, which is also known as fundamental or pure research, is theoretical and is focused on improving or expanding the knowledge base of a particular concept. It is a systematic investigation that aims to achieve a better understanding of a phenomenon and not to solve a specific problem. Since business and management is mainly an applied science, pure basic research is quite difficult. Most basic research emerges from other disciplines such as education, health and psychology. For example, studies on how the human memory works is basic research in education but informs business and management, especially when considering consumer behaviour.

On the other hand, applied research is a systematic enquiry that aims to provide practical solutions to a specific problem. It is a form of investigation that entails solution-oriented inquiries into a phenomenon and analyses empirical evidence as seen in the case of Litburn (i.e Case 1.1). As you can see from the earlier definition, business and management research mainly has an applied orientation and is conducted to address a particular issue and proffer a solution to a problem.

While the distinction between basic and applied research is useful in describing research, there are few aspects of research that apply only to basic or only to applied research (Zikmund et al., 2013). These are mostly within a basic to applied research continuum. The research is of direct and immediate relevance to managers and addresses issues that they see as important closer to the applied spectrum (Saunders et al., 2012).

Nevertheless, we argue that regardless of the specificity of purpose and relevance (i.e. basic or applied), a key aspect of any research project is **rigour.** In ensuring that your study has been conducted rigorously, it is important that you follow the research process. More detail will be provided in the discussion on the research wheel.

Case 1.1   Conducting research

Emeka was faced with a big issue. He is the chairman of Litburn, a chain of hotels that had been operational since 1909. This is a family-owned business and has been passed from generation to generation. Before the pandemic, the hotel chain was sought after and attracted a wide range of visitors especially tourists. But this has changed in the last two years and the hotels have struggled to remain functional. Employees are demotivated and scared that the company will go under and they will be made redundant.

It seems that customers' taste and priorities have changed, and it has become difficult to attract them. Emeka has recruited Anu (who is a researcher) to conduct research and proffer solutions to the present predicament facing his company. He is optimistic that Anu will be able to communicate her findings and use them to solve the pertinent problem.

Questions

- How do you think Anu should go about conducting her research?
- Based on the specificity of the research purpose, where should this intended study be categorised (i.e. basic or applied)?

* This is a fictional case. Names, characters, places and incidents either are products of the author's imagination or are used fictitiously. Any resemblance to actual persons, living or dead, or actual events is purely coincidental.

1.5 The qualitative research process

Understanding the qualitative research process is central to the success of any research project. One's ability to capture and accurately identify a research topic, undertake a review of literature, select the appropriate methodological choices and analysis define the research process. As captured in a variety of research texts, these are the key steps a researcher must follow to address pertinent research issues. While several texts have laboured to distinguish between the qualitative and quantitative research process (Bell, E. et al., 2018; Easterby-Smith et al., 2019; Myers, 2020; Gray, 2020), it must be emphasised that neither qualitative nor quantitative supersedes the other. Scholars have often demonstrated a strong preference for either or both methods, although methodological choices are a matter of principle and in most cases, dependent on philosophical positions.

Quantitative research is number-based and seeks to understand the causal or correlational relationship between variables while qualitative research is interpretation-based and seeks to obtain richer information about a phenomenon. The term qualitative implies an emphasis on the constructed nature of reality, and the intimate relationship between the researcher and what is studied (Denzin and Lincoln, 2003; Omeihe, 2019). Qualitative studies are more likely to obtain unexpected information, as it allows for the emergence of new concepts that were not found previously in the literature. Qualitative research can be used in studying the meaning of people under real-world situations; and is effective in the representation of the views and perspective of participants in a given study (Yin, 2011). In this book, ten interconnected, specific considerations underpin the qualitative research process. We treat these as phases which the researcher must incorporate to address the pertinent research questions. Here the researcher enters the research process through a wheel that permeates the distinct phases of the research process. Indeed, it is at this juncture that we will address a key question:

> What is the qualitative research wheel and how does this connect the series of stages which one must pass?

Decisions about qualitative research questions can be located within the 'research wheel' – *which is the lens through which a variety of considerations can be made regarding data collection and analysis techniques.* Importantly, the research wheel best defines the boundaries of the research process. It locates the stages a researcher must pass through when developing an effective qualitative methodology. Indeed, it helps shed light on the different decisions a researcher must make while considering ostensibly different options. The excerpt below draws from the experience of a research student who has just completed her research project. Here she describes the research process and the difficulties she faced as she moved in each phase.

An interview with a research student on the research process

For me the research process was not an easy feat. First, I had no idea about how to undertake research. In fact, I had never undertaken research before. But given that I had to pass my research project, I knew I had to be prepared mentally for the task ahead. Identifying the research topic was the most gruelling part. I spent a considerable amount of time deciding a topic that appealed to me. At times, I was almost in tears because I found it difficult connecting the right dots in this case. But after extensive reading and guidance, I realised that the research process can be exciting and difficult at the same time. But upon reflection, I now know that a good research process involves understanding the research problem, developing good research questions, reviewing literature related to the research problem and selecting the appropriate methodological choices.

From the above, one of issues which the student faced was understanding how to undertake good research. For the student, she required a general vantage point to plan her research and ensure that her choices connected well with her research purpose. This is where the research wheel comes in – that is, to illuminate the various stages of research activities needed to address the research aim. Figure 1.1 provides a snapshot of our research wheel. The views captured in our research wheel below are by no means the only views that can be considered while conducting the research process.

However, in the context of this present edition, its implication is very useful in guiding the researcher's methodological choices. In our research wheel (see Figure 1.1), we do capture several existing concepts and proceed to explain how they shape the research process. For us, it is important to note the four underpinning building blocks namely: (1) research topic; (2) research aim, objectives and questions; (3) literature review – narrative or systematic; and (4) theoretical or conceptual framework that form the foundational components of the research process. In fact, a good understanding of these initial elements provides the link to connect the remaining boundaries of the ten methodological choices. The structure of the research wheel provides the lens through which one can make the right choices when undertaking a given research.

This involves (1) the research philosophy; (2) the research approach; (3) research strategy; (4) research methods; (5) time horizon; (6) sampling technique; (7) interview; (8) data analysis; (9) criteriology for quality; (10) ethical consideration. We contend that these are the main elements to be captured in the methodology section of any research project. Linking the ten elements with the four building blocks mentioned earlier forms the basis of an effective research process. This will further be explained in Chapter 8.

In our interactions with students, we have always been asked if there are any distinctions between the research methodology and research methods. Our answer has always been an emphatic 'Yes.' In our view, methodology involves the entire research process. It involves the ten listed elements and can best be described as the theories and conventions that underpin a researcher's approach to any given research. Put succinctly, methodology can be defined as the collection of methods through which research is undertaken (Somekh and Lewin, 2005).

Method on the other hand implies the process or technique through which data is collected before analysis. For us, there are three main methods, mono-methods, mixed methods and multi-methods. Mono-method research involves using a single research approach or data collection method, relying solely on one type of data (e.g., surveys, experiments, interviews) to investigate a research question or problem. Mixed method research combines both qualitative and quantitative data collection and analysis techniques. Here, researchers use various methods to gain a comprehensive understanding of their research question, allowing for triangulation to validate findings. Multi-method research goes beyond mixed methods and incorporates multiple approaches beyond just qualitative and quantitative methods. It involves using a diverse range of data collection methods (surveys, interviews, observations, experiments) to explore a research problem from various angles, aiming to enhance the overall validity and reliability of the research findings.

As this book focuses on qualitative research, we will primarily be concerned with the mono-method of qualitative research. Other elements of the research wheel will be considered later in this book.

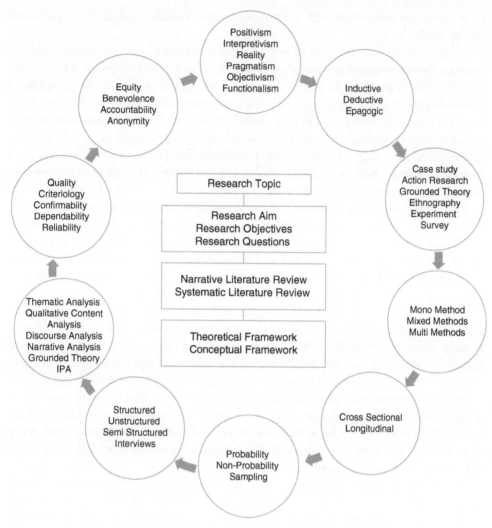

Figure 1.1   **The Research 'Wheel'**

1.6 The structure and essence of the book

Essence

Higher education has become much more diverse in the last decade, and this has thrown up challenges regarding how we support students. Students have become so diverse that it is less and less effective to apply a specific intervention to address a perceived deficit amongst a specific group of students. Instead, we recognise that all students are individuals with multiple identities, attitudes, aptitudes, cultures and backgrounds.

In this book, we see the need to reflect our multicultural society and embrace diverse perspectives and scholarship. Our book is written using inclusive language which is free from bias and stereotypes. By committing to this, we believe our text makes a significant contribution to the decolonisation of curricula and to supporting diversity, equity and inclusion in society. Our examples and case studies experiment with the boundaries of interpretation, linking research to a diverse audience, capturing elements of cultural nuances to understand more fully the relationship of qualitative research across contexts. It offers a broader knowledge base by including conceptual and theoretical work from non-western sources and further provides opportunities for practice in diverse cultural contexts.

We build on experiential learning so that students can experience and reflect on the intercultural aspects of their learning alongside core disciplinary learning. Examples within the book are geographically diverse and include non-western countries. It embeds contributions internationally and includes further readings from international textbooks, journals, reports and websites that present non-western views, thereby developing students' international and intercultural perspectives.

A glossary on commonly used concepts, terms and acronyms is provided. Tables, illustrations and diagrams are used to offer non-verbal information to suit the different learning styles of the students. The ultimate aim is to better equip students with the knowledge and skills they will need in their future careers as well as to generate and pluralise knowledge. This is apt in projecting the book's relevance to a diverse readership.

Much of what we have set out to accomplish in this book draws from the limitations of previous qualitative textbooks. We do not intend to produce a long and intimidating text, rather we want a book that would serve as a study companion – one that is friendly, clear and easy to understand. It is helpful to note that this book is designed with two distinct types of potential readership in mind:

First, the book will be of benefit to undergraduate and postgraduate students in business and management. In particular, it will be useful for undergraduate and postgraduate students as they enter the magical realm of empirical research. It is also relevant for students across a range of disciplines, including finance, leadership, human resource management, international business, marketing, strategic management and accounting.

Second, for faculty members, practitioners, managers and more experienced researchers, the book would be useful in gaining insights into modern techniques and approaches needed to yield the best results. On this basis, the expectation is that the potential readership can build on this book to uncover new and original ideas that are ignored or under-explored in existing textbooks.

In this circumstance, our differentiator is based on the modification of three key elements: content, process and product. This modification is guided by our understanding of students' readiness, interests and learning profiles. For content, we recognise that our book's content must embrace the knowledge, understanding and skills required by students to learn. Consequently, we have provided appropriate scaffolding when designing our content to demonstrate the ways through which facilitators can present content to students in the classroom.

However, this book differs through the scope of its coverage and the sophistication of topics. For example, the book captures elements of originality as we bring new evidence to bear on old issues. We focus purely on business research to look at areas that previous scholars have not examined before. For example, our articulation of the epagogic approach which is closely associated with social problems, has more general applicability than the inductive and abductive approaches to reasoning. Although it bears similarities to both approaches in respect to the meshing of theories and data collection, our approach will spur you to a further reasoning reflection, by building on the weaknesses of existing **research approaches**.

It should also be noted that our depiction and introduction of the stage model of the systematic literature review, research strategies, research wheel, codebook analysis and our emphasis on ethics fits concepts together in such a way that previous texts haven't done.

Our intention is to provide you with clear insights and a range of skills needed to navigate the empirical world of qualitative research. In doing so, our case studies and examples cut across national boundaries, gender, race, paradigms and disciplines.

Structure of the chapters

As a field of inquiry, qualitative research is often difficult to define. This is because it cannot be reduced to a set of stages or techniques, but is rather a dynamic process that ensures the linkage of theories, methods and social problems. Each of the subsequent chapters follows the research outline highlighted in Figure 1.2. In this section, the content to be covered within the chapters is explained.

Chapter 2 is written to assist you in identifying a research topic. Research is a form of systematic enquiry that contributes to knowledge. In the process of conducting research, the identification and examination of a suitable topic hold significant importance. The chosen research topic should be of personal interest, offer a foundation for further exploration, and most importantly, contribute to knowledge in the relevant field. However, many individuals encounter challenges when it comes to generating research topics and transforming abstract ideas into viable subjects for examination. This chapter presents effective strategies and step-by-step guidance on how to convert ideas into well-defined research topics ready for exploration.

Planning a research project is important to ensure that the milestones set are achieved. It provides a clear sense of direction of all stages to be followed for the project. One of the core stages in planning a research project is the research question formulation. A research question is a focused and concise question that relates to the purpose of the study. It shows the general intentions and paints a picture of the research project. This chapter explores how to formulate the appropriate research questions for a study.

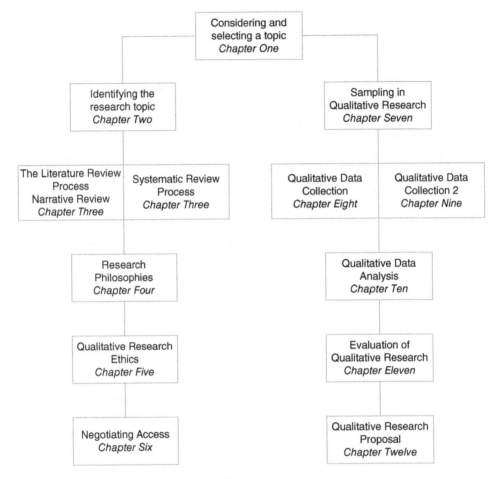

Figure 1.2   **The Qualitative Research Outline**

Furthermore, research objectives are important in every research project. Objectives are the steps taken to answer research questions or a specific list of tasks needed to accomplish the goals of the project. These objectives need to be framed as tightly as possible to make it feasible to achieve. The steps to be employed in drafting the appropriate research objectives will be examined in this chapter.

Chapter 3 discusses the literature review process. The literature review process is central within any form of academic enquiry and provides a key tool for management research. It is a selective analysis of existing research relevant to a topic matter and shows how it relates to the proposed project. The aim of conducting a literature review is to enable a researcher to map and assess the existing intellectual territory and to specify research questions and objectives to contribute to the existing body of knowledge. It shows the reader what scholars have written about the topic, the methods and approaches adopted and the theories that underpin the issue.

In this chapter, we will look into the conceptualisation of a literature review and its significance in qualitative research. We will explore two forms of literature review: the narrative and the systematic literature review. A narrative literature review entails collecting and evaluating sources related to a specific topic. It offers a comprehensive overview, typically used to gain insights into a subject and potentially identify gaps in the existing literature. Essentially, it serves as a starting point that summarises and synthesises the body of work on a broad topic. Throughout this chapter, we will thoroughly examine the narrative literature review and demonstrate the process of scanning studies during this undertaking.

While the narrative literature review has found widespread use in qualitative research, it has faced criticism for being overly descriptive and susceptible to researcher bias. In certain cases, it lacks critical analysis due to dealing with a vast and potentially unmanageable volume of information. As a response, the systematic literature review has emerged as an alternative to the traditional narrative review. The systematic literature review follows a replicable, transparent and scientific process. It employs a meticulous approach to minimise bias, involving exhaustive searches of both published and unpublished studies, while also providing an audit trail of the reviewers' decisions, procedures and conclusions. This method is recognised for generating reliable knowledge by adopting an evidence-based approach.

In order to develop the level of discussions, this chapter examines the traditional narrative literature review with its strengths and limitations. It then proceeds to explore the systematic literature review process and provide a new conceptualisation of the process. Authors such as Tranfield et al. (2003) and Denyer and Tranfield (2009) have provided ideas for the systematic literature review process. This chapter rethinks the systematic literature review to propose a more robust model of the process.

Chapter 4 examines research philosophies and approaches. Much of this chapter is concerned with the nature of philosophical perspectives, the nature of research approaches and their relevance to research methodologies. We found in the first chapter that decisions about qualitative research questions can be located within the 'research wheel' – which is the lens through which a variety of considerations can be made regarding data collection and analysis techniques. These key decisions are what we focus on in this chapter.

The focus lies on two fundamental aspects: ontological issues, which pertain to the nature of the social world and assumptions about social reality, and epistemological issues, which concern the nature of knowledge and how we understand the social reality. The subsequent discussion is dedicated to exploring the concept of research philosophy.

At first, this might seem perplexing, but it needn't be. In simple terms, research philosophy refers to the beliefs about how data should be collected, analysed and utilised. It refers to the philosophical reasoning and stance that the researcher adopts during the study.

Our discussions will demonstrate that such commitments are not solely dependent on the research being philosophically informed, but rather on how researchers reflect upon and justify their specific philosophical choices. The chapter also demonstrates the relationship between theory and research. Here, we recommend the consideration of an appropriate set of theoretical perspectives before deciding whether theory informs research (deductive) or is an outcome of research (inductive/abductive). Our introduction of the epagogic approach is closely associated with social problems but has more general applicability than the inductive and abductive approaches to reasoning.

As with debates and concepts introduced in this book, we contend that although it bears similarities to both approaches in respect of the meshing of theories and data collection, this approach will spur you to reflect more by building on the weaknesses of existing research approaches to reasoning.

Chapter 5 addresses ethics in qualitative research. The ethical practice of business research involving human participants is a complex and demanding responsibility for any researcher. As in all aspects of business and human interactions, ethical issues exist in research. It is imperative that all parties in qualitative research exhibit ethical behaviour. Ethics is a set of rules, norms, attitudes or behaviour that guides our methodological choices. This chapter considers the need for ethics in qualitative research. It is important that while conducting qualitative research, no one is hurt and suffers adverse consequences. Research should expand knowledge and provide findings that people can trust.

For every qualitative research, ethical codes and principles need to be considered and adhered to. Principles such as: non-maleficence and beneficence; autonomy; justice, **confidentiality** and **anonymity**; honesty and integrity are important. This chapter examines how to maintain these principles while conducting a qualitative study. It explores the various ethical issues that may emerge and how these issues can be addressed. In summary, it provides a thorough examination of the ethical implications of qualitative research.

Chapter 6 focuses on the complexities of negotiating access to research sites and participants, a challenging aspect of qualitative research. The lack of comprehensive guidance on this matter often leaves qualitative researchers unprepared, leading to difficulties in gaining and maintaining access to participants, sometimes resulting in project abandonment. Given the essential need for human interaction in most qualitative studies, establishing rapport with participants becomes paramount. Identifying key figures and gatekeepers, foreseeing potential obstacles, and defining mutual benefits are crucial steps to ensure the success of the qualitative research project.

The chapter provides a comprehensive overview of the steps required to negotiate access effectively, emphasising the significance of accessing research settings and sites. Common access problems and issues encountered during qualitative research are also thoroughly explored, accompanied by strategies to address these challenges.

Chapter 7 examines **sampling** in qualitative research. This chapter goes further to identify and describe the various types of sampling techniques and suggests practical approaches for overcoming pitfalls inherent in the process. Indeed, much mystery surrounds the way in which researchers select their sample sizes. In this matter, we acknowledge that the logic behind the selection of informants requires having an information rich sample. Hence, to achieve the best explanations of the phenomenon, the discussion in this area contends that samples must be determined according to the needs of the study.

We also devote attention to how a range of sampling techniques enables one to consider data from certain sub-groups rather than capturing data from an entire population. This is because it is not feasible to interview or survey an entire population. Emphasis is on the connections between the main types of probability and non-probability sampling, the issues involved in making sampling decisions and the need to justify how participants were chosen to provide the breadth, depth and saliency of sample data for reporting and authentic analysis.

Chapter 8 explores the first part of qualitative data collection. Data collection methods such as observation, participant observation, ethnography, diary studies/methods, visual methods and archival research are examined in detail. This chapter is useful for uncovering the meanings and interpretations people attach to their social reality.

Chapter 9 goes further to examine more qualitative data collection methods namely, surveys, interviews, focus groups, critical incident technique, Delphi method, case study and action research. Interviews are core to qualitative research as they provide a clear picture of people's experience as socially constructed and peculiar to them. When complex issues are to be covered, qualitative interviews are the best means of collecting data. This chapter also explores the strategies, competences and skills required in conducting qualitative interviews.

Chapter 10 discusses qualitative data analysis. It is important to provide a detailed examination of data management and a range of approaches to qualitative data analysis. In this chapter, we recognise coding as the main feature of data analysis, and we offer extended insights into its nature and the common pitfalls, since it tends to fragment data. Similarly, in terms of data analysis, we refer to the decisions one has to consider when employing computer-aided qualitative data analysis software (CAQDAS). The chapter concludes with some general discussion on analysis procedures themselves.

Chapter 11 focuses on the evaluation of qualitative research. Research methods should not only be viewed in terms of the aims and contexts of the research; priority should also be given to the quality of the study. Research, whether qualitative or quantitative, requires rigour to ensure that findings are trusted and believed. It is imperative to subject research to critical scrutiny, to evaluate the robustness of the findings. By so doing, the confidence of the academic community can be satisfied regarding the credibility of the findings.

Specifically, in qualitative research, it is important that methodological rigour is ensured. Previous studies have adapted the quantitative concepts of reliability and validity in evaluating qualitative research. Such conceptualisations are not suitable for qualitative research and only lead to the debate about the degree of rigour of qualitative research. Specific evaluation criteria which are more attuned to qualitative research exist and provide a scrupulous approach.

This chapter puts forward the relevant criteria for evaluating qualitative research. Criteria such as credibility, dependability, confirmability and transferability are examined. This framework is important in ensuring methodological rigour and should be adopted by qualitative researchers and practitioners.

Finally, **Chapter 12** explores writing good qualitative research proposals and the dissertation process. Among the very popular texts devoted to qualitative research methodology have been those which provide writing up accounts, where they have discussed ways in which researchers can present their research. Yet, even in these texts, it is important to note that it is the writing styles that are provided, with some insights into how research projects are structured. One of the main strengths of this chapter is highlighting, with exemplars, the ways in which one can design research proposals and dissertations. We recognise this will have a bearing on your success.

The research proposal is a fundamental part of any proposed study. It is an articulate synopsis of a proposed research dissertation. It sets out the central issues to be addressed and provides a strong justification of where the intended project lies within the current state of knowledge. Most importantly, it demonstrates the originality of the proposed study. It is expected that the proposal will progress to a qualitative dissertation. This chapter examines what is expected in a research proposal and how such proposals can be progressed to the dissertation phase.

To assist you in constructing your research, we present the characteristics of good qualitative research dissertations, which should have the power to convince and persuade examiners. This chapter is designed to support our community of students in spotlighting good practice through a review of the ways in which dissertations are structured. Our attempt is to locate the production of research dissertations, by examining the assumptions and tasks of writing, which are built into research dissertations. It is our hope that participants are keen to use this understanding to evaluate the extent to which they can be applied to produce a reliable knowledge stock.

1.7 Summary

- This book is written to help you embark on your research project, whether you are an undergraduate or postgraduate student of business and management or across any discipline.
- It is valuable for researchers, managers and practitioners to gain insights into conducting research needed to yield the best results.
- Research is a form of systematic enquiry undertaken to contribute to new knowledge or expand the existing knowledge base. It involves the systematic collection and analysis of information to increase understanding of a topic and provide solutions to an existing issue.

- Business and management research as a systematic enquiry is undertaken to contribute to knowledge within the field of business and management and to know more about the phenomena.
- Research could be viewed as either basic or applied depending on its purpose.
- Basic research, which is also known as fundamental or pure research, is theoretical and is focused on improving or expanding the knowledge base of a particular concept. It is a systematic investigation set to achieve a better understanding of a phenomenon and not to solve a specific problem.
- Applied research is a systematic enquiry that aims to provide practical solutions to a specific problem. It is a form of investigation that entails solution-oriented inquiries into a phenomenon and analyses empirical evidence.
- While the distinction between basic and applied research is useful in describing research, there are few aspects of research that apply only to basic or only to applied research. These are most times within a basic to applied research continuum.
- In ensuring that your study has been conducted rigorously, it is important that you follow the research process. In this book, the research process is presented as our research wheel.

Self-check questions

1. What is research?
2. What is the difference between basic and applied research?
3. Provide an example of basic research and applied research.

Self-check answers

1. Research is a form of systematic enquiry undertaken to contribute to new knowledge or expand the existing knowledge base. It involves the systematic collection and analysis of information to increase understanding of a topic and provide solutions to an existing issue.
2. Basic research, which is also known as fundamental or pure research, is theoretical and is focused on improving or expanding the knowledge base of a particular concept. It is a systematic investigation set to achieve a better understanding of a phenomenon and not to solve a specific problem. On the other hand, applied research is a systematic

(Continued)

enquiry that aims to provide practical solutions to a specific problem. It is a form of investigation that entails solution-oriented inquiries into a phenomenon and analyses empirical evidence.

3. Some examples of:

   a. Basic Research includes:

      - A critical analysis of branding strategies in product placement
      - An investigation into the role of employee motivation
      - Enablers of resilience in the healthcare supply chain

   b. Applied Research includes:

      - A study into branding strategies to improve customer retention in Costa
      - A study of how to improve employee motivation of the staff in McDonalds
      - Development of a resilience framework for healthcare supply chain of the NHS during a pandemic

Questions for review and discussion

1. What is the purpose of business and management research?
2. Think about research you would like to undertake, is it basic or a more applied form of research? Discuss.
3. A consultant is conducting research to investigate the ways of improving employee motivation in a supermarket in the UK. Is this basic or applied research? Explain.

Further reading

Blumberg, B., Cooper, D. S. and Schindler, P. S. (2011) *Business Research Methods.* 3rd ed. Maidenhead, Berkshire, England: McGraw-Hill Education.

Bryman, A. and Bell, E. (2011) *Business Research Methods.* 3rd ed. Oxford, England: Oxford University Press.

Saunders, M., Lewis, P. and Thornhill, A. (2012) *Research Methods for Business Students.* 6th ed. Edinburgh gate, Essex, England: Pearson Education Limited.

Zikmund, W.G., Babin, B.J., Carr, J.C., and Griffin, M. (2013) *Business Research Methods.* Cengage learning.

2

Identifying the Research Topic

Learning outcomes

By the end of this chapter, you should be able to:

- generate and transform initial ideas into a suitable research topic
- identify and select relevant research topics using appropriate criteria
- understand the key components of a good research topic
- generate clear research aims, objectives and research questions
- design a research proposal for research project.

2.1 Introduction

In this chapter, we will examine research topics and explore ways by which one can identify suitable topics. Chapter 1 helped to conceptualise the nature of qualitative research and explain the different stages of a research process. This is essential for laying foundations for a good research topic. Generally, research projects or dissertations are compulsory courses to be undertaken at the university level. Every university or school will have specific requirements regarding the design of dissertations. This often includes the structure, components, word length and page margins to mention a few. It is always useful to follow the recommended format provided by your institution. This is good practice and very important to the dissertation's success. We do recommend that students start early rather than waiting to consider possible avenues for exploration. This entails contemplating various approaches to thinking and designing such projects.

A first approach will involve formulating the research idea – and what students often believe is the most difficult facet of the research project process. In choosing research topics, we always recommend that students consider topics that are relevant and perhaps, one that fits with their passion and career interests. We have seen instances where project supervisors are decided by supervisors. This is not welcomed nor encouraged. A good start in the right direction is for students to decide topics themselves. However, a point of caution relates to the supervisory process. We have seen instances where students have failed to maximise the opportunities of the student-supervisor relationships. Supervisors are intended to help students progress towards the completion of their dissertation. We strongly recommend that students fully leverage on their supervisor's expertise. The supervisor's role is to *help* students throughout the research process, and to advise them on the standard of their work. The supervisor will give advice to the best of their ability but will not tell students what to do. The final responsibility rests with the student and not the supervisor. Table 2.1 provides an exemplar student-supervisor relationship.

Table 2.1   Student-supervisor role and remit

Supervisor's role and remit	Student's role and remit
• The supervisor's role involves providing support and guidance to students throughout the research process, as well as offering feedback on the quality of their work. • The supervisor will provide advice to the best of their abilities, but they will not dictate the students' actions. The ultimate responsibility for the project lies with the students, not the supervisor. • Students are expected to meet or have regular contact with their supervisor during the dissertation process. • Students should make appropriate arrangements to ensure they can fully focus and engage during supervisory meetings. • Supervisors should be accessible to provide advice on problems, given reasonable notice. • Supervisors will provide verbal feedback on selected written work and may include handwritten or typed comments as appropriate. • Throughout the process, supervisors should be supportive and offer constructive criticism to help students improve their work.	• Students should keep their supervisors fully informed about their progress and any challenges they encounter. It is advisable to prepare questions in advance for supervisory meetings. • Students should submit drafts ahead of scheduled meetings with enough time for the supervisor to provide comments and engage in discussions. • It is the student's responsibility to arrange meetings with their supervisor or attend the scheduled ones agreed upon in consultation with the student. • Since supervisors are likely overseeing multiple projects, students should not assume that the supervisor can immediately recall every previous discussion. • The dissertation largely relies on self-management. Students must take the initiative in organising the research project, seeking advice from the supervisor, and addressing any problems or difficulties that arise.

Students need to formulate topics that will sustain their interests and engagement with the subject matter. This is the starting phase of any given research study. The research process becomes more interesting and relevant when students have a particular devotion to their topic. We do recommend that research topics should be unique in order to highlight one's skills and strengths. By doing this, students will be able to explore and integrate knowledge in a way that satisfies the project requirements.

But again, identifying a good research topic can be a challenging effort. Below, we have captured some tips to support students in the identification process. These tips are summarised in Box 2.1.

Box 2.1   Common tips for selecting a topic

Tip One: Ensure the ideas lead to a topic that is specific. Very broad topics limit the ability to undertake quality research.

Tip Two: Familiarise yourself with closely related topics by reading relevant journal articles and recommended text. This enhances your ability to limit the scope of your research.

Tip Three: Use mind maps as an impressive way to identify and develop a research topic. Brainstorm and organise elements of a proposed topic to identify main categories and ideas, utilising keywords to articulate ideas effectively.

Tip Four: Think of a topic that is achievable, both within the recommended time frame and with manageable data collection uncertainties.

Tip Five: Utilise probing questions – who, what, why, and how – to refine your topic. This involves asking:

- Why was the topic chosen?
- What are the key questions that the topic will seek to address? What is the problem statement? What are the current issues?
- Who will need the information or results? Scholars, practitioners, policy makers?
- How relevant is the proposed topic to current debates?

The five tips summarised in Box 2.1 are certainly not the only ones to consider when choosing a research topic, but they hold significant importance and usefulness. In the context of this book, these recommendations should be evident and beneficial for navigating the challenges one might encounter in the process. We acknowledge that formulating a research topic can be a daunting task. Once this initial step is carefully thought through, the next phase involves refining and generating the research process. As a result, we will describe below how to explore ways to generate good research ideas.

2.2 Generating research ideas

What is a research topic? Although there is no perfect definition, we define a research topic as an area or issue that a researcher is focused on when undertaking a particular research area. It is often drawn from the knowledge of the existing literature familiar to the researcher and demonstrates some relevance and importance to the field.

This definition highlights that a research topic involves a process of exploration, refinement and discovery, which commences with the generation of ideas. In short, research ideas are a good source of research topics. There are several reasons why generating good ideas is important to achieving a suitable research topic. But a good question is, where do research ideas come from? A useful way to think about this answer is to ask how inventors like Elon Musk or scientists create new products, concepts or services. In most cases, credible links have been found between prior experiences and the environments around them. Many good minds have found that environments provide them with ample sources of ideas and the production of new ideas. In this sense, the environment enhances one's creativity and productivity. Conversations and interaction have also been identified to be an invaluable source of idea generation. Interesting conversations that facilitate robust and stimulating discussions often lead to inspirational sparks which evolve into areas worth exploring.

For students as a group, different sources of ideas have been recognised as useful for the creative and productive identification of research topics. The sources are the student's experience, reading literature and using mind maps. Each will be discussed in turn. First, research ideas are drawn from personal experiences that can be useful for the exploration and identification of a research problem. Students often find inspiration for their research topics from a variety of places. For instance, through personal experiences. Everyday experiences have been recognised to be a very good source of research ideas. Previous dissertation students have mentioned that they often critically draw from personal experiences related to their personal life, previous school projects, and experiences within their communities to decide on the research topics.

Another good source of research ideas is through reading and reviewing prior dissertations or existing research related to their area of interest. This provides an opportunity to navigate current problems before deciding on an appropriate topic. On our part, we agree that this is a unique approach and contend that scanning existing literature provides valuable sources of research ideas. One of the ideal elements of scanning relevant literature for ideas is that it helps identify understudied topics. Also, it captures existing gaps and often doing this can encourage students to consider whether similar studies can be conducted across a different context. For example, a previous study may have examined the challenges facing taxi drivers in Scotland. This may point another student to examine a cross country comparison of Scottish taxi drivers and taxi drivers operating in the UAE. Overall, this approach points students towards areas that deserve to be examined, providing them with opportunities to contribute to existing knowledge.

Further along these lines, mind maps are also a good source of idea generation. They are an excellent visual thinking method often employed by creative thinkers. Experienced scholars and business strategists acknowledge that mind maps provide a logical visualisation of ideas in such a way that information is structured until a potential opportunity is identified. Slightly more than half of the students we engaged with utilised the **mind mapping** process. Mind maps are often used during a brainstorming process or for strategic analysis. These are graphical representations of ideas and concepts.

It is a visual thinking tool for structuring information, helping you to better understand, remember and generate new ideas. By using mind maps students can define patterns of interactions between their ideas drawn from their own thinking. This can be done individually or collectively with a group of friends. The process involves identifying initial assumptions before proceeding to explore alternative ideas or areas of inquiry.

We cannot stress enough that to complete a credible and realistic piece of business research, students must consider the purpose of the study, its feasibility, the associated issues, themes and topics, and the likely groups that their dissertation would impact. Hence, starting your dissertation with a good mind map allows you to map out your initial ideas on a topic. One of the key advantages of mind mapping over other standard approaches, is that its open-flow format appears to support the natural thinking process, which is thought to go on randomly and in a non-linear way.

Mind map exercise

For the mind mapping exercise, students should visually organise their topics such that their themes are identified and connected along three key components:

Key Objective: Identify some of the key outcomes to be derived from the potential dissertation.

Key Buzzwords: Identify buzzwords that relate to the area that you will seek to explore. This may be drawn from conversations, prior reading and literature search, environments, news or reflections.

Key People: Identify key individuals and groups associated with your study.

To locate your thinking process on the mind map, the proposed topic should be placed in the centre of the page. This should be followed by branches connecting key buzzwords linked to the topics. Branches and further sub-branches capturing secondary ideas will then be used to fit the brainstorming frame. The principle is that ideas should move from the abstract to the concrete.

2.3 What makes a good research topic

To date, identifying good research topics in business management has been of interest to both undergraduate and postgraduate students alike. Being able to undertake an effective research project involves choosing a topic that satisfies the requirements of the school's examination body. This implies that consideration should be given to a topic that addresses the core problems and issues which the research seeks to address. Undeniably, students will have to consider that the research topic shapes the direction of the dissertation. We recommend that students engage with their research topic from the onset. This is the first step towards producing a good piece of research worthy of achieving excellent grades. And as such, consideration should be given to what makes a good research topic. So, what are the attributes of a good research topic?

Attributes of good research topic

Research topics should be clear and feasible

Whatever the situation, it's worth noting that a research topic must be clear and researchable. Every good research topic should be based on the factor of clarity. This ensures that the topic is easily understood by the readership, which in this case would be an examiner, or anyone who comes across the project. But more importantly the topic must be clear to the researcher themselves. Unclear research topics create bottlenecks to achieving the research aim and objectives. Having an unclear research topic can often lead to unfavourable research outcomes. We recognise that it often takes students a while to capture clarity and an acceptable focus. But again, students must see the dissertation as a continuous process of making unclear aspects clearer. The situation would involve developing the key words in the topic to be more understandable so that they reveal the researcher's intentions. Clear research topics should be free from ambiguous words and must be succinct in nature. A good way to achieving clarity in the research topic is by using the right words which provide a sense of purpose. This helps in setting the focus of one's research.

Research topics should be achievable

After achieving some clarity, it is highly advisable to ensure that dissertation topics are achievable. The feasibility of a topic can be assessed through various means. For instance, we have observed students who embarked on topics that cannot be completed within the required dissertation time frame. Additionally, some students have chosen broad topics that hinder their access to relevant data, such as critical secondary sources, key stakeholders, necessary facilities and suitable organisations. Identifying the necessary resources for the research is also crucial, as certain dissertations may require travel, access to specific software and equipment, or attendance at additional workshops. Topics likely to encounter challenges related to these bottlenecks are best avoided in favour of more feasible ones.

To assess these factors effectively, you can ask yourself the following questions as outlined below in Table 2.2.

Research topics should be located within the student's capabilities

The situation becomes worse when students engage in topics that appear to be beyond their skill set. Capability in this sense implies the ability to address the proposed research topic, conduct credible research and provide solutions that address the research problem. Capability involves the student's ability to execute the dissertation or achieve the

Table 2.2   **Six Reflective Questions**

Six Reflective Questions
1   Will I be able to gain access to the right stakeholders or gatekeepers?
2   What type of access would I require?
3   Will I get the resources to achieve the research objectives?
4   Do I understand my topic, and will it be clear to anyone who reads it?
5   Will my research require primary or secondary data or complement both sources of data?
6   Will I be able to complete this dissertation within the required timeframe?

relevant dissertation outcomes. For example, choosing a research topic that involves quantitative analysis, whereas the researcher has little or no skills to engage in the research analysis. A good way to address achievability in this sense would be by probing to see if they will be supported to achieve such skills. However, it's important to note that students will be provided with the opportunity to develop their research capability during the dissertation. Course lectures, tutorial workshops and research clinics are usually provided to support students to develop relevant skills needed to make contributions to their field of practice.

Research topics must be timely, interesting and presented in an engaging way

Dissertation supervisors frequently emphasise the importance of selecting research topics that are timely and address contemporary issues. These topics are often referred to as "hot topics" because they relate to current events or issues in the present time and are relevant to the current context. For instance, during the Covid-19 global pandemic, numerous students conducted research on Covid-19 and its impact on society. The rationale behind choosing timely topics lies in their potential to contribute by addressing current problems within society. Justifying the timeliness of a topic is crucial as it helps identify current gaps in existing knowledge and indicates that the research investigation deserves attention. This approach provides fresh insights into the research problem.

The importance of designing an engaging research topic cannot be overstated in the progress of a dissertation. It is crucial for students to identify research topics that address pertinent research problems deserving of explicit answers. Interesting research topics not only set expectations and provide clues to the readership about the research's direction but also establish the tone for capturing the study's essence. Moreover, they serve as a reliable yardstick to assess the success of the dissertation. It is worth emphasising that interesting topics also offer motivation to the students themselves. We recommend that students pursue research aligned with their career goals (Saunders et al., 2023). This approach provides students with excitement and valuable opportunities to enhance the skill set required for their employability.

Table 2.3 presents a summary of the attributes of good research. It is essential to highlight that these attributes form a composite picture, reflecting a collective perspective rather than solely our viewpoints.

Table 2.3   What makes good research topic?

Attributes of a good research topic	
Accessibility	When choosing topics, issues around access to resources must be considered. Resources could include: <ul><li>access to relevant software</li><li>access to primary and secondary data</li><li>access to stakeholders such as gatekeepers</li><li>access to finance needed to undertake field trips or workshops</li></ul>
Clarity	<ul><li>Topics should be clear and easily understandable.</li><li>Topics should easily capture the essence of the study.</li><li>Topics should be established based on a credible study.</li></ul>
Problem-solving	<ul><li>Topics should be seen to be addressing a particular issue, with the goal of providing a viable solution. This implies that the topics would provide actionable measures which contribute theory, policy and practice.</li><li>Interesting and compelling topics always provide well-articulated solutions.</li><li>Topics should highlight a potential problem and the likely chance of addressing it through credible evidence.</li></ul>
Achievability	<ul><li>Topics should be designed such that they can be completed within the given time frame.</li><li>Topics should have a workable methodology and an appropriate method of data collection.</li></ul>
Fit with career aspirations	<ul><li>Topics should be designed to link with ones' career aspiration and interests.</li></ul>
Well located	<ul><li>Topics should be well located within a student's capabilities.</li></ul>

2.4 Uncovering the research proposal

In the previous section, we concentrated on identifying good research topics. You will have seen that there are advantages to developing research topics by considering the right attributes. But what happens next after identifying a good research topic? Usually, upon commencement of the research courses, students are asked to identify specific topics which they will base their research on. Once the topics have been identified and approved by the supervisors, the next stage would be the development of a research proposal. A good question in this light is, what is a research proposal?

Let's consider this scenario: two movie producers in Nollywood are seeking funds from potential investors to finance their blockbuster movie project. A consortium of powerful entertainment investors expresses interest in investing in the proposed movie. However, one investor remains cautious due to the inherent risks in the movie industry. To mitigate these risks, the investors ask the producers to provide a business proposal outlining key details, such as a movie summary, background, track record of actors and producers, movie cost, marketing plan, contingency estimates, proposed financial returns and timelines. Essentially, they require a well-structured document that explains what movie the producers intend to create, why it's worth investing in, and how the movie will be executed.

Relating this to the research process, the fundamental underpinnings of any research proposal are the answers to the "why", "what", and "how" questions. The "why" addresses the justification or rationale for undertaking the research, the "what" explains the essence of the research (i.e., what the research entails), and the "how" pertains to the practicalities of the research, including how the research problem will be investigated.

In simple terms, a research proposal can be defined as a structured, concise, and coherent document that lays out the central issues (what, why, and how) a given research seeks to address. Research proposals are used in proposing research projects, just like the movie producers presented their business proposal to secure funding. In academia, a research proposal provides a comprehensive explanation of the chosen research topic and its significance.

2.5 Writing the research proposal

Up until this point, we have established that the research proposal document serves as the intended plan for the research. It should be regarded as a crucial planning document, as poor execution can render the research meaningless. In academia, the

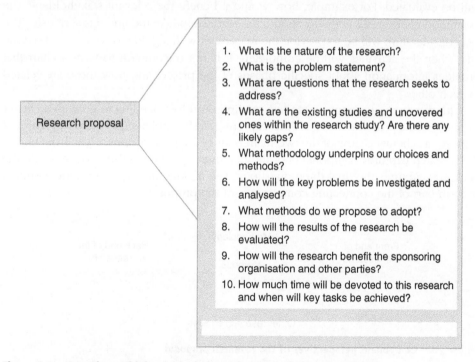

Figure 2.1   **Questions which a typical research proposal aims to address**

research proposal outlines the nature of the research, specifying its key aspects, and is used to persuade the readership, typically the supervisor or dissertation examiner.

At the undergraduate and postgraduate levels any research project begins with the development of a research proposal. It proves highly valuable in assisting students to articulate and navigate through the steps of their research projects. We emphasise that proposals should be structured in a manner that is easily comprehensible to the recipients, as good research proposals aid students in making intelligent and ethical research decisions (Mitchell and Jolley, 2020).

To address these points effectively, we have compiled several key aspects that a typical research proposal should cover (see Box 2.3).

As a starting point, we recommend that to develop a research proposal, consideration should be given to addressing the ten questions listed in Figure 2.1. First, what is the nature of the research and what is the existing problem that demands action? Third, what are the questions that the research seeks to address? This is followed by probing to uncover the existing studies within the context of the research. It is obvious enough that this can uncover under-researched pathways also known as research gaps. Following this is the justification of the methodology and methods, which form a fundamental part of the research process. In research, one needs to make it clear how the knowledge of the existing problems will be attained. This is often recognised as a pivotal part of the research process. The final questions related to the research results will be evaluated. For example, how would it benefit the relevant stakeholders? The assumption here should be why should the readership take the findings seriously? The last consideration will be to provide the researcher with a guide to what must be done and when the activities will be completed. It is not uncommon to have a chart that provides information about specific phases of the project and how these are related to each other.

With these ten questions expanded, we find ourselves needing to go with a clearer structure of the proposal. But this time, capturing the basic elements carefully. Figure 2.2 captures a schematic view of the two main parts of a typical proposal. The front end of the research captures components of the first three questions raised above, while the back end captures the final three questions. The middle three questions are assumed to form part of the connecting components of the proposal.

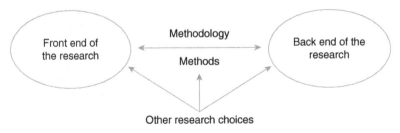

Figure 2.2   **Component perspectives of the research proposal**

2.6 The contents of a good proposal

The research proposal topic or title page

The starting point of the research proposal is the research topic or title. This describes in a few words the main ideas shaping your study. A very good topic captures at a quick glance the content of the proposed study. It is important to note that the proposal topic should be seen as dynamic rather than static. In this vein, the proposal topic may evolve as the researcher becomes familiar with more readings and in most cases a richer understanding of the topical issues. Once this has been captured, the next phase will be to develop an abstract.

The abstract

The abstract serves as a condensed version of the research proposal, offering the readership a concise summary of the entire study. It is often regarded as a miniature representation, briefly describing the research study problem. The typical outline of an abstract includes an introduction, body and conclusion. In the introduction, the initial sentences provide a general overview of the study. This is followed by a clear statement of the research problem and an identification of the research purpose, along with potential theoretical foundations. The subsequent section of the abstract should summarise the methodological choices, including the selected methods and the likely process of data analysis. The final part captures the conclusion. It is worth noting that although the abstract is the first section of any study, it should be the last to be completed. This is because the abstract aims to succinctly summarise the completed work without delving into extensive details. Additionally, a well-structured abstract should consist of well-developed paragraphs, ensuring clarity for any reader who comes across it.

Introduction

The introduction holds significant importance in a research proposal. In this section, the topic of the research is described, but it goes beyond that. It provides a brief but informative explanation of why the study is being conducted, with a focus on highlighting the research gaps. These gaps refer to questions or problems that prior studies within the field have not addressed. Additionally, good introductions can include definitions of core concepts and offer a preview of the main sections of the first chapter.

The primary aim of the introduction is to provide an outline of the proposal or planned study, giving readers a sense of direction. Considering the limited word count of most proposals (typically 2,500 to 3,500 words), it is recommended to keep the introductory section to less than one page. However, the key is to ensure that the introduction is sufficiently detailed, building upon insightful discussions to address the study's aim and objectives effectively.

Background

The background section of the research proposal serves as the foundation that captures the essence of the study. Several key points should be considered when crafting this section. It should effectively encompass a review of the research area, current information on the issue, previous studies related to the problem, and relevant historical context. Ideally, this section sets forth the history and background information related to the dissertation problem. It should also provide a synopsis of existing studies to demonstrate the existence of a problem worth investigating. One effective approach is to present a chronological indication of the problem, tracing its development from inception to its status.

Furthermore, the background section should set the tone for the main study's expectations and clue the reader in on the research's objectives. Specifics in this section will serve as criteria for judging the success of the proposal. Similar to the introductory section, the background should address the gap in knowledge that the study aims to fill. And it should provide insights into the gap and how the research intends to define and contribute to the broader research area. The recommended length for this section is approximately one to one and a half pages, considering the word count limitations of the proposal.

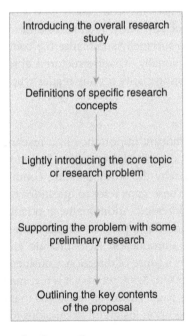

Figure 2.3 **Outline of the introduction section**

Box 2.2   Tips for the background section

Top tips for writing an engaging research proposal:

1. Start with a powerful opening: Begin your proposal with a compelling statement that captures the attention of the readership. Consider using an interesting statistic to support the importance of the problem you intend to investigate. This will convey the significance of your research right from the start.
2. Build on recent activities: Develop the foundations of the problem by referencing recent activities in the field from the last three to seven years. This demonstrates that your research is current and relevant to the current state of the field.
3. Use general statements: Clearly state the broad concept of the problem, the research focus and the research gap. This provides a clear framework for your proposal and helps readers understand the scope of your study.
4. Utilise identifiable keywords: Incorporate key terms and phrases that precisely convey the research problem. These keywords make it easier for readers to grasp the central theme of your study and align it with their interests.

Research aim and objectives

Research aim

The research aim and objectives are two distinct yet interconnected sections in a research proposal. It is essential not to combine them but to address each separately. The research aim expresses the overall intention of the planned research study. It should be a concise statement summarising what you aim to achieve at the conclusion of the research project. When determining the research aim, it is crucial to make it specific and phrased in a way that allows for clear identification of its achievement.

A key step in this process involves summarising in a single sentence what the research intends to accomplish at the end of the research dissertation. The box below provides tips for formulating the research aim.

Box 2.3   Tip for the research aim section

Top tips

A good practice is to provide a concise statement which serves as the link between the problem being addressed and the focus of the study. This is because the research aim should

(Continued)

describe the focus or intention of the research study. This should be limited to 20-25 words at the maximum.

The aim of this research is to examine the ....

This research aims to ....

The research:

- presents a core topic or discipline area
- uses a general action word
- indicates the context investigated: geographic, cultural or organisational.
    - Geographic: This refers to the physical location or area of focus for the research. Different regions may have unique characteristics, resources, or challenges that can influence the research. Climate, infrastructure, and accessibility are examples of geographic factors that may affect the study.
    - Cultural: Cultural considerations involve recognising the beliefs, values, customs, and behaviors of the individuals or communities being studied.
    - Organisational: This pertains to the structures, policies, and practices within the organisations relevant to the research.

Provide a concise statement that serves as the connection between the problem being addressed and the focus of the study. A research aim expresses the intention or an aspiration of the research study; it summarises in a single sentence what you hope to achieve at the end of a research project. Your aim should be specific and phrased in such a way that it is possible to identify when it has been achieved.

- Around 20–25 words maximum

Research objectives and research questions

It is crucial to understand that research objectives and questions define the 'what,' 'why,' 'who,' 'when' and 'how' aspects of a study. Regularly checking and reviewing your research objectives throughout the project is a good practice to stay focused and make necessary revisions if needed. The research objectives should be specific and clearly phrased to enable easy identification of their achievement.

In essence, research objectives describe the expected outcomes of the study and should be articulated in lay terms, making them understandable not only to the researcher but also to the examiner. Importantly, research objectives should be closely aligned with the statement of the problem, breaking down the research aim into specific parts. For instance, if the study's aim is to investigate the low utilisation of antenatal care services, the general objectives could be:

RO1. To identify the reasons for the low uptake and explore ways to improve it.

RO2. To investigate the benefits of antenatal care.

When setting research objectives, it is advisable to have four to five objectives, but not more than five and not less than three, to ensure a focused and comprehensive study.

When formulating research objectives, it is essential to use specific action verbs that can be measured. Action verbs such as 'to compare,' 'to calculate,' 'to assess,' 'to determine,' 'to verify,' 'to investigate' and 'to describe' are recommended. Avoid using vague non-active verbs like 'to appreciate,' 'to understand,' 'to believe,' 'to study,' etc., as they can be challenging to evaluate in terms of achievement.

For example:

To address the research aim, four key research objectives were developed and are outlined as follows:

To identify...

To critically examine...

Research question

A research question is a clear and explicit statement presented in the form of a question that outlines what the researcher intends to investigate. It not only defines the scope of the investigation but also guides the research methodology (Bell et al., 2022). Selecting a research question holds significant importance in qualitative research. Well-crafted research questions aim to enhance knowledge on important topics and are typically focused and specific.

The choice of a research question will influence the data collection and analysis methods, as qualitative studies seek to understand the 'why' or 'how' of a phenomenon. Thus, the researcher's inquiry should be directed towards exploring the 'what,' 'why' or 'how' aspects of the research topic. When crafting a research question for a qualitative study, it is crucial to formulate questions that address the 'what,' 'why' or 'how' of the topic under investigation.

Box 2.4   Tips for the research questions

Top tips

Research questions play a huge role in realising the project in a practical sense. Some initial questions aid in the:

- Focus of the aim
- Outlining of the objectives
- Method to be used

Some questions require:

- A wider population sample (typically Quant-based)
- Specific contexts or groups (typically Qual-based)

Literature review

In this context, it is essential to consider what makes a good literature review. To put it simply, a well-crafted literature review should provide a comprehensive examination of current literature related to the study topic and chosen methodology. It should explore how researchers in the subject area have approached the problem, outlining the strengths and weaknesses of their work. By reviewing and synthesising studies under distinct headings, the literature review aims to present what is known about the study topic, identify areas of controversy, and highlight gaps in the existing literature that warrant further investigation.

One common difficulty faced by students when conducting the literature review is the challenge of synthesising insights from multiple studies. Rather than simply summarising individual studies one after another, a good review should demonstrate a deep understanding of theory and key issues. Arguments presented in the review should be convincing, particularly when they relate to the crucial elements of the study.

Moreover, a strong literature review should be critical, showcasing the ability to extract essential and overlapping ideas from different sources to support one's independent argument. To achieve this, a wide array of academic sources should be utilised, forming a strong foundation for the literature review's content. Further insights on the literature review will be discussed in Chapter 3.

> ### Box 2.5   Top tips for writing a comprehensive literature review:
>
> - Use clear and academic language: Ensure that your literature review is well-written with coherent paragraphs, statements and paraphrased discussions. Minimise the use of direct quotations.
> - Move from general to focused: Describe the broad aspects of your topic and gradually transition into more focused discussions. Compare and contrast key arguments to provide a nuanced understanding of the research field.
> - Adopt criticality and reasoning: Engage in critical analysis and thoughtful reasoning of the key arguments and discussion points within your chosen field. This showcases your ability to evaluate and synthesise the existing literature.
> - Cite published, peer-reviewed sources: Base your literature review on reputable academic sources, including articles, textbook publications, books, conference proceedings, relevant media and credible online sources.
> - Organise into sections and sub-sections: Structure your literature review with clear sections and sub-sections, either thematic or otherwise, to present a coherent flow of ideas and information.
> - Reference similar themes: Discuss and refer back to similar themes or findings within your own research field or topic, highlighting the connections between your study and existing literature.

Methodology

The significance of this section lies in the researcher's ability to make informed and explicit choices to address the research problem effectively. Justification is the key principle that underpins the selection of some specific and relevant choices over others. Here, the different types of choices, reflecting the researcher's understanding of the field, demonstrate how methodological decisions were made. Hence, several crucial considerations should be considered. It is essential to provide clear and robust justifications for your methodological choices, such as the philosophical position (positivist or interpretivist), research approach (deductive, inductive, or abductive), research method (quantitative or qualitative), sampling technique (convenience, purposive, etc.), interviews (structured, semi-structured, unstructured) and analysis method (**thematic analysis**, etc.).

Let's consider the sampling section as an example. Following the introduce, identify and justify approach, the first step is to define what sampling means and provide descriptions of the available types of sampling. Subsequently, a justification for the

Table 2.4   **Methodological process**

Research philosophy	Research approach	Research method	Sampling	Data collection	Data analysis	Ethics
Introduce	Introduce	Introduce	Introduce	Introduce	Introduce	Introduce
Identify	Identify	Identify	Identify	Identify	Identify	Identify
Justify	Justify	Justify	Justify	Justify	Justify	Justify

chosen sampling strategy should be presented, explaining the specific procedures for drawing the sample. It is advisable to provide a comprehensive description of the proposed sampling frame, including inclusion and exclusion criteria. This should involve a thorough explanation of the planned recruiting procedures and how demographic information will be collected.

Ethical procedure

Since research is bound by ethical considerations, it is crucial to outline plans in the proposal that adhere to the ethical guidelines set forth by the university's ethics advisory board. A well-crafted proposal should demonstrate how it was guided by a clear understanding of the underlying ethical principles. In this book, we will focus on three key ethical principles: non-maleficence and beneficence; confidentiality and anonymity; justice and autonomy. These principles will be thoroughly discussed in Chapter 5 to ensure a comprehensive understanding and application of ethical considerations in the research process.

Research timeline: The use of a Gannt chart

The relationship between projects and their timeline is a critical concern for various stakeholders, including project managers, contractors, business owners, government practitioners and researchers. Similarly, for students undertaking a research project, neglecting to consider the various activities and deadlines can lead to significant issues in completing the project or dissertation. This underscores the importance of effective time management – the ability to manage work efficiently, allowing for monitoring and control of the dissertation's progress.

A practical and straightforward approach to achieve this is using a Gantt chart. Developed by Henry Gantt, the Gantt chart helps to allocate time for each stage of the project. It facilitates the creation of intermediate goals or milestones with specific dates, enabling you to stay on track and assess if you are adhering to the schedule. The Gantt chart not only allows for timely responses and adjustments but also provides a comprehensive overview of the project's progress as a whole, offering a clear advantage in managing the entire research process effectively.

Moreover, the Gantt chart offers a clear and visual representation of your research project plan, organising the various stages of the project against a time base. The example below provides a similar format to what is typically used when creating a timeline for your research proposal. It presents a simple visual representation of the tasks or activities involved in the project, aligned with a proposed timeline. This enables you to easily grasp the sequence and duration of each activity, providing a valuable tool for effectively managing and monitoring the progress of your research.

Table 2.5   **Gantt chart for a hypothetical study**

Activity / Week Number	September	October	November	December	January	February	March	April	May	June	July
Topic selection	▓										
Topic approval		▓									
Identifying research objectives and questions		▓									
Commence reading	▓	▓	▓								
Literature review			▓	▓							
Commence reading for methodology				▓	▓						
Consider approaches to reasoning				▓	▓						
Develop planned data collection techniques							▓	▓			
Data analysis											
Draft proposal chapter								▓	▓		
Supervisor feedback										▓	
Revise and submit											▓

2.7 Summary

- In choosing research topics, we always recommend that students consider topics that are relevant and perhaps, one that fits with their passion and career interests.
- The supervisor's role is to *help* students throughout the research process and to advise them on the standard of their work. Supervisors will give advice to the best of their ability but will not tell students what to do.
- Mind maps are a useful way to identify and develop a research topic. They can be used to brainstorm and organise elements of a proposed topic so that you are able to identify the main categories and ideas underpinning a particular topical area.
- Being able to undertake an effective research project involves choosing a topic that satisfies the requirements of the school's examination body.
- A research proposal documents the nature of the research, specifying the key aspects used to convince the readership.
- Gantt charts help you to identify how much time you can spend on each stage of your project. It is very useful in creating intermediate goals/milestones that inform you if you are on schedule or not.

Self-check questions

1. Why is an abstract important?
2. What is the difference between a research aim and the research objectives?
3. What are the attributes of a good research topic?
4. What are the reputable sources for relevant literature? Provide six examples of literature review sources.
5. Why is critical reading and writing important?
6. Perform some 'quick' online search on entrepreneurship using the university's databases to see how much research has been published in this area.

Self-check answers

1. An abstract provides a concise summary of the research paper, allowing readers to quickly ascertain the purpose, methodology, findings, and implications of the study. It acts as a snapshot that helps readers decide whether the research is relevant to their interests or needs, facilitating quicker engagement with the material.
2. The research aim articulates the broad goal of the study, providing a clear direction or purpose. In contrast, research objectives break down the aim into specific, actionable steps or targets that the research intends to achieve or explore. While the aim provides a general direction, objectives offer measurable outcomes that guide the research process.

3. A good research topic should be clear, focused, and researchable. It should address a gap in the existing literature, have practical relevance, and contribute to the field's body of knowledge. Additionally, it should be feasible in terms of available resources, time, and scope.
4. Reputable sources for literature include academic journals, books, conference proceedings, university repositories, government publications, and reputable online databases. Six examples are: JSTOR, Google Scholar, ScienceDirect, Wiley Online Library, SpringerLink and PubMed.
5. Critical reading and writing are vital in research as they enable the researcher to engage with the literature thoughtfully, identify gaps, assess the validity of arguments, and synthesize findings. This critical engagement fosters deeper understanding and contributes to more rigorous, well-argued, and insightful research outputs.

Soso Clothing: a case study of luxury brand development in Lagos

Introduction

This case study looks into the remarkable journey of Soso Clothing, a leading luxury brand in Lagos, Nigeria. Founded in 1999 by Obinna Omeihe, Soso quickly gained recognition for its contemporary tailoring and menswear, setting new standards in the industry. The study explores the company's progression from its humble beginnings to becoming a prominent player in the competitive fashion market.

Background

In 1999, Obinna Omeihe launched Soso in Lagos, as part of the Soso Group, before embarking on his university education. The company's vision was to offer a fresh and progressive take on bespoke tailoring, rejuvenating traditional cuttings with a modern touch. Starting with a single store in Surulere, Lagos, a neighbourhood with a rich tailoring history spanning almost five decades, Soso has rapidly gained a reputation for exceptional craftsmanship and contemporary menswear. Over the years, the business expanded its presence and influence, opening a flagship luxury store in the capital, Abuja. Today, the company is a thriving family business, with Christopher's brothers, Azu Omeihe as the CEO of Soso Africa and Creative Director in Abuja, and Michael Omeihe serving as its Global Chair. Although the founder Obinna Omeihe has diversified into other fields, he continues to provide valuable advice and strategic guidance when needed.

Company philosophy

Soso is driven by a commitment to creating classic clothing of unrivalled quality. The brand pushes the boundaries of design, colour and cut, offering an unmatched luxury experience

(Continued)

to its customers. Service and expertise are integral to the company's success, with close collaborations with skilled artisans and renowned mills in Lagos and Abuja. These partnerships enable Soso to design and produce exclusive fabrics and handmade accessories, adding to its uniqueness in the market.

Success and recognition

Since its establishment, Soso has achieved remarkable success, solidifying its position as a leading luxury brand in Lagos and Abuja. Being the first of the 'New Establishment' bespoke tailors in the city, Soso takes pride in its role in reviving traditional tailoring techniques with a progressive approach. Lagos, renowned worldwide as a fashion capital, embraced Soso's contemporary style, attracting a diverse clientele of discerning customers.

Future aspirations

As Soso continues to flourish as a quintessentially African luxury brand, it envisions further expansion. Plans are underway to launch an online service, enabling customers to access its exquisite offerings globally. Additionally, Soso aims to explore international opportunities through strategic collaborations with worldwide stockists. Led by its Creative Director, Azu Omeihe, the brand is poised to make a mark on the global luxury fashion scene.

Conclusion

The case study of Soso Fashion House exemplifies the success story of an exciting African brand that, along with an unwavering commitment to craftsmanship and innovation, propelled a brand to the forefront of the fashion industry. By seamlessly blending timeless traditions with contemporary trends, Soso Clothing has etched its place in the luxury market, setting new standards for bespoke tailoring and menswear.

Figure 2.4   Soso Clothing

Figure 2.5 **Soso Clothing**

What is the purpose of a research proposal?

1. Think about research you would like to undertake and consider why it is important to have a good research topic. Discuss.
2. A consultant is conducting research to investigate the ways Soso can launch its online service, enabling customers to access its exquisite offerings globally. Additionally, Soso aims to explore international opportunities through strategic collaborations with worldwide stockists.

You are expected to undertake the following:

Task One: Design a proposal title and develop one research question and/or research objective and an introduction for the Soso group.

Task Two: Distinguish between the broad aim of your research and specific research questions/objectives. One objective/question is sufficient to show that you understand this distinction and to inform the rest of the assignment

Task Three: Undertake a short literature review. Summarise key theory and evidence relevant to your research and show the importance or benefit of your study question/objective.

Task Four: Explain your research philosophy, strategy and methodology. In particular, comment on what makes your research positivist, phenomenological or any other philosophy you choose or a hybrid of approaches.

Task Five: You will need to think carefully about both your research question/objective and your research philosophy/strategy/approach, as these will influence your choice of research technique in Task 6.

Task Six: Tests your ability to explain your research strategy and methodology in terms of an appropriate selection from the range of concepts introduced in the lecture course: e.g., positivist/phenomenological research; deductive/inductive approaches; theory-testing/theory-building; quantitative/qualitative data; research sample frame/sample size and so forth.

Task Seven: Discuss and reflect on the ethical implications of your research.

Further reading

Creswell, J.W. (2014) *Research design: Qualitative, quantitative, and mixed methods approach*. Sage Publications.

Saunders, M., Lewis, P., and Thornhill, A. (2019) *Research methods for business students*. Pearson.

Yin, R.K. (2017) *Case study research and applications: Design and methods*. Sage Publications.

3

The Literature Review Process

Learning outcomes

By the end of this chapter, you should be able to:

- understand the concept of a **literature review**
- explain the importance and purpose of a literature review
- search the literature and engage critically with the ideas of other scholars
- conceptualise the systematic literature review process
- reference the literature found correctly
- evaluate the structure and features of a good literature review.

3.1 Introduction

The literature review is an important component of any academic enquiry or research project. As part of your studies, you are always expected to embark on a review of the literature in that area or field. Indeed, a literature review plays a critical role in any undergraduate or postgraduate dissertation and is fundamental in providing the information that justifies the need of the intended research project.

Several books have tried to conceptualise the process of conducting a literature review. Despite such attempts, it remains a daunting task for students, researchers, scholars and practitioners. In this chapter, we simplify the process and make it easier to understand. We start by providing a clear description of what it means to review the literature. The purpose and objectives of undergoing the task are explored. We also provide an elaborate examination of the literature review process and how you can structure your literature review. In addition, we explore the systematic literature review that has been advocated as an alternative to the traditional narrative review. Finally, we examine the role of referencing the work of others which is an important academic convention in structuring a literature review.

3.2 What is a literature review?

Structuring your research through the lens of existing knowledge is the building block of all academic enquiry especially within the discipline of business and management. In business and management research, several scholars have attempted to define the literature review. Fink (2010) defines the literature review as a survey of books, scholarly articles, and any other sources relevant to a particular issue, area of research, or theory, which provides a description, summary and critical evaluation of these works in relation to the research problem being investigated. It is the selection of available documents on the topic, which contain information, ideas, data and evidence written from a particular standpoint to fulfil certain aims or express views in relation to the research being proposed (Hart, 2009). It means locating and summarising the studies about a topic (Creswell, 2014). In general, it is broadly described as a systematic way of collecting and synthesising previous research.

However, these definitions do not give a complete picture of the process. A literature review does not only provide a survey of scholarly sources on a specific topic and summary of the sources. It proffers an overview of the current and existing knowledge which helps to identify relevant gaps, methods and theories in the field. It analyses and synthesises the literature in the field to give a clearer picture of the state of knowledge of the topic. Through the literature review, you can demonstrate an engagement with prior scholarly work based on your reading and understanding. It shows your reader that you have an in-depth grasp of the topic and that you are aware of where your research fits and can add to the existing body of knowledge. It affirms your credibility as someone who is knowledgeable in the chosen field and topic area.

The literature review is integral to the success of any academic enquiry or research project, so a more encompassing definition is needed. We define a literature review as *the selective analysis, synthesis and critical evaluation of the existing literature in your chosen topic area so as to identify the relevant gaps, theories and methods which inform your proposed project and justify the significance of your study.*

3.3 Purpose of a literature review

In the earlier section, we provided a more holistic definition of a literature review. However, why do we need to review the existing literature in the first place? Why is this an essential part of the research process and enquiry? To answer these questions, it is important for us to know its purpose.

Whether it is an undergraduate, postgraduate, doctorate or broader research project, we can say that a literature review serves the following eight purposes:

1. To know what other scholars have written about in that area.
2. To understand the nature and context of the problem.
3. To learn about the related theories and ideas that have been applied to the chosen topic.
4. To identify the important variables relevant to the subject.
5. To learn about the research methods, approaches, designs and strategies that have been adopted in studying this area.
6. To rationalise the significance of the problem.
7. To demonstrate the originality and novelty of your research project.
8. To show how your work will contribute to the chosen area and field.

To know what other scholars have written about in that area

This is one of the major reasons for conducting a literature review. It is important that you know what other scholars have written about in your chosen area or topic so that you do not reinvent the wheel. By knowing what others have embarked on, you can avoid repeating works that have been carried out already. For example, if a research paper has examined employee motivation within Amazon in the UK, it might not be valuable for you to conduct the same study in the same context since it would be just a repetition of a prior study.

Beyond avoiding reinventing the wheel, it will make you more familiar with the current research and debate in the area. The researcher will become more knowledgeable about the scholarly work in the domain and the research other scholars have conducted. By examining what other scholars have written you are able to discover specific recommendations for further research which will build your rationale for conducting your research project. For example, in entrepreneurship research, many scholars have proposed the need for taking a dual perspective when examining entrepreneurs as they tend to have an exaggerated conception of their abilities (Busenitz and Barney, 1997; Harrison et al., 2018). Your project could take on this recommendation and obtain data from not just a singular perspective but also that of the follower.

You also must remember that the literature review is not just for you and others will also want to read it, including your supervisor, scholars, colleagues etc. It will show your audience what has been done previously and how knowledgeable you are about the field. In every topic, there are usually researchers who have written the most on a particular topic and are therefore probably experts in the area.

Someone who has written about ten papers or more in a particular area would be considered to be more knowledgeable than a person who has written only one paper, for example. In addition, the number of times such writers have been cited by other scholars also serves as an **index** for the relevance of their work. The starting point for students and researchers who may want to examine entrepreneurial leadership will be to use such scholarly work as a key resource for consultation.

To understand the nature and context of the problem

As stated in the first chapter, the essence of most research, especially in business and management, is to address a particular issue and offer a solution to a problem. Before you can do that effectively, it is important that you understand the nature and context of the problem. Such insights can only be provided by a good literature review. It allows the reader to gain a much better understanding of the issue that the study addresses and how it relates to previous studies in the domain.

Conducting a literature review is very similar to completing a jigsaw puzzle. Jigsaw puzzles are fun but can also be difficult if the right approach is not taken. One critical part of the puzzle is locating pieces and setting them together. Once they are put together, you can see clearly where the missing pieces are and what they look like. After doing this, you can then go looking for the missing pieces, which is the literature that informs the study.

In finding the missing pieces, it is important to note that some problems in business and management may go beyond the discipline and it is often important to familiarise oneself with existing knowledge in other disciplines. For example, if you want to examine ethical leadership within the National Health Service (NHS), not only will you need to draw on ethical leadership, but you would also need to have a good grasp of ethics, leadership and the health sector. This is not to say that you must read all the papers in all the highlighted domains, but it is important to justify the perspective that you will undertake and how the articles have informed your study.

To learn about the related theories and ideas

It is important to examine the relevant theories and concepts that provide the foundation for your research. For example, if your project is on the contingency approach to leadership, you will need to explore models and theories that focus on this area such as Fiedler's contingency model. If your study is looking at employee motivation, theories such as Maslow's Need Hierarchy Theory, Herzberg's Motivation Hygiene Theory, McClelland's Need Theory, McGregor's Participation Theory, Urwick's Theory, Argyris's Theory, Vroom's Expectancy Theory, Porter and Lawler's Expectancy Theory etc. should be considered. Through your literature review, you might argue for the applicability of a specific theoretical approach or combine various theoretical concepts to create a framework for your research.

Importantly, a good literature review is the first vital phase towards identifying the relevant conceptual frameworks, theories and models. What we have noticed over the years is that many students lack the required theoretical foundation and as a result they are not able to develop a conceptual framework from the review. A conceptual framework is generally developed based on a literature review of existing studies and theories about the topic and will be discussed more elaborately in the next section.

To identify the important variables relevant to the subject

A literature review is critical in identifying the important factors relevant to the subject. A good way to view these variables and their relationship within your subject area is by developing a conceptual framework. It is defined as a representative structure of factors which best explains the phenomenon to be studied. It is often referred to as a generative framework that reflects the thinking of the whole research process. It is generally developed based on a literature review of existing studies and theories about the topic. It clarifies the key terms and suggests how those terms fit together.

Example

Imagine that you want to examine leadership skills as a project. Based on your literature review, you may have noticed that there are three key skills namely, technical skills, human skills and conceptual skills. The use of a conceptual framework can be employed to explain, either graphically or narratively, these key skills and their presumed relationships. This framework can now serve as the investigator's current map of the territory being investigated. For quantitative research, which draws more on a deductive approach, you may decide to develop and test hypotheses after generating the conceptual framework. However, in qualitative studies, which adopt a more inductive and abductive approach, the conceptual framework will inform an empirical-based model after your fieldwork. In this text, we define the conceptual framework as a network of linked assumptions that represent an understanding of the research phenomena.

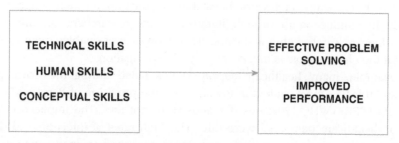

Figure 3.1   **A conceptual framework on leadership skills**

To learn about the research methods, approaches, designs and strategies

One of the major reasons for conducting a literature review is to identify the research method, approaches, designs and strategies that have been adopted by scholars in studying the topic. The use of prior methodological choices of scholars provides credibility and could be a strong justification for adopting such methodological stance for your study.

For example, several previous studies on entrepreneurial leadership such as Harrison et al. (2018); Omeihe et al. (2020) etc. have adopted qualitative techniques and specifically semi-structured interviews as a mode of data collection. If you decide to adopt a qualitative stance in examining entrepreneurial leadership, it will give your study more credibility. The credibility of your research is enhanced when well established methods are adopted (Shenton, 2004).

Although it provides credibility by using established methods, a literature review could also show that such an approach might not be best, and you may propose a new methodological approach to study that phenomenon. For example, in entrepreneurship studies, which is replete with positivism and quantitative research, some scholars have argued that it has led to fragmentary research looking narrowly at aspects of entrepreneurship. It creates a one-dimensional view which is atomistic and consequently loses much of the **richness** and idiosyncrasy that characterise the more comprehensive picture of what we mean by entrepreneurship (Anderson and Starnawska, 2008). Hence, although a majority of scholars have explored the topic from a quantitative stance, you could argue that a qualitative approach is more suited for your study. In the end, the most important decision is to adopt a methodological view that fits the purpose of your study and will satisfy your research objectives.

To rationalise the significance of the problem

In business and management research, as discussed in Chapter 1, the emphasis is often on applied rather than basic research. As a result, most studies in this field have a problem-focused approach. A critical component of this process is the literature review, which serves as a framework for establishing the importance and significance of the study. By conducting a thorough literature review, researchers can rationalise the need for their research within a specific field. Moreover, it enables them to demonstrate that the chosen topic is indeed worthy of investigation.

For example, many healthcare supply chains failed during the Covid-19 pandemic, and this was most evident in the strain on the provision of Personal Protective Equipment (PPE) (WHO, 2020) as demands were not met. The implications of this failure on healthcare personnel were dire. The high rates of infection and death of healthcare professionals and patients are partly attributed to inadequate access to PPEs. In order to prevent similar issues from reoccurring in the future, your research may seek to analyse the resilience of healthcare supply chains to disruptions and the implications of these on the well-being of the healthcare staff.

To demonstrate the originality and novelty of your research project

Originality is a major criterion used to evaluate academic scholarship. According to Guetzkow et al. (2004, p. 190), originality in research may involve any, or all, of the following criteria:

- using a new approach, theory, method, or data
- studying a new topic
- doing research in an understudied area
- providing new findings.

In research, the intent is not to replicate what others have done but to add to it in some way, no matter how small, to the existing body of knowledge (Hart, 2009). As a result, a literature review provides evidence of what scholars have done and have not done within the particular area.

For example, in reviewing the literature on entrepreneurial leadership, you may note that:

- Most research has focused on individual leaders.
- There is an increasing interest in entrepreneurial leadership skills.
- There is no skill-based framework for entrepreneurial leadership teams.

This is a gap that you could address in your own research and could justify the originality and novelty of your study.

Originality may also be based on a new context. As Phillips and Pugh (1994) state, trying out something in one country that has previously only been done in other countries is one of the ways in which research can claim originality. From reviewing the literature, you may realise that the topic you want to investigate has only been explored in a particular region, sector, country etc. It will be of great value to your readers and the academic community if you decide to explore your topic in a new sector. For example, in reviewing the literature on distributed leadership, you may note that the majority of prior research has focused on the education sector. Research in a new sector such as tourism, health etc. could be a new area of focus within this field.

To show how your work will contribute to the chosen area and field

In addition to originality, a literature review shows how your work will contribute to the chosen area and field. Many times, we tend to hear that research ought to contribute to knowledge, and this is not far from the truth. Every piece of research should strive to bring something significant and new to the conversation. Contributing to knowledge means creating new or adding to the existing body of knowledge in an area or topic by carrying out rigorous research. This is usually based on prior studies and work conducted in that topic. Contribution to knowledge is an important factor in any thesis whether it is a doctoral, postgraduate or undergraduate. However, there is more emphasis on contributing to knowledge at the doctoral level. Phillips and Pugh (1994, p. 34) point out that a contribution to knowledge 'does not mean an enormous breakthrough which has the subject rocking on its foundation.' However, the findings in a dissertation or thesis should be proof that the researcher has a good grasp of how such activity is done in the relevant field (Cryer, 2006). By reviewing the literature, you are able to show that you have a good knowledge of prior scholarly work and the gaps that other studies have not filled. Through this, you can contribute and fill those gaps in the field.

Contribution to knowledge could be in the form of an empirical nature, where you provide a novel account of an empirical phenomenon that challenges existing assumptions about the world or reveals something previously undocumented (Ågerfalk, 2014). It could also be of a theoretical nature, where you advance an existing theory or develop a new theory. Finally, it could be methodological, where you use different methodological traditions that past studies have not used to examine a phenomenon or concept.

3.4 Systematic literature review

Lately, there has been a lot of focus on systematic literature reviews. Such an approach to reviewing literature has its root in the health sciences and is linked to evidence-based practice. The first example of a systematic review was conducted in 1753 by James Lind, in his work titled *A Treatise of the Scurvy*. For him, it was important to provide an unbiased view of what had been published on scurvy and it was necessary to remove a great deal of rubbish (Lind, 1753).

Therefore, the uncovering of rubbish remains the focus of systematic reviews (Clarke and Chalmers, 2018). The traditional narrative literature review approach has been criticised for lacking criticality (Tranfield et al., 2003), and a systematic approach to reviewing literature has been proposed to counter this. Systematic literature reviews are now widely accepted as the most reliable source of knowledge from research. Scholars agree that systematic reviews allow us to refute poorly conducted research that provides a biased, inaccurate and unreliable presentation of evidence.

Although systematic reviews have been associated with health sciences, they have also been applied to the fields of business and management. Similar to health sciences there is now a strong demand in business and management for evidence-based approaches and solutions. As a result, a systematic literature review is seen as the answer to this conundrum.

Several scholars have proposed definitions for the systematic review of literature. A systematic literature review (SLR) has been defined as 'a replicable, scientific and transparent process; in other words, a detailed technology that aims to minimise bias through exhaustive literature searches of published and unpublished studies, and by providing an audit trail of the reviewer's decisions, procedures, and conclusions' (Tranfield et al., 2003, p. 209). According to Wright et al. (2007), a systematic review is a review of the evidence on a clearly formulated question that uses systematic and explicit methods to identify, select and critically appraise relevant primary research, and to extract and analyse data from the studies that are included in the review.

We define a systematic review as a comprehensive, transparent and unbiased assessment of the literature to answer clearly formulated review questions with an explicit and reproducible methodology. It involves planning a rigorous search strategy which identifies all relevant studies (both published and unpublished) that have a specific focus on the review questions. This is usually conducted over multiple databases and the findings reproduced by other scholars. The final intent of the systematic review is to extract, analyse and synthesise the findings from the studies obtained through the process.

Stages in a systematic literature review

A successful review involves three stages:

- Stage 1: Organising the review
- Stage 2: Carrying out the review
- Stage 3: Reporting the review

Stage 1: Organising the review

The first step in the organising stage involves identifying the need for the review. To do this, a scoping study of the literature in the field is required. It is important to consider whether a systematic literature review is needed before you embark on your project. Has someone already conducted a systematic literature review in your chosen topic? For example, two systematic literature reviews have been conducted on entrepreneurial leadership namely, Harrison et al. (2016) and Clark et al. (2019). If you intend to conduct a systematic review in this topic, you will need to ask yourself what is new I want to address that has not been provided by these two previous studies? If a systematic review answering your question has been conducted, you may need to refine your question if you plan to embark on the project.

Secondly, in order to reduce the risk of bias, an expert panel can be consulted at this stage. This usually comprises experienced scholars in the topic and can be a valuable resource in justifying the need for the systematic review and most importantly in developing and validating the review questions and protocol. You might ask people that have a good knowledge of the literature about their views of the research gap and current debates in the field based on the scoping study. This will be instrumental in the next phase which is the formulation of the review questions.

Formulating the review questions is a vital part of the organising stage in a systematic literature review. The review questions should be clear, concise and focused on your research. For example, what are the attributes of an entrepreneurial leader? It should not be too broad in scope, which could make it difficult to select a manageable number of studies. For example, what is leadership? This review question is too broad and will provide millions of studies that cannot be reviewed. Alternatively, it should not be so narrow that very few studies can be obtained from the search. For example, what are the attributes of an entrepreneurial leader in Hamilton, Scotland? This is too narrow and you will be lucky if you get any article that has examined this area.

As a result, identifying the right review questions can be an iterative process. Brereton et al. (2007) suggests using pre-review mapping to identify subtopics when preparing your review questions. This involves carrying out a quick mapping procedure to identify the nature of research activities related to the review questions.

However, we propose that you follow these steps. First, you need to select a topic that you intend to examine, e.g. entrepreneurial leadership. Carry out a scoping study of the literature on this topic. After this, you engage in a critical analysis about the topic and start asking questions about the area such as how has entrepreneurial leadership been studied in the last 30 years? Based on your critical analysis, you may come up with draft review questions after which you evaluate them by asking yourself the following:

- Are the questions clear?
- Are the questions focused?
- Are the questions concise?
- What will be my contribution to this topic area?

The final step in the organising phase is developing and validating the review protocol. A review protocol is a detailed plan which provides the rationale and methods to be adopted in conducting the systematic literature review. It is critical because it reduces the possibility of bias in data selection and analysis (Xiao and Watson, 2019) and can be used by other researchers to repeat and verify the study.

The review protocol should include:

- the rationale for the study
- the review questions
- inclusion and exclusion criteria

- databases and grey literature that will be used for your search
- search strategy
- quality assessment criteria
- strategies for data extraction, synthesis and reporting.

It is important that the review protocol is validated before use. This is one of the key roles of the expert panel that we discussed earlier. They play a key part in validating and amending the review protocol to ensure that it is fit for purpose.

A key component of the review protocol as stated above is the inclusion and exclusion criteria. This is an important part of the organising stage and provides the boundaries of the systematic review. One of the main factors that distinguishes a systematic literature review from a traditional narrative review is the provision of criteria for including and excluding studies in the review. In a narrative review, the criteria for selection are not explicitly put forward as is the case in systematic reviews.

The inclusion and exclusion criteria employed should be based on the purpose of the study and review questions. Studies that are not related to the intent of the review should be excluded. For example, you may decide to exclude papers that do not address one or more of the review questions that you have formulated for your study. It is also important that your inclusion criteria are not too broad or narrow as it may affect the outcome of the review process. The inclusion criteria should be able to identify the appropriate studies that would inform your project.

The inclusion and exclusion criteria can also be based on your research design and methodology. Depending on what you want to find out, you may decide to exclude studies that do not meet your design or methodological criteria. For example, a researcher who is investigating entrepreneurial intentions of university students in a developing country, might decide to exclude studies that have focused on developed countries.

Finally, beyond the purpose of the study, review questions, research design and methodology, other pragmatic criteria may be adopted. For example, you may exclude publications based on language. Studies in a language that you do not understand will not be relevant to you. It is very common in systematic reviews conducted by researchers in English speaking countries that English language is an inclusion criterion and publications written in other languages an exclusion criterion. Furthermore, the date range of publication can also be employed as a criterion for inclusion and exclusion especially if the date is important to your study. For example, the first study on entrepreneurial leadership was in 1987 and it is not surprising that the systematic literature reviews conducted within this topic had a starting date range of 1980.

Stage 2: Carrying out the review

This involves conducting an unbiased and extensive literature search of selected academic research databases using a search strategy.

Databases for the review

A research database is a catalogue with an organised collection of information or data such as journal articles, books, book chapters, essays and other professional resources. The databases you search depend on your review questions and the subject area/field. Typical databases used in business and management include Sage, Emerald, Web of Science, Taylor & Francis, Science Direct, SpringerLink and ABI/PROQUEST. In addition, Google Scholar is a very useful search engine and can be used to obtain additional literature especially that which is produced outside of the traditional publishing and distribution channels commonly known as grey literature.

Grey literature is literature that is not formally published as journal papers or books. Examples of grey literature include conference proceedings/abstracts/papers, websites, policy papers etc. Though they are not easily obtained from electronic academic databases they could be very valuable depending on the focus of your study and review questions. For example, if your study is focused on social media privacy, typical academic literature will not be sufficient. You may want to consider legislation such as The Data Protection Act 2018 and other policy reports.

It is important to keep note of the databases you will be employing in your research and the date range your search will encompass. The number of databases you need to search will also depend on what is used within your field. However, about eight are considered appropriate for a rigorous review in business and management (Harrison et al., 2016).

Depending on the topic, searching may go beyond databases and involve consulting key scholars and known experts in the subject area. You may decide to consult an expert to evaluate the databases and the search strategy (see below) to ensure that the process is rigorous and unbiased. This is similar to what we discussed earlier about validating the review protocol as the databases used are an important component of the protocol.

When using the databases, key literature that emerge from the search is selected, but it is important that a backward and forward search is also conducted to ensure that no relevant study is missed. A backward search involves looking at the references of the papers selected to see if there are studies that might be valuable in your work. The forward search involves flipping the coin and you are instead looking at the studies that have cited the papers you have identified. Google Scholar is quite useful in citation searches. The literature obtained from both searches will be added to your review.

Search strategy

It is important to conduct a scoping study before you commence your literature review. This will help you identify the key studies in the domain. You also need to take note of the keywords you used to retrieve those studies. These keywords will be useful in shaping your search strategy and strings for your systematic review. A search string is a combination of keywords, Boolean operators, truncation and wild cards that you use for the literature search. If the search strings you develop later are not able to retrieve these studies, it implies that your strings need some amendment.

In developing your search strategy, the keywords and search strings are critical. The keywords are usually developed from your review questions. For example, if your review question is 'what are the attributes of an entrepreneurial leader?' the keywords here could be attributes, entrepreneurial leader, leader. For each of these keywords, you will need to consider all the different terms that could be used to explain them. You also need to think about their synonyms, abbreviations, alternative spellings and plurals when coming up with your search strings.

Some keywords could retrieve too much or too little literature. For instance, using the keyword entrepreneurial leadership on Google Scholar will retrieve about 1.48 million results. This is not manageable, and you will need to amend the keyword. One way of modifying keywords is by using Boolean operators, truncations and wild cards.

Boolean operators are simple words such as AND, OR, NOT which are used as conjunctions to provide a more focused search. The Boolean operator AND provides literature with several words. For example, a search on Entrepreneurship AND attributes will offer results containing both words. The Boolean operator OR provides synonyms and will include at least one of the search terms. For example, a search on Challenges OR Abilities OR Capabilities OR Attributes OR Competencies OR Skills will only retrieve any of the above. While NOT is usually used to narrow the search. For example, Entrepreneurial Leadership NOT Transformational Leadership will retrieve literature only focused on entrepreneurial leadership.

Many electronic databases are configured to allow the use of Boolean operators. The success of the search strategy is dependent on how well you construct your search strings and use your Boolean operators. A good example of a search string using a couple of Boolean operators discussed is found below.

Entrepreneurial leadership AND challenges OR abilities OR capabilities OR competencies OR skills NOT traits NOT characteristics

Truncation and wild cards are also important in constructing your search strings. Truncations are used to retrieve various spellings of words. You place the symbol * after the root of the word and it will retrieve a couple of searches. For example, you might want to examine entrepreneurship, but some scholars might have referred to it as entrepreneur. To avoid losing such relevant literature, the root word Entrep can be used

Entrep* will retrieve entrepreneurship, entrepreneur, entrepreneurial etc.

For wild cards, you insert the symbol into your words. This is commonly used for variants of the words. These words have similar meaning but different spelling. For example, utili#e will retrieve utilize, utilise and utility. However, the symbols for trun-cation and wild cards may vary depending on the databases (i.e. *, #, ?) so it is best to verify before using on the databases.

Once the search strategy and the databases have been agreed, it is very important to document the date of the search, the databases employed, the search strings, the procedure and the number of results obtained. This will allow for other researchers who may be interested in your work to conduct the same search and reproduce your findings.

During the search of various databases, you will realise that some articles may emerge more than once. These are called duplicates. This does not necessarily mean that your search is not good, but it implies that the studies are quite relevant to your work based on the search strings and keywords constructed. You will need to take note of the duplicates and eliminate them when collating the cumulative number of articles to be reviewed.

Furthermore, as stated earlier, the citations (forward search) and the reference list (backward search) should also be used to retrieve more literature for your systematic review. You need to keep note of the articles obtained from both processes.

Screening for inclusion

Screening studies is an important part of conducting the review. It involves select-ing the literature that will be part of the review. The inclusion and exclusion criteria provided in the review protocol should be used to sift out the relevant studies and literature. Each article obtained from the search process must be assessed based on the inclusion and exclusion criteria.

Though it can be conducted by one person, more rigour is shown when it is done by two independent reviewers to avoid bias. If both reviewers disagree during the screening process about the literature to be included or excluded, a third independent reviewer should be assigned to resolve it and make the final decision.

The manuscripts obtained go through two levels of screening. The first phase is the abstract screening where the abstracts are examined to eliminate irrelevant studies. By having a quick read of the abstract, you will be able to decipher if the paper is related to your review questions and important to the overall purpose of your study. For example, you may notice that after the manuscripts have been retrieved through your well-developed search strings on entrepreneurial leadership from your databases, the abstracts of some of the papers do not show any relationship to the topic. It might have only been referred to in the title but the abstract, which is the snapshot of what has been written within the paper, does not allude to this. As a result, those papers must be excluded.

After the papers have gone through the abstract screening, you may then proceed to read the entire paper to ensure that it meets the inclusion criteria. If after reading the paper, you realise that it is not relevant to your study, it then needs to be excluded. Finally, the list of all excluded papers should be kept, ensuring validity and reproducibility.

Quality assessment

After you have selected the literature to include in your review, the next phase is quality assessment. This is the process of checking whether the papers selected have met the expected methodological quality. Different names such as checking internal validity have been used by other scholars (Petticrew and Roberts, 2008). Nevertheless, this stage is important as it ensures that the study is internally valid and free from methodological bias (Xiao and Watson, 2019). It is critical in finalising the collection of studies that will proceed for data extraction and synthesis.

Depending on the nature of the study (i.e. qualitative or quantitative), we propose that you ask the following questions and use as a check list for assessing the quality.

- Does the study report unambiguous findings based on evidence and argument?
- Has the research been conducted in a way that ensures minimum bias?
- Is the study relevant to your review question?
- Is the paper appropriately referenced?
- Is the sample strategy adopted by the study free from bias?

Similar to the screening process, we recommend that you have two independent reviewers who will assess the quality based on the criteria and if there is a disagreement then a third reviewer may serve as an arbitrator and make the final decision.

After the quality assessment phase is completed, all the papers that are deemed fit to be of an acceptable standard are recorded and the date of completion of the systematic review is noted.

Data extraction and synthesis

Once you have finalised the identity and number of the papers for the review, the next phase is extracting the data. A data extraction form should be used in this stage to make the process easier. Most researchers tend to use Microsoft Excel or other spreadsheets/software to facilitate this process.

The nature of the data to be extracted depends on your review questions and the synthesis method to be employed. If a meta-analysis which focuses on the quantitative aspect of the systematic review is to be used, then more quantitative data is extracted from the studies. However, if a thematic analysis is the synthesis approach to be adopted, which is more qualitative and inductive, then there will be more emphasis on coding.

We advise that for a comprehensive and rigorous systematic review, data should be extracted based on geographical distribution, type of study, method of data collection, number of publications, literature source, number of citations and most importantly the review questions.

Once the data extraction is complete, the next phase is to synthesise the data. This is where you address the review questions that you have proposed in your systematic review. There are three methods for synthesising data. The first is the descriptive analysis. The descriptive analysis is usually focused on quantitative and numerical data. This often requires a combination of tables, pie charts and bar charts to illustrate the relationship and to depict the key findings from the review in the form of geographical distribution, type of study, method of data collection, number of publications, literature source and number of citations. There is no limit to what the researcher can seek to provide in the form of descriptive analysis. The choice is dependent on what you deem important and relevant to your topic. However, we expect that every rigorous systematic review should provide a descriptive analysis.

The next form of synthesis is more connected to quantitative analysis and goes a step further to produce a forest report which is a graphical representation of the results of multiple studies that investigated the same questions and outcomes. This form of analysis is a meta-analysis. A meta-analysis is a research process used to synthesise systematically the findings of single independent studies using statistical methods to calculate an overall effect (Xiao and Watson, 2019). It involves the statistical combination of results from various studies. Data from different studies are weighed depending on the sample size and relevant criteria and evaluated to produce a cumulative outcome. It is not expected that every systematic review should proceed to a meta-analysis. This is more common in quantitative research.

The last form of synthesis is qualitative analysis. This method synthesises the findings from different types of studies using coding and eliciting themes. The review questions are addressed from the findings of the data and the themes are developed from the studies. A common approach adopted is the thematic analysis discussed in Chapter 10 which involves primary coding, explanatory coding and developing central themes. When all the information has been analysed and synthesised, it leads to the commencement of the final stage which is the reporting of the review.

Stage 3: Reporting the review

This involves writing and providing a summary of the available evidence. How you report your review will depend on your discipline and the methodological focus of your study. In the health sciences, a unique style of reporting is adopted; this can be seen in the Cochrane handbook. However, despite the discipline, it is expected that you produce a report with sufficient guidance and detail about the process. This is important to ensure that other researchers can reproduce and verify your findings. The report should include the review protocol employed, the inclusion and exclusion criteria, quality assessment criteria and all steps involved in conducting the systematic review. The report should provide directions for future research and the limitations of the systematic review process should be identified. A conclusion which draws on the findings of the review is required. Finally, every systematic review needs to be updated to ensure that it is quite recent, hence the researcher needs to take this into consideration.

3.5 The literature review process

The previous section provided an elaborate examination of the systematic review process. However, it might not always be the best approach to take because of the time-consuming nature of the process. Sometimes, very stringent inclusion and exclusion criteria may sift out some relevant literature especially grey literature. Furthermore, some philosophical positions such as interpretivism and methodological standpoints such as qualitative research may be more suited to a narrative review.

Narrative reviews offer a wider scope and are less focused. It is an examination of the literature to enhance the understanding of the subject area providing a vast impression of the topic. If your approach to theory and research is inductive rather than deductive or abductive, then a narrative review may be more suitable. As a result, it is not surprising that many qualitative studies which draw from an interpretivist philosophical stance tend to adopt a narrative literature review.

Regardless of whether you conduct a systematic or narrative literature review, we propose that every literature review should be critical. A critical review of the literature will provide strong foundation for your research. According to Saunders et al. (2012, p. 58), a critical review will need

- to include the key academic theories within your chosen area of research
- to demonstrate that your knowledge of your chosen area is up to date
- through clear referencing, to enable those reading your project report to find the original publications you cite.

The literature review you write should therefore be a critical analysis and evaluation of previous scholarly work. When writing your literature review, you need to focus on the purpose of the study and the research questions.

First, it should commence as a scoping study providing an initial impression of the literature before proceeding to the research aim, objectives and questions. It should then provide an outline of the key themes and draw on previous studies of the key scholars in the topic area. From these studies, you then discuss the relevant findings taking note of their methodological considerations and highlighting the gaps in their studies. After this, you propose where your own research can address these gaps. A typical literature review structure should reflect the above.

Searching for relevant literature

There are several literature sources which are important in your literature review to provide a good understanding of the subject area. There are three categories of literature namely, primary, secondary and tertiary literature.

Primary literature is usually articles or studies based on original research. For example, an empirical journal paper that examines how a university was able to address the challenges of the Covid-19 pandemic in their teaching delivery can be classified as a primary source. Primary literature includes journal articles, conference papers, dissertations, technical reports etc. that provide original findings and data.

Secondary literature is usually summaries of primary literature. It involves summarising and reviewing the findings of the original research reported in the primary literature. Examples of secondary data include review articles, systematic reviews, edited volumes, books. Secondary literature uses primary literature as its main source.

Finally, tertiary literature is summaries of mostly secondary sources and is used to provide a general overview of the subject. Examples include textbooks, encyclopedias, dictionaries and handbooks.

In conducting your literature, all these categories of literature will be important depending on the focus of your study. For example, if your study is on the motivation of employees, you might want to look at a book that examines the different types of motivation and theories to have a good understanding of the subject area before commencing the examination of primary literature. You might also want to look at review articles to identify the primary literature that has been identified in the subject area.

Nevertheless, regardless of the type of literature you focus on, a successful literature review is based on the search strategy that you adopt to sift out the relevant literature.

Identify the databases

A fundamental part of a literature review is a literature search, and this involves the use of catalogues and research databases. These catalogues and research databases provide access to information in the form of journal articles, books, book chapters and essays giving you an opportunity to probe deeper into your research. First, you need to identify the appropriate databases for conducting your research. The Internet has made it easy, and many journals can be obtained online, and you do not need to access them as hard copies in your library. Your library is usually a good starting point as they have online catalogues that can be used to identify the different categories of literature in that subject area.

However, many library catalogues are limited and do not have access to all the important databases. As a result, we recommend that you use it as a starting point and follow up by using other databases that are relevant to your discipline. Some of the popular business and management databases are listed in Box 3.1.

Box 3.1   Relevant databases

ABI/INFORM Database: A database comprised of ABI/INFORM Global, ABI/INFORM Trade & Industry, and ABI/INFORM Dateline. The collection features thousands of full-text journals, dissertations, working papers, key business and economics periodicals.

EBSCO: A database covering over 3,000 business and management journals. It provides vast access to industry and market reports.

ECONLIT: A database covering more than 1,000 economics publications. It is professionally classified, updated weekly, and includes over 1.6 million records.

EMERALD: A database of over 3,300 eBook titles and a portfolio of over 300 journals authored by renowned academics and industry leaders from over 150 countries.

GOOGLE SCHOLAR: It is not a database but a search engine. However, it is very useful in finding academic sources ranging from books, journal papers, to conference proceedings etc.

INGENTA CONNECT: A database covering about 5 million articles from 13,000 publications.

JSTOR: A database that provides access to more than 12 million journal articles, books, images and primary sources in 75 disciplines.

PSYCINFO: A database with over 2,250 journals covered in American Psychological Association (APA).

SAGE: A database with more than 900 journals and over 800 new books each year, spanning a wide range of subject areas.

SPRINGERLINK: A database covering over 1,200 peer-reviewed journals and 25 published book series containing a variety of topics in the sciences, social sciences, and humanities.

SOCIAL SCIENCES CITATION INDEX (SSCI): A database that contains over 3,400 journals across 58 social science disciplines, as well as selected items from 3,500 of the world's leading scientific and technical journals.

(Continued)

TAYLOR & FRANCIS: A database that has over 2,700 journals, including social science and humanities journals published by Routledge.

WEB OF SCIENCE: A database that contains over 21,100 peer-reviewed, high-quality scholarly journals published worldwide in over 250 sciences, social sciences, and arts & humanities disciplines.

Formulating an effective search strategy

For all these online relevant databases identified, you will need to work out a search strategy to apply. Please refer to the section on generating keywords in the systematic literature review. The success of the literature search will be based on the keywords and search strings used in the database. Extremely narrow keywords will provide very limited results while very broad ones will proffer an unmanageable number of studies. Keywords are the terms that guide the search for the relevant literature. They are usually based on the research aim, objectives and questions of your study. While generating keywords, you may use tertiary literature such as encyclopedias, dictionaries, textbooks and handbooks which provide an initial impression of the topic. This will be useful especially if you are unfamiliar with the topic area. You may also use secondary literature such as review articles that have summarised the primary research in the subject area. Your subject librarian, supervisor, lecturers, colleagues and other scholars may also be a valuable resource in developing and shaping your keywords.

While developing your keywords, you need to think of the synonyms, abbreviations and alternative spelling of the words. For example, enterprise development may be presented as entrepreneurship development in some publications. It is important that you can adapt and amend your keywords to enable more relevant findings. In most databases, the keywords can be maximised by using Boolean operators, truncations and wild cards (see section 3.4. on search strategy in systematic literature review).

Conducting your search

After the keywords have been generated you may then apply them within the databases identified. For systematic reviews, it is expected that you have inclusion criteria with a review protocol to help select the appropriate literature. However, in every literature review we suggest that parameters are produced to guide the search process. These parameters should include the type of publication (e.g., journal articles, conference papers, books etc.), publication period/timeframe and the focus on the research topic.

It is important that all the literature obtained from the search is recorded. Saunders et al. (2012) advise that for journal articles, the following should be noted:

- author or authors of the article
- date of publication
- title of the article
- title of the journal
- volume and part number of the journal issue
- page numbers of the article.

For other types of literature, it is important that you keep note of the relevant bibliographical details. This is discussed later in this chapter in section 3.6 on referencing.

Similar to systematic reviews, abstract screening is important. To ensure that you are obtaining the relevant literature, it is critical that you read the abstract to find out whether the article is relevant to your question. For example, a search on mental well-being might retrieve numerous studies especially from the health sciences; a quick abstract screening will be able to sift out the irrelevant articles. When you find a useful article, book or paper you may also check the reference list to find other relevant sources and take note of them. In addition, a citation search using Google Scholar is also a valuable resource and will help identify other studies that have cited the literature that you found.

Evaluating your literature

If the number of studies obtained is manageable after scanning through the abstracts, reference lists and citations, the next step is to evaluate the sources. This is very important as it ensures that the literature to be employed is relevant to your work. The most important criteria in your evaluation are your research aim, questions and objectives. It is important that the literature that will serve as the core of your review should contribute to it. We suggest that in your final selection of the literature, you ask yourself the following questions:

- Is this study relevant to my research aim, objectives and questions?
- Does this article or chapter provide an important contribution in terms of theoretical background?
- Are the methodological approach and design applied appropriate?
- Does the study report unambiguous findings either empirically or conceptually?
- How recent is the article or chapter?
- Has the article been cited severally by other scholars?
- How does the article or chapter support or contradict my arguments?

After you have evaluated the literature based on the questions and criteria above, then you can eliminate literature that does not meet your criteria. The literature that meets the criteria is noted and most importantly, read. While reading the article or chapter, you should be guided by the following questions:

- What is the focus of the article or chapter?
- What are the relevant theories underpinning the work?
- What methodological considerations and approaches were adopted?
- What were their findings?
- What were the gaps or weakness of their study?

After reading, we advise that you summarise each article or chapter as they pertain to your study taking into consideration these questions. The reason for this is to ensure that you carry out a critical analysis based on the literature. We suggest that after evaluating the articles you reflect on the following questions.

- What are the strengths of the themes of my chosen topic?
- What are the gaps and weaknesses in the literature?
- What are the recent developments and arguments in the literature?
- How do my research aim, objectives and questions contribute to the debate?
- Why is my proposed research important?
- What are the appropriate methodological approaches to adopt for this study?
- What are the limitations of my study?

Writing the literature review

A literature review is more than just providing a summary of the literature selected. Many students make that mistake and produce an exhaustive list of previous studies in the subject area. The presentation and structure of the literature review is important. The structure of your literature review will depend on the focus of the study. Some literature reviews may take a chronological perspective where the emphasis is on timeline and how later studies have built on earlier studies. This is only advisable if the subject area has few development paths as numerous paths may lead to chaos using this structure (Blumberg et al., 2011). You may also structure your review based on thematic categories and outcomes. If you have found some recurring themes, you can organise your literature review into sections that address them. For example, if you are reviewing literature about the challenges of enterprise development, key themes might include infrastructure issues, government support, cultural attitudes, finance barriers, family support etc. The review could also be structured based on the methodology. It involves discussing literature that has applied a variety of research methods and comparing their findings. Finally, the most common approach is adopting a theoretical structure where a conceptual framework is a product of the literature review. In this case, you discuss various theories, models and concepts that are important in your study.

Nevertheless, no matter what structure you decide to adopt, it is expected that every literature review should consist of an introduction, a main body and a conclusion.

- **Introduction:** The introduction should define the topic and state the intent of the literature review. It is important that you state the reason for conducting the literature review. Beyond your reason, it is critical that you also emphasise the significance of the topic. For example, the Covid-19 pandemic affected humanitarian supply chains; if you intend to focus on this area, you may want to accentuate its significance and importance. Within the introduction, you can also highlight the gaps in the literature evaluated. For example, you may have noticed that there are limited studies that have investigated employee well-being post-pandemic in the hospitality sector; this could be highlighted in the introduction. Finally, the introduction should also explain the organisation and sequence that the review will take.
- **Main Body:** This is the crux of the literature review and is usually divided into sections. The sections used will depend on the approach taken as discussed in the earlier paragraphs. The sections could be in chronological events, themes, methods or theories. Within the body of the literature review, it is expected that you synthesise the important parts of the literature and provide an overview of the main points. For example, what are the key things that scholars within this subject area have examined? It is vital that you analyse the literature and provide insight into the link between your chosen topic and prior studies. Finally, you will need to highlight the strengths and weaknesses of these literature sources to justify the importance of your study.
- **Conclusion:** In the conclusion, you summarise the key findings and significant facets of the literature to evaluate the current state of the field. Within the conclusion, you identify the gaps in existing knowledge and how your research will address them. You many then draw the literature review to a close by highlighting the areas for future research.

3.6 Referencing

Referencing is an important aspect of any academic enquiry. It shows that you are aware of the research within the field and most importantly, the contribution of other researchers within this space. When the idea is not yours you need to acknowledge the sources that it was obtained from. By so doing, you are recognising the intellectual right and contribution of that researcher.

Within your dissertation, research project or thesis, it is important that you provide reputable and quality references and citations. This is because the references show that you have a good understanding of the topic. It also demonstrates that you have examined the subject vastly to justify the gaps that your study will address. Furthermore, it shows that you have a good understanding of the methodological stance of prior studies and how yours fits within this area.

Every institution and subject discipline tend to have a recommended style of referencing. However, there are three widely used referencing styles namely Harvard, American Psychological Association (APA) and Modern Humanities Research Association (MHRA) system.

Harvard System

This is the most common referencing system in business and management. It was first widely used by Harvard University, hence its name. It involves placing the surname of the author(s) and the year of publication in parenthesis immediately after the idea or argument of the author in your work. If the idea has not been paraphrased and is stated the same way it was put forward by the author, then it must be put in quotation

Case 3.1   In-text citations using Harvard style

These are some fictitious examples of in-text citations based on the number of authors.

Table 3.1   Examples of in-text citations based on the number of authors

One author	Two authors	Three authors	Four or more authors	Corporate author
Motivation and trust are fundamental to successful leadership (Harrison, 2018).	Motivation and trust are fundamental to successful leadership (Harrison and Omeihe, 2018).	Motivation and trust are fundamental to successful leadership (Harrison, Omeihe and Clark, 2018).	Motivation and trust are fundamental to successful leadership (Harrison et al., 2018).	Motivation and trust are fundamental to successful leadership (BBC, 2018).
OR	OR	OR	OR	OR
Harrison (2018) argues that motivation and trust are fundamental to successful leadership	Harrison and Omeihe (2018) argues that motivation and trust are fundamental to successful leadership	Harrison, Omeihe and Clark (2018) argues that motivation and trust is fundamental to successful leadership	Harrison et al. (2018) argues that motivation and trust is fundamental to successful leadership	BBC (2018) argues that motivation and trust are fundamental to successful leadership

marks. In this case, the page number is included in addition to the author's surname and year of publication. For example, 'Entrepreneurial leadership is a type of leadership capable of identifying and exploiting opportunities in an entrepreneurial environment' (Harrison, 2018, p. 57). If there are more than three authors, et al. is used. More information about Harvard referencing is found in Case 3.3 and Case 3.4.

The references provided within the body of the work are usually referred to as citations. However, at the end of your dissertation, research project, thesis or paper, you are also supposed to provide full bibliographical information of the sources used in form of a reference list. The full bibliographical information provided depends on the type of literature that is being cited e.g. journal papers, books, book chapters, conference proceedings, internet sources, websites etc. It must be arranged in alphabetical order by the author(s)' surnames.

At times, you might be expected to present a bibliography and many students struggle to know the difference between a reference list and a bibliography. A reference list only includes sources you have referred to in the body of your text while a bibliography includes sources you have referred to in the body of your text and sources that were part of your background reading that you did not use in your work. Hence a bibliography usually contains more scholarly work than a reference list. However, it is recommended that a reference list is provided in the first instance and not a bibliography.

Case 3.2   Reference list using Harvard Style

These are some reference list guides of how Harvard referencing is used across different sources of literature

Book

Surname, Initial. (Year of publication) Title. Edition. Place of publication: publisher.

Chapter in edited book

Surname of chapter author, Initial. (Year of publication) 'Title of chapter', in Surname of book editor, Initial. (ed.) Title of book. Place of publication: publisher, Page number(s).

Journal article

Surname, Initial. (Year of publication) 'Title of article', Journal name, volume number (issue number), page reference. doi: doi number if available OR Available at: URL (Accessed date).

(Continued)

Newspaper article

Surname, Initial. (Year of publication) 'Title of article', Title of Newspaper, Day and month, Page number if available. Available at: URL (Accessed: date).

Webpage

Surname, Initial. (Year that the article/site was published) Title of web page. Available at: URL (Accessed: date).

Website

Organisation (Year that the page was last updated) Title of web page. Available at: URL (Accessed: date).

American Psychological Association (APA) System

This system is mainly used within the education, social and behavioural science field. It was introduced in 1929 by the American Psychological Association and is very similar to the Harvard system. It involves putting the author(s) surname, date of publication, page or page numbers at the end of the idea or argument of the author. One of the key variations from the traditional Harvard style is the citation of websites. It is not compulsory to include an access date when the page content is not going to change over time. Apart from this, most of referencing requirements for both systems are the same.

Modern Humanities Research Association (MHRA) System

This system is mainly used in the field of humanities. It was introduced by the Modern Humanities Research Association. Unlike the Harvard and APA system that uses parenthesis for referencing, this approach uses superscript numbers in the text. A superscript number is placed closed to the idea or argument by the author and the full reference list is then placed at the foot note or the end of the page. An example of the MHRA system is:

[1] Kingsley Obi Omeihe, Amon Simba, David Rae, Veronika Gustafsson, Mohammad Saud Khan, 'Trusting in indigenous institutions: Exporting SMEs in Nigeria', *Journal of Small Business and Enterprise Development* 28: 7 (2021), 1117–1142 (p. 1119).

Finally, there is numerous software that is available to assist with referencing and retrieving the full bibliographical details of the literature that you cite. EndNote, Medeley and Zotero are very popular and are widely used reference management software. Your university may have the licence for one of these software so always consult your subject librarian in the first instance.

3.7 Summary

- A literature review is an important component of any academic enquiry or research project. It is the selective analysis, synthesis and critical evaluation of the existing literature in your chosen topic area which helps you to identify the relevant gaps, theories and methods that inform your proposed project and justifies the significance of your study.
- Literature reviews are conducted for a range of purposes, and they affirm engagement and knowledge of previous scholarly work in the field.
- Systematic literature reviews are now widely accepted as the most reliable source of knowledge of research and are a good way to refute poorly conducted studies.
- Narrative reviews have been critiqued for their lack of criticality but regardless offer a wide scope and can be used to provide a vast impression of the topic.
- Regardless of the type of literature review, it is important that it is critical. It should be a critical analysis and evaluation of previous scholarly work and should focus on the purpose of the study and the research questions.
- There are several literature sources which you need to consider in your review and they include primary, secondary and tertiary literature.
- Every successful literature search is dependent on the catalogues, databases and keywords employed so it is important that you formulate an effective search strategy.
- Evaluating your literature is important to ensure that the literature to be examined is relevant to your work. The most important criterion in your evaluation is the focus on your research aim, questions and objectives.
- The presentation and structure of the review is critical. The structure of your literature review will depend on the focus of the study. Nevertheless, it is expected that every literature review should consist of an introduction, main body and a conclusion.
- Referencing is an important component of any academic enquiry and referencing styles such as Harvard, APA and MHRA are useful in recognising the intellectual rights and contributions of other scholars.

Self-check questions

1. What is a literature review?
2. Why do you conduct a literature review?
3. What is a systematic literature review?
4. What are the pros and cons of conducting a systematic literature review?
5. What are the main reasons for conducting a narrative review?
6. In what type of research is the narrative review more appropriate?
7. What are primary, secondary and tertiary literature?
8. When evaluating literature what should you consider?
9. Why is referencing important to your work?
10. What are the three most common referencing styles used in any academic enquiry?

Questions for review and discussion

1. Discuss how you would conduct your systematic literature review using the three-stage process discussed namely, organising your review, carrying out the review and reporting the review.
2. Think about the research topic that you would like to undertake and formulate an effective search strategy to retrieve the relevant literature.
3. Write a critical review on a research topic employing the literature process discussed in this chapter.

Self-check answers

1. A literature review is the selective analysis, synthesis and critical evaluation of the existing literature in your chosen topic area so as to identify the relevant gaps, theories and methods which informs your proposed project and justifies the significance of your study.
2. A literature review serves the following eight purposes:

   o   To know what other scholars have written about in that area
   o   To understand the nature and context of the problem
   o   To learn about the related theories and ideas that have been applied to the chosen topic

    o   To identify the important variables relevant to the subject

    o   To learn about the research methods, approaches, designs and strategies that have been adopted in studying this area

    o   To rationalise the significance of the problem

    o   To demonstrate the originality and novelty of your research project

    o   To show how your work will contribute to the chosen area and field.

3. A systematic review is a comprehensive, transparent and unbiased assessment of the literature to answer clearly formulated review questions with an explicit and reproducible methodology. It involves planning a rigorous search strategy which identifies all relevant studies (both published and unpublished) that have a specific focus on the review questions.

4. Systematic reviews allow us to refute poorly conducted research that provides a biased, inaccurate and unreliable presentation of evidence. It is a very reliable source of knowledge as the process is transparent, unbiased and replicable. However, it might not always be the best approach to take because of the time-consuming nature of the process. Sometimes, very stringent inclusion and exclusion criteria may sift out some relevant literature especially grey literature.

5. Narrative reviews offer a wider scope and are less focused. They are an examination of the literature to enhance the understanding of the subject area providing a vast impression of the topic.

6. If your approach to theory and research is inductive rather than deductive or abductive, then a narrative review may be more suitable. As a result, it is not surprising that many qualitative studies which draw from an interpretivist philosophical stance tend to adopt a narrative literature review.

7. Primary literature is usually articles or studies based on original research. For example, an empirical journal paper that examines how a university was able to address the challenges of the Covid-19 pandemic in their teaching delivery can be classified as a primary source. Primary literature includes journal articles, conference papers, dissertations, technical reports etc. that provide original findings and data. Secondary literature is usually summaries of primary literature. It involves summarising and reviewing the findings of the original research reported in the primary literature. Examples of secondary data include review articles, systematic reviews, edited volumes and books. Secondary literature uses primary literature as its main source. Finally, tertiary literature is summaries of mostly secondary sources and is used to provide a general overview of the subject. Examples include textbooks, encyclopedias, dictionaries and handbooks.

(Continued)

8. When evaluating the literature, the following questions should be asked:

    o   Is this study relevant to my research aim, objectives and questions?
    o   Does this article or chapter provide an important contribution in terms of theoretical background?
    o   Is the methodological approach and design applied appropriate?
    o   Does the study report unambiguous findings either empirically or conceptually?
    o   How recent is the article or chapter?
    o   Has the article been cited severally by other scholars?
    o   How does the article or chapter support or contradict my arguments?

9. Referencing is an important aspect of any academic enquiry. It shows that you are aware of the research within the field and most importantly, the contribution of other researchers within this space. When the idea is not yours you need to acknowledge the sources from which it was obtained. By so doing, you are recognising the intellectual right and contribution of that researcher.

10. Every institution and subject discipline tends to have a recommended style of referencing. However, there are three widely used referencing styles namely Harvard, American Psychological Association (APA) and Modern Humanities Research Association (MHRA) system.

Further reading

Harrison, C., Paul, S. and Burnard, K. (2016) Entrepreneurial leadership: a systematic literature review. *International Review of Entrepreneurship*, 14(2), 235–64 https://www.senatehall.com/entrepreneurship?article=544

Hart, C. (2009) *Doing a Literature Review*. 8th ed. London: Sage.

Sawyerr, E. and Harrison, C. (2019) Developing resilient supply chains: lessons from high-reliability organisations. *Supply Chain Management: An International Journal*, 25(1), 77–100 https://doi.org/10.1108/SCM-09-2018-0329

Shorten, A. and Shorten, B. (2013) What is meta-analysis? *Evidence-Based Nursing*, 16(1), 3–4.

Tranfield, D., Denyer, D. and Smart, P. (2003) Towards a methodology for developing evidence-informed management knowledge by means of systematic review. *British Journal of Management*, 14(3), 207–22.

4

Research Philosophical Perspectives and Approaches

Learning outcomes

By the end of this chapter, you should be able to:

- understand key philosophical research assumptions
- identify and determine the meaning and relevance of various philosophical perspectives
- identify and differentiate between the three main research approaches.

4.1 Introduction

In this chapter, we will examine research philosophies and approaches. Here, we will attempt to capture how one can suitably distinguish between the underpinning assumptions shaping research. Much of this chapter is concerned with the nature of philosophical perspectives, the nature of research approaches and their relevance to research methodologies. If you recall in the research wheel (see Chapter 1), we acknowledged that decisions about qualitative research questions can be located within the 'research wheel' – which is the lens through which a variety of considerations can be made regarding data collection and analysis techniques. The discussions over the past years have often commenced with consideration of the research philosophy, its meaning, and the various types. We will also commence here, shifting later to examining research approaches.

4.2 Distinctions of research philosophies

In the context of social sciences, historically, much emphasis has been placed on three essential ontological, epistemological and axiological issues. Ontological issues pertain to our understanding of the social world and the assumptions we make about the nature of social reality. Epistemological issues are concerned with the nature of knowledge and the methods used to learn about social reality. Axiological issues, on the other hand, revolve around the role of values in the research process. These three perspectives play a crucial role in shaping how we approach research philosophy.

However, the concept of research philosophy itself requires further exploration, and that is the primary objective of this chapter. In simple terms, research philosophy refers to the researcher's beliefs about how data should be collected, analysed and used. It encompasses the philosophical commitments that underpin the researcher's perception of the world. These beliefs serve as the foundation for the researcher's actions and guide their choice of research strategy and methods.

In essence, research philosophy is a set of fundamental beliefs that influence how researchers view the world and seek to attain true knowledge about it. Every research study is built upon these underlying philosophical assumptions, regardless of whether the researcher explicitly acknowledges them. Thus, understanding and articulating one's research philosophy is crucial as it shapes the overall approach to conducting the study and justifies the chosen methodologies. It is the cornerstone that grounds the researcher's inquiries into the nature of reality and the quest for knowledge.

The term philosophy alludes to the set of assumptions and beliefs that underpin the development of a particular study (Saunders et al., 2016). It refers to the philosophical commitments which embody the perception of the researcher. Such commitments are not contingent on the research being philosophically informed, but on how the researcher reflects and justifies certain philosophical choices in relation to other available alternatives. In stimulating concerns about philosophical commitments, Easterby-Smith et al. (2015) provide four important reasons for understanding the philosophical issues.

First, the investigator can understand the key issues of epistemology, thus revealing the reflexive role of the investigator in the research method. It will be argued that in relation to knowledge, such clarity is essential to making a creative contribution to the field of study. Second, an in-depth understanding of the adopted philosophy enables the clarification of the research design. Such clarifications will be shown to reflect good answers to the central questions being investigated. Third, by having knowledge of the philosophical commitments, researchers would recognise which designs would be most appropriate for their study. Lastly, it helps researchers identify and develop designs that may be outside their prior experience, thereby allowing for an adaptation of the research design to the constraints of different knowledge structures or subjects.

Accordingly, there exist enduring debates about research philosophies. To understand the philosophical viewpoints, it is important to be aware of the assumptions under which each philosophy is based. Such an appreciation ensures that the researcher is aware of the assumptions which distinguish research philosophies.

The central argument among philosophers is focused on matters concerning ontological and epistemological assumptions. Central to the ontological assumption concerns the essence of the phenomena being investigated (Blumberg et al., 2014; King and Horrocks, 2012; Shane and Venkataraman, 2000). This includes the nature of the social world and the way it would be investigated. Burrell and Morgan (2005) assert that researchers are faced with basic ontological questions which probe whether reality is a product of the researcher's cognition; or if reality is a given 'out there' in the world. Associated with the philosophical nature of research is a second set of assumptions referred to as epistemology. This refers to a theory of knowledge that enables the researcher to understand the most unique way of enquiring about the nature of the social world (Easterby-Smith et al., 2015). Epistemology concerns assumptions about what constitutes legitimate and valid knowledge, and how this can be communicated to others (Burrell and Morgan, 2005; Saunders et al., 2016). This includes what forms of knowledge can be gathered, and how the researcher validates between the dichotomy of 'true' or 'false.'

Further associated with the ontological and epistemological debates is a third set of assumptions concerning axiology. Axiology refers to the role of ethics and values in the research process. This includes how researchers deal with their own values and those of the research participants (Heron and Reason, 1997; Saunders et al., 2016). The three sets of assumptions described above have a direct effect on the methodological nature of any study (Burrell and Morgan, 2005). At this juncture, researchers are inclined to draw from various ontological and epistemological assumptions when deciding the choice of methodology. This is pertinent as knowledge of key philosophies is necessary for accomplishing a given research.

The central point is that philosophy encompasses three main components:

- Epistemology: *asks, how do we know the world?*
- Ontology: *queries the nature of reality*
- Axiology: *focuses on how knowledge of the world is acquired*

In the next section, we introduce them as the three major ways by which a researcher can consider the research process.

Epistemology

Epistemology – or the theory of knowledge – is a philosophical perspective simply concerned with knowledge. In philosophy, knowledge implies having a clear or complete idea of someone or something, which may include any of the following: *'facts* or *knowing that'* (propositional knowledge), *'objects* or *knowing by acquaintance'* (acquaintance knowledge) and *'skills* or *knowing how'* (procedural knowledge) (Bengson and Moffett, 2011). Although knowing how or skills and knowing by acquaintance and objects have been invoked in a variety of epistemological contexts, the emphasis on epistemology is particularly concerned with propositional knowledge or what constitutes acceptable facts. In this sense, propositional knowledge is usually expressed in an indicative or declarative manner. 'I know that cows and wolves are mammal' is paradigmatic.

One way to make the distinction clearer is to indicate that epistemology refers to assumptions about what should be regarded as acceptable facts or knowledge in a given discipline. A similar but more elaborate version is that epistemology refers to theories about what is known, or what we can know (Bell et al., 2022). It should be noted that epistemologists seek to capture the essential but defining constituents of knowledge. Their central questions focus on the origins of knowledge, where the experience is generated, the relationship between knowledge, certainty and the impossibility of error and the changing forms of knowledge. The typical epistemological questions as Woleński (2004) argues, revolve around the following: what does knowledge mean? can it be achieved? is it based on reason or sense? what are its limits? Nevertheless, any profitable discussions on epistemology must do well to recognise that its mission as the theory of knowledge is to clarify what knowledge involves, its application, and an explanation of why it has the features it does (Rescher, 2003). This is because it relates to how one has access to the right information. This, however, can happen in various ways. In general terms, a pertinent question in this context is whether or not the social world can or should be studied according to the same principles as the natural sciences (Bell et al., 2022). It must be noted that two contrasting positions stand out; these are positivist and interpretivist philosophies (also referred to as phenomenology). Both philosophies are perceived as two opposite ends of a continuum. Between both positions lie realism and pragmatism, which incorporate principles from both philosophies. The position that affirms the stance of the natural scientist is invariably associated with an epistemological position known as positivism. We will deal with this in the next section.

Positivism

Positivism traces its history to great theorists such as Auguste Comte and Émile Durkheim. From the 1930s through to the end of 1960s, it remained the dominant epistemological perspective. Its central argument was that reality is out there to be studied, captured and understood (Denzin and Lincoln, 2003; Gray, 2020). This focal concept contends that the social world exists externally, while its properties should be measured objectively rather than through reflections (Crotty, 1998; Easterby-Smith et al., 2015; Saunders et al., 2023). As a matter of fact, the principle of positivism reflects the stance of the natural scientist who, in generating a research strategy for the collection of data, would likely use existing theories to develop a set of hypotheses.

From a positivist position, it is assumed that reality exists independently and thus the job of the researcher is to eliminate alternative explanations using experiments. This can be measured precisely through a verification of a predetermined hypothesis. With the positivist view, the research process commences by identifying causalities and testing to determine if such causalities can be generalised. In fact, this explains why most positivist studies often neglect other aspects of a phenomenon, by singling out one explanation (Blumberg et al., 2014). The logic of the positivist is deductive because it replicates the process of experimentation adopted in physical sciences (Bryman and Bell, 2015).

Table 4.1   **Assumptions shaping Positivism**

Philosophical Assumptions of Positivism: *Summary*

- Reality consists of what can be seen, smelt and touched. Only knowledge confirmed through the senses can be considered as knowledge.
- There is reality out there to be studied, captured and understood.
- Enquiries should be based on scientific observations.
- Researchers should be independent and must progress through hypothesis and deductions.
- Knowledge is attained through the gathering of facts tom provide the basis for laws.
- All explanations should show causality. The goal here is to identify casual explanations that explain human social behaviour.
- Research should be conducted in an objective manner.
- Concepts need to be defined such that they can be measured.
- The researcher must be independent of what is being observed.

Realism

Another epistemological position worth exploring, relates to realism. It aims to provide an account of the nature of scientific practice. A striking position is that the picture which science captures of the world is accurate and valid. For realism, this implies that there is reality which is independent of the mind. It assumes similarities with positivism in its approach to knowledge development. In fact, it shares two distinct features with positivism. The first assumes that similar approaches to data collection and explanation can be applied to social and natural sciences, while the second feature contends that there exists another reality different from our description of it (Bell et al., 2022). Viewed in this perspective, let us proceed to examine two forms of realism: (a) critical realism and (b) direct realism.

a. *Critical realism:* contends that the way the world is viewed depends to a large extent on one's beliefs and expectations, and as such, may hinder the emergence of the complete truth (Gray, 2020). The nature of critical realism has been articulated to suggest that our experiences are unreal and perhaps, mere figments or illusions shaped by our sensations. Critical realists argue that we would be able to understand and change the world, when we can identify the specific structures that generate the events and discourses. However, these structures would only be identified via the practical and theoretical work of the social sciences (Bhaskar, 1989). The main message here is that in critical realism, there is the thing itself and the sensation it conveys and secondly, there exists the mental processing that continues much longer after the sensation catches up with the senses (Saunders et al., 2023). Overall, critical realism recognises that social conditions have consequences whether observed by social scientists or not, however it acknowledges that concepts are products of human constructions (Easterby et al., 2015).

b. *Direct realism:* At this stage, it is useful to address the second form of realism. Indeed, we have so far understood that critical realists make a case that what we would normally experience are mere sensations, which are indeed images of the things in the real world, but not the things directly. Direct realism on the other hand, implies that what you see is what you get. This suggest that what is experienced through our senses, portrays the world in its real sense. Yet, the question naturally arises as to how direct realism differs from critical realism. As Saunders and colleagues have appositely remarked, the direct realists believe that the world is unchanging and operates at a certain level (the individual, the group or the organisation). However, the critical realist, on the other hand, recognises the essence of multi-level studies (for example, at the level of the individual, the group and the organisation). Unlike the critical realist, a direct realist would argue what we call illusions are because one has insufficient information available.

Interpretivism

Consequently, interpretivism that emerged in critique of the positivist philosophy emphasises a richer interpretation of social contexts. As an alternative to the positivist orthodoxy, it subsumes the views of scholars who have been critical about the application of scientific experiments to the study of the social world. Unlike positivism, interpretivism is underpinned by three basic principles: (1) the social context is constructed and given meaning subjectively; (2) The investigator is part of what is observed; (3) the research study is driven by interests. Interpretivists share the view that aspects of the social world should be described through a detailed account of specific social relationships or settings (King and Horrocks, 2012). One thing that is clear is that the researcher can uncover the experiences and understanding of people from vantage points. This implies that the researcher can reflect on the distinctiveness of the respondents.

Historically, interpretivism draws on ideals of the German intellectual tradition of Verstehen in sociology and hermeneutics, and critiques of positivism and scientism. At the root, this implies that interpretivism is all about a contextualised meaning. As rightly pointed out by Schwandt (1999), interpretivists argued for the uniqueness of human inquiry. They assume that social reality should be socially constructed and should be based on the process of interpreting and re-interpreting the intentional, meaningful behaviour of actors – with the researcher inclusive. By taking an interpretivist stance, what is important to know is that one shares the belief in the limitations of positivism, because it provides grounds to uncover surprising findings outside the context being investigated.

On our part, we do agree that interpretivism offers explanations of the social world which are often reflected in one's motives and beliefs. This is because it involves openness and dialogue. Indeed, the knowledge drawn from interpretivism is value laden because it represents an intertwinement of facts and values. Particularly worth stressing is the notion that interpretivism reveals dimensions of lived experience, but more importantly it recognises that reality is perceived through multiple mental constructions shared among individuals (Lincoln and Guba, 2000).

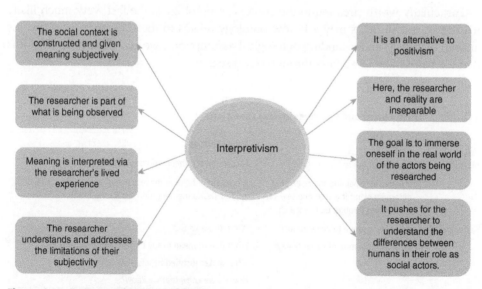

Figure 4.1   Features of Interpretivism

Ontology

The discussion presented in the earlier part of this chapter leads to the known fact that the central argument among philosophers is focused on matters concerning ontological and epistemological assumptions. While epistemology seeks to understand '*what it means to know,*' ontology on the other hand, seeks to uncover '*what is.*' A noteworthy depiction is aptly pointed out by Marsh and Stoker (2002: 11) who state that 'ontology is concerned with what we can know about the world and epistemology is concerned with how we can know it.' However, it is worth noting that the central ontological assumption concerns the essence of the phenomena being investigated. In particular, the nature of the social world and the way it would be investigated.

Clearly what the above discussion tends to demonstrate is that ontology is concerned with the nature of reality and assumptions made about what it means for something to exist. As a matter of fact, it raises the essential question about the nature of reality. And more importantly, it seeks to know the form of reality and what can be known about it. As echoed by Bell et al. (2018), an important query addressed by ontology is whether the social phenomenon that one seeks to uncover should be understood as existing objectively, external to observers, or made real by the interpretations which observers attach to them. Acknowledging this much, Burrell and Morgan (2005) assert that researchers are faced with basic ontological questions which probe whether reality is a product of the researcher's cognition; or if reality is a given 'out there' in the world. These are the basic assumptions a researcher makes about the nature of reality.

Particularly worth stressing in the context of ontology is the fact, very much likely to persist, that students may ask how ontology relates to their research. The obvious answer is that by understanding ontological assumptions, we can determine what it is that we would like to address through our research.

Table 4.2   **Ontological and Epistemological Questions**

	Ontology	**Epistemology**
Meaning	Focuses on the nature of reality	Focuses on the theory of knowledge
	It is useful in helping the researcher determine what it is that one seeks to understand through their research.	It is useful in helping the researcher understand the best approaches to inquiring into the nature of the world.
Assumptions	What is out there to know about?	What do we know?
	What is the nature of social reality?	What does it mean to say that we know something?
		What makes justified beliefs justified?
		How do we know that we know?

Further, understanding ontology can be largely effective because it enables us determine how to uncover the true nature of reality. Nevertheless, an understanding of ontology would be incomplete with an understanding of its two main aspects. It is relevant to point out that these two ontological aspects have, over the years, been the primary field of interest to scholars. The central argument relates to whether social entities can exist in reality to social actors connected with their existence (*objectivism*); or whether social phenomena are created from the social perception and action of actors connected with their existence (*subjectivism*). We will discuss in more detail the differences between objectivism and subjectivism.

Objectivism and subjectivism

The ontological position of objectivism contends that social phenomena exist beyond the influence of social actors. It holds that reality does exist independently of the consciousness of the social actor. It bears emphasis that we should strive to eliminate all subjective elements about one's perception about reality. This portrays that an objective reality exists externally to social actors. As pointed out by Bunge (1993), objectivism does not imply the rejection of reality, rather it encourages one to study it objectively. It is immediately apparent that for subjectivism, social phenomena are formed from the perception and deeds of social actors.

Table 4.3 Ontological Positions and meanings

Ontological positions	Meanings
Objective	Holds that reality does exist independently of the consciousness of the social actor. It bears emphasis that we should strive to eliminate all subjective elements about one's perception about realty.
Subjective	Holds that the world is a creation of knowing the subject and draws on the explanations of differences in opinion

More precisely, subjectivism is of the view that the world is a creation of knowing the subject and draws on the explanations of differences in opinion. To put this in perspective, a statement can be acknowledged to be subjective if it involves one's feelings or beliefs. On the other hand, a statement can be recognised as objective if it is impersonal and proceeds to predict or explain facts occurring in the external world by relying on the works of others. For example, '*The pound sterling lost its value last week*' is an objective statement, whereas '*The loss in value of the pound sterling make me sad*' is a subjective one.

Figure 4.2   **Two contrasting ontological positions**

Both positions are accepted as producing valid knowledge

Pragmatism

Derived from the Greek word *pragma*, loosely translated to mean action, is the source of derived words such as practice and practical (James, 2000). As a contending philosophical position, pragmatists generally reject the claim that a true statement or otherwise believed, is one that captures the world as it really is (Godfrey-Smith, 2015). As a matter of fact, it is a striking feature in the discussions about pragmatism that the nature of knowledge, meanings and beliefs should be considered in terms of their practical usage and successes. Consequently, proponents of pragmatism argue that knowledge and understanding should be sourced from direct experience.

The way pragmatism is usually presented suggests that it does not recognise that people can construct their truth out of nothing, nor does it recognise that there are predetermined truths that underpin knowledge and truth (Easterby-Smith et al., 2015). There are admittedly several key points that must be noted here: first, for pragmatism, specific beliefs and general methods of inquiry should be judged by their usefulness in achieving set goals. Secondly, our knowledge is interpretive and shaped by how people cope within the contexts in which they find themselves (Carlsen and Mantere, 2007). Note carefully that for pragmatism, an ideology can be accepted as true only if it works or produces positive societal consequences such as promoting peace, equality and freedom (Gray, 2020).

In recent times, there has been a growing call for scholars to move beyond traditional mono-method approaches, such as solely relying on qualitative or quantitative methods, and to embrace more mixed method approaches. The rationale behind this shift is the recognition that mixed methods can address research questions in ways that singular approaches may not fully achieve (Pansiri, 2005). For researchers who are unfamiliar with the concept of pragmatism, it is important to consider its value when research questions do not explicitly align with either positivist or interpretivist philosophies, or when it is challenging to separate them from both. Pragmatism can serve as a useful framework in such cases (see Figure 4.3). The core idea of pragmatism is that knowledge claims emerge from actions and social situations that are socially constructed through institutionalisation and socialisation processes. Therefore, perception plays a central role in the inquiry.

Since philosophical debates can often be endless, adopting pragmatism as a philosophical position allows researchers to employ strategies that effectively address research questions rooted in both positivist and interpretivist perspectives. By embracing a pragmatic view, scholars who favour mixed methods can navigate the complexities of research questions that encompass a range of philosophical underpinnings.

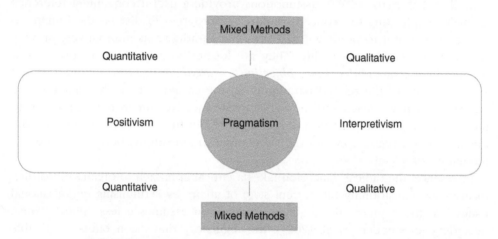

Figure 4.3   **Pragmatism as choice**

Research paradigms

Over the past few decades, the concept of paradigms as belief systems guiding actions has gained significant attention. Paradigms are seen as principles resulting from human constructions, shaping our understanding of the world, our place in it, and the possible relationships we have with it. As Guba and Lincoln (1994) aptly point out, paradigms represent a worldview that defines our perception of reality. Some beliefs within paradigms are accepted on faith, as they cannot be proven in conventional ways or verified for their truthfulness.

The discourse surrounding paradigms has been spurred by diverse perspectives. Guba and Lincoln, for instance, present a comprehensive framework that includes three essential elements of paradigms: epistemology (how we know the world), ontology (questions about the nature of reality), and methodology (how we acquire knowledge about the world). Additionally, the work of Burrell and Morgan (1979) contributes to the understanding of paradigms by identifying four distinct paradigms: functionalist, interpretive, radical humanist and radical structuralist. These paradigms are characterised by their meta-theoretical assumptions, which prove valuable in approaching social theory.

A key aspect emphasised in this discussion is that paradigms serve as useful tools for understanding social phenomena and providing comprehensive explanations. Each paradigm offers a unique lens to view the world, allowing for a distinctive and valuable perspective on social-scientific reality.

Given these insights and in spite of what seem to be contrasts in perspective, Burrell and Morgan's (1979) assumptions provide a useful convenient reference point for explicating the concept. Before we progress to discuss the four paradigms, it is useful to point out that the four paradigms as alternatives, provide different views of social reality. They are located and arranged to match four unique dimensions (*subjectivist, objectivist, radical change and regulation*) that subsume each of the related paradigms. In the earlier part of this chapter, you will recall that we discussed the subjectivist-objective dimension in relation to the nature of science. However, largely ignored in the scholarly debates are the dimensions on regulation and radical change. Interestingly, both are related to the nature of society.

In essence, the radical dimension takes a critical approach to organisational life, focusing on transforming the current state of affairs by scrutinising organisational issues. On the contrary, the regulatory dimension assumes a less critical stance. According to Saunders et al. (2023), the regulatory dimension offers a valuable understanding of how organisations are regulated and offers recommendations for their enhancement.

It is noteworthy that in terms of dimensions, the quadrant map in Figure 4.4 shows that although each paradigm shares joint features with others on the vertical and horizontal axis, they are assumed to be distinct entities as they offer differing viewpoints about social phenomena. This makes them mutually exclusive. Let's work through the paradigms below.

The functionalist paradigm

As per Burrell and Morgan's (1979) framework, the functionalist paradigm holds a dominant position rooted in the objectivist perspective and is closely associated with sociology. Its pragmatic orientation makes it highly effective in offering practical solutions to societal issues while generating knowledge. In essence, the functionalist paradigm is best suited for providing explanations of social order, status quo, solidarity and actualisations. Within the quadrant, it lies between the objectivist and regulatory dimensions.

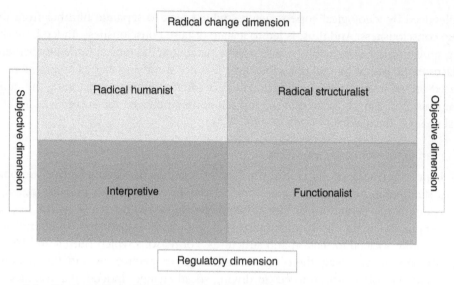

Figure 4.4   Four paradigms for the analysis of social theory

Source: Adapted from Burrell and Morgan (1979: 22), *Sociological Paradigms and Organisational Analysis.*

The interpretive paradigm

The first thing to point out in this respect is that the interpretive paradigm is subjective in nature. It is thus relevant as it seeks to understand the fundamental nature of the world through a subjective lens. This is particularly true given the fact that it views the world as a product of an emergent social process developed by the concerned individuals. And even to the extent that by being located within subjectivity and individual consciousness, it seeks an understanding of the participant rather than the observer of the action. In keeping with Burrell and Morgan (1979), the interpretive paradigm challenges the essence of ontological assumptions that underpin functionalist approaches to the study of organisations. This is because it views the ontological status of the world as problematic and questionable. The interpretive paradigm is located in the bottom left-hand corner within the subjectivist and regulatory dimensions.

The radical humanist paradigm

In the same vein, it may be remarked that the radical humanist paradigm is defined by its subjectivist standpoint. It is evident that it shares much in common with the interpretivist paradigm as it views the social world from an anti-positivist and nominalist lens. As Burrell and Morgan (1979) point out, the radical humanist paradigm espouses the importance of transcending the limitations of social arrangements. Precisely for this reason, this paradigm is underpinned by the consciousness that a person is influenced by ideological superstructures which seek to separate him/her from their true consciousness. And thus, is led to a state of false consciousness. Indeed, by sharing similar foundations with the interpretive paradigm, the radical humanist paradigm places emphasis on human consciousness. It is not surprising that its assumptions are based on the inversion of the functionalist paradigm. Within the quadrant, the radical humanist paradigm is located in the top left corner, between the subjectivist and radical change dimensions.

The radical structuralist paradigm

An important feature of the radical structuralist paradigm is that it advocates an objectivist standpoint. Although it shares some similarities with the functionalist paradigm, its assumption is centred upon structural relationships within a realist world. In effect, this emphasises that radical structuralists seek to provide explanations of interrelationships within societal formation and structures. For reasons which Burrell and Morgan (1979) have made clear, there exist conflicting perspectives within the paradigm regarding the role of social forces in driving social change. Indeed, the argument for some focuses on deep-seated contradictions. Among others by contrast, it is focused on the structure of power relations. Nonetheless, the consensual view across the board is that society is shaped by conflicts which lead to radical changes through economic and political issues. The assumption here is that emancipation from social structures occurs via such conflicts. Within the quadrant, the radical structuralist paradigm is in the top right corner, located between the radical change and objective dimensions.

Research approaches

A major characteristic of the relationship between theory and research is the consideration of two contrasting approaches to reasoning: *deduction* and *induction*. Both approaches raise questions concerning the design of the chosen research project. They inform the researcher of the research strategy and appropriate choices needed for research.

Deductive reasoning

Deductive reasoning involves the development of a theory testing process which seeks to examine whether the theory can be applicable to specific instances. This occurs when certain conclusions are derived logically from a set of premises, such that the derived conclusions follow from the earlier premise (Harrison, 2002; Ketokivi and Mantere, 2010). Essentially, it is a form of inference which purports to be conclusive. This implies that likely conclusions would necessarily follow from the reasons given (Blumberg et al., 2014). As pointed out by Myers (2020), when using deductive reasoning, the researcher commences with a general theory about a given topic, which will then be operationalised into a set of hypotheses for testing. It may be noted that once empirical data is collected and analysed, the hypotheses and theory will either be confirmed or not. Another point deserves to be made. Deductive reasoning is concerned with quantitative studies and involves the use of experiments. Such experiments are subjected to rigorous testing through series of propositions.

Inductive reasoning

In contrast, inductive reasoning involves a movement from the empirical observations of the real world to constructing theories of what has been observed (Gill and Johnson, 1997; Hyde, 2000). The point indeed is that the inductive approach is an outcome of empirical findings. The emphasis here is that empirical findings are fed back into the stock of the theory. It is no doubt true that inductive reasoning involves the collection of data and development of theory as an outcome of the data analysis. It is

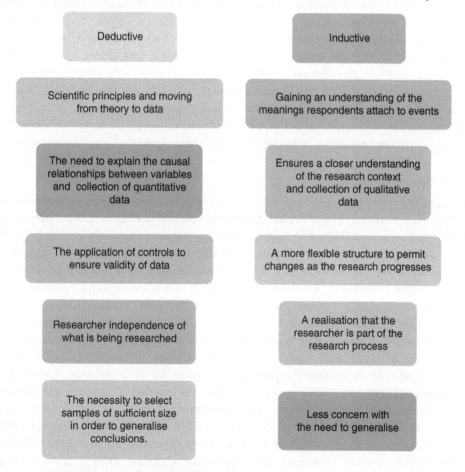

Figure 4.5   Deductive and Inductive approaches

immediately apparent that no theoretical or conceptual basis can be developed prior to it. That's why inductive researchers rely on an approach that involves drawing inference out of observations. Unlike deductive reasoning which requires a larger sample size, the inductive approach is appropriate for smaller sample studies.

Figure 4.5 summarises the key distinctions between the deductive and inductive approaches.

Comparing research approaches

In highlighting the distinctions between both approaches, scholars such as Yin (2011) argue that inductive reasoning leads to the emergence of concepts while the deductive approach provides for a definition of the relevant data that needs to be collected. It is no doubt true that deduction involves a movement from theory to findings; while induction on the other hand, moves from findings to theory. To put this into perspective, qualitative research is inductive in approach and on the other hand, the deductive approach has a positivist leaning and is associated with quantitative methods. This being said, note that the deductive approach enables a cause-effect link between particular variables but lacks a clear understanding of the way the human world is interpreted. On the other hand, the process of inductive enquiry depends on the process of linking data and investigating the context where events occur. Thus, such a researcher can establish different views of phenomena through a variety of qualitative methods.

Abductive reasoning

In recent years, the abductive approach to reasoning has become very popular among qualitative researchers. The abductive approach emerged in response to the limitations of the deductive and inductive approaches. For instance, Bryman and Bell (2015) argue that a weakness associated with deductive reasoning is its reliance on a strict logic of theory testing as there is a lack of clarity on how to select the theory to be tested. On the other hand, the inductive approach to qualitative inquiry is often seen as protracted and time consuming. In effect, an abductive approach combines the deductive and inductive approaches to reasoning. The abductive approach has strong ties to inductive reasoning with regard to the social perspectives of the participants.

Across studies, scholars argue that the perspectives of respondents are better described through an abductive reasoning rather than an inductive one. With abductive reasoning, Bryman (2016) reminds us that the researcher grounds the theoretical understanding of the contexts and participants involved, in the meaning and perspectives that form their view of the social world. It involves selecting the best interpretation of data (Mantere and Ketokivi, 2013); as new discoveries are revealed in a logical and methodological way (Reichertz, 2007; Bryant and Charmaz, 2007). It enables a cognitive logic of discovery, as its strength lies in its approach to uncovering deep insights and new knowledge. This remains crucial as abductive reasoning ensures that the researcher is open to the possibilities of new findings from their data, rather than confirming pre-understandings (Alvesson and Kärreman, 2007; Bryman and Bell, 2015).

It can therefore be agreed that abduction is broadly inductive, but richer in terms of its reliance on explaining the social perspectives of the respondents. Since abduction consists of the discovery and interpretation of data for which there is no appropriate explanation, the argument in favour of an abductive approach allows for profound insights into a given phenomenon.

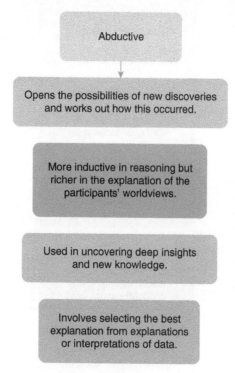

Figure 4.6　**Key features of the abductive approach**

The case for retroductive reasoning

In this book, we have chosen to reintroduce retroduction and propose it as a replacement for abductive reasoning. While there have been debates that distinguish abductive and retroductive concepts, we go back to the foundational roots to argue that abduction is actually misunderstood as retroduction. Charles Peirce, in the late nineteenth century, coined the term retroduction as a form of logical inference. He emphasised that retroduction is based on the idea that social reality consists of interconnected structures and objects, and understanding their social reality requires developing fundamental concepts beyond empirically observable questions (Meyer and Lunnay, 2013). Similar to abduction, retroduction encourages the emergence of knowledge, where researchers remain open to new findings from their data rather than confirming pre-existing understandings.

Peirce identified three types of reasoning: Deduction, which relies on confidence in analysing the meanings of signs; Induction, which depends on the confidence that a series of experiences will not change abruptly without prior indication; and

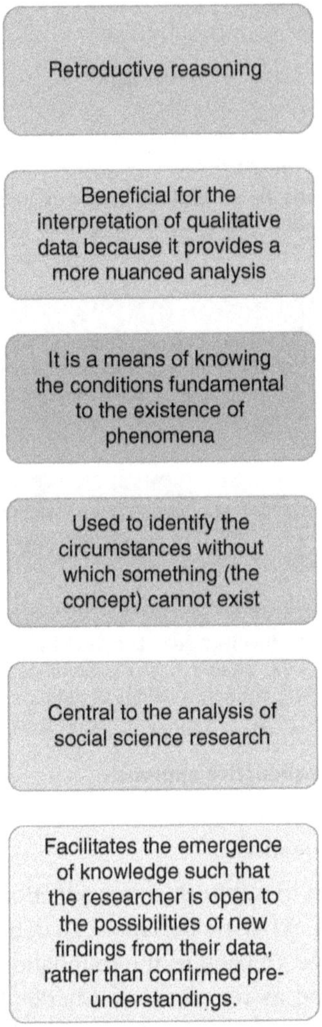

Retroductive reasoning

Beneficial for the interpretation of qualitative data because it provides a more nuanced analysis

It is a means of knowing the conditions fundamental to the existence of phenomena

Used to identify the circumstances without which something (the concept) cannot exist

Central to the analysis of social science research

Facilitates the emergence of knowledge such that the researcher is open to the possibilities of new findings from their data, rather than confirmed pre-understandings.

Figure 4.7   **Key features of retroductive reasoning**

Adapted from Meyer and Lunnay (2013).

Retroduction, which relies on the hope of eventually guessing the conditions under which a specific phenomenon will manifest. According to Peirce, retroduction is the most crucial reasoning because it opens up new possibilities and is the least complex form of reasoning. It helps in understanding the conditions fundamental to the existence of a given phenomenon.

We argue, following Meyer and Lunnay (2013), that like abductive reasoning, retroductive reasoning is valuable for interpreting qualitative data as it allows for a more nuanced analysis. It can also be utilised to extend an analysis of research that may not be theory-driven, thereby adding clarity to the method of analysis. Retroduction, as we propose, brings a fresh perspective to understanding social reality and exploring new avenues of research.

4.3 Summary

- Ontology in social sciences has to do with the social world and assumptions about the nature of social reality.
- Epistemology is concerned with the nature of knowledge and ways of learning about social reality.
- Axiology is concerned with the role values play in the research process.
- Research paradigms represent a worldview that defines the nature of the world, the individual's place in it and a range of possible relationships to the world.
- Deductive reasoning involves the development of a theory testing process which seeks to examine if the theory can be applicable to specific instances.
- Inductive reasoning involves a movement from the empirical observations of the real world to constructing theories of what has been observed.
- The abductive approach has strong ties to inductive reasoning with regard to the social perspectives of the participants.
- Retroduction facilitates the emergence of knowledge such that the researcher is open to the possibilities of new findings from their data, rather than confirmed pre-understandings.

Self-check questions

1. Outline the differences between positivism and interpretivism. How important are they in your consideration?
2. Outline, using examples of your own, the difference between the types of approaches to reasoning.

(Continued)

3. What are the differences between the four paradigms and how do they influence research?
4. Define interpretivism and why is it important?
5. What does research philosophy mean?
6. If you had to conduct a research project, which research philosophy would you adopt and why?

Self-check answers

1. Positivism is an approach that assumes reality is stable and can be observed and described from an objective viewpoint without interfering with what is being observed. It often involves quantitative methods. Interpretivism, on the other hand, suggests that reality is subjective and constructed, requiring the researcher to interpret elements of the study, thus often involving qualitative methods. These philosophical stances are crucial as they underpin the research design, methodology, and analysis approach.

2. & 3. Deductive reasoning starts with a general hypothesis or theory and moves towards specific observations to confirm or falsify the theory. For example, if all businesses aim to increase profit (general theory) and Company X is a business, then Company X aims to increase profit (specific observation). Inductive reasoning works the opposite way, starting with specific observations and moving towards general conclusions. For instance, observing that Company X and Company Y, both tech firms, invest heavily in R&D, one might conclude that tech firms generally invest heavily in R&D.

4. Interpretivism emphasises the subjective meaning of human experiences and the context in which they occur. It's important because it allows researchers to explore and understand the complexity of human behaviour, social processes, and cultural phenomena, providing depth and insight that may be overlooked by more objective methods.

5. Research philosophy refers to the underlying belief system or set of principles that guide a researcher in their approach to understanding and investigating their research topic. It influences the choice of methodology, data collection, and analysis methods, shaping the overall direction and integrity of the study.

6. The selection of a research philosophy depends heavily on the nature of the research question, the objectives of the study, and the context in which the research is situated. If my research aimed to explore complex, context-dependent human behaviours or social phenomena, I would likely adopt an interpretivist philosophy. This approach would allow me to understand the subjective experiences, motivations, and meanings that individuals ascribe to their actions and interactions, providing a rich understanding of the research context.

Case study   Interpretivism in action

'We don't deal with courts': *Cooperation and alternative institutions shaping exporting relationships of small and medium-sized enterprises in Ghana*

In their study focusing on small and medium-sized enterprises (SMEs) in Ghana, Amoako and Lyon adopted an interpretivist approach to capture the richness and diversity of the Ghanaian context. Their empirical research focused on 12 exporting SMEs operating in Ghana and trading across West African markets. These SMEs represented various sectors, including agriculture, services and manufacturing, and were drawn from both formal and informal sectors, with a balanced representation of male and female-led enterprises.

The findings of their study revealed several important insights.

Ghanaian SMEs had a strong perception of corruption, especially concerning commercial disputes, which they acknowledged as prevalent both within the domestic market and in the West African markets. SMEs in Ghana tended to rely on personal relationships built on trust to address trade disputes, rather than seeking recourse through formal legal channels.

Instead of resorting to the courts, SMEs in Ghana utilised culturally specific relationships and practices to resolve trade disputes, indicating a reliance on informal mechanisms.

Amoako and Lyon concluded that despite the lack of institutional support commonly found in many Western economies, SMEs in Ghana have managed to develop and maintain relationships that enable successful internationalisation across the West African region. Their study sheds light on the adaptability and resourcefulness of Ghanaian SMEs in navigating the challenges of cross-border trade and illustrates how cultural factors play a significant role in shaping business practices in the region.

Source: Amoako and Lyon (2014) *International Small Business Journal*

Questions

- What is the central tenet of interpretivism, and how does it differ from positivism in social research?
- How did Amoako and Lyon adopt an interpretivist approach in their study of SMEs in Ghana and why was this approach suitable for capturing the richness and diversity of the Ghanaian context?
- What are the main characteristics of interpretivist research methods, and how do they align with the research design used by Amoako and Lyon?
- Discuss the advantages and limitations of using an interpretivist approach in studying SMEs and understanding their experiences and perceptions in the Ghanaian context.

(Continued)

- Analyse the findings of Amoako and Lyon's study regarding Ghanaian SMEs' perception of corruption and their preferred methods of resolving trade disputes. How do these findings reflect the interpretivist lens used in the research?
- How do cultural factors influence the behaviour of Ghanaian SMEs, particularly in their approach to internationalisation and relationship-building within West African markets?
- In the context of interpretivism, how can the reliance on personal relationships and trust-based mechanisms be understood as a form of 'sense-making' for Ghanaian SMEs in navigating business challenges?
- Compare and contrast interpretivism with other research paradigms, such as positivism and critical theory. What unique insights does interpretivism offer in understanding social phenomena and organisational behavior in Ghanaian SMEs?
- Discuss the implications of Amoako and Lyon's study for policy makers and practitioners aiming to support the growth and internationalisation of SMEs in Ghana. How can understanding interpretivism contribute to designing more effective strategies for supporting SMEs in the region?
- Reflect on the ethical considerations associated with conducting interpretivist research, particularly in a cross-cultural context like Ghana. How can researchers ensure respect for participants' perspectives and cultural values while conducting qualitative research?

Further reading

Creswell, J.W. (2017) *Research Design: Qualitative, Quantitative, and Mixed Methods Approaches*. Los Angeles: Sage

Denzin, N.K. and Lincoln, Y.S. (eds) (2011) *The SAGE Handbook of Qualitative Research*. Sage.

Giddens, A. (1979) *Positivism and Its Critics: Philosophical Issues in Social Science*. University of California Press.

Leavy, P. (ed.) (2014) *The Oxford Handbook of Qualitative Research*. Oxford University Press.

Saunders, M.N.K., Lewis, P. and Thornhill, A. (2019) *Research Methods for Business Students*. Pearson Publishers.

Thorne, S. (2016) *Interpretive Description: Qualitative Research for Applied Practice*. Routledge.

5

Ethics in Qualitative Research

Learning outcomes

By the end of this chapter, you should be able to:

- define research ethics
- explain the importance and need for ethics in research
- apply the ethical codes and principles in conducting research
- anticipate the ethical issues that emerge during research and how they can be addressed
- conceptualise the process of obtaining **ethical approval.**

5.1 Introduction

Research is about addressing questions and providing solutions to a range of issues and problems. While conducting research, there is always an element of risk to people who participate in the study or even to the society or environment in which the study takes place. As a result, there is a need that all research should be conducted ethically and morally. Anyone who embarks on research must be sensitive to and mindful of ethical principles and considerations. Especially in qualitative studies, where human interactions are commonplace, ethical issues are very existent and need to be given full attention.

In this chapter, we first start by exploring the different ways research ethics has been conceptualised. Within this, we examine the importance and need for carrying out research ethically. We then explore the different codes and principles to be considered while conducting research. In the following section, we analyse the ethical issues that occur while conducting research and offer several strategies to address such issues. Finally, we examine the process of obtaining ethical approval which is important in every research study.

5.2 What is research ethics?

When people think of ethics, they think of rules that define right and wrong. However, what does it mean to be right or wrong? For example: Is it acceptable for a doctor to engage in mercy killing when a terminal patient begs to be put out of misery? Is it acceptable to lie to your colleague about how your boss perceives him or her to spare them the pain of knowing the truth? Ethics is more than doing the right thing. You also need to understand why decisions are made. Societies have laws that govern behaviour but ethics tend to be broader than laws. In general, ethics and laws are not the same. An action may be illegal but ethical, or legal but unethical, as seen in the earlier examples provided. Indeed, ethics can be defined as moral principles that govern a person's behaviour and guide their choices.

While ethics remain a somewhat elusive topic, what is clear is that it cuts across several disciplines and people have various ethical standards and orientations. Within the context of research, ethical concerns will emerge from the design of your study, data collection and how the data is analysed and reported. Research ethics is the study of the right behaviour and addresses the question of how to conduct research in a moral and responsible way (Blumberg et al., 2011). It relates to questions about how we formulate and clarify our research topic, design our research and gain access, collect data, process and store our data, analyse data and write up our research findings in a moral and responsible way (Saunders et al., 2012). Conducting empirical research often requires that the methodological stance adopted is sound and morally defensible to all those involved. We define research ethics as *the moral principles that guide how researchers should carry out their study. It involves the application of fundamental ethical principles to guide how research is designed and conducted.*

There are many approaches to ethics. However, within the field of business and management, there are two established philosophical standpoints namely, deontology and teleology. In deontology ethics, emphasis is placed on the principles of the decision or action itself and not on the outcome or consequence. Hence, the outcome never justifies the use of unscrupulous means or approaches. For example, in covert observation where deception may be used to obtain data based on the justification that being honest may affect validity and reliability. Such an approach to data collection is not acceptable and considered unethical from the lens of deontology.

In contrast, teleology focuses on the end rather than the action. If the outcome of an action gives rise to benefits, then that action is said to be morally right. Conversely, if the action causes harm, then the action is morally wrong. This approach to ethics, though popular in the field of business and management, causes some major problems. First, it implies that the approach taken to achieve a particular outcome, if positive, could be ethically questionable. Second, the cost and benefit relationship may not be that simple. For example, the study may be problematic to the respondent but beneficial to the researcher. How is it possible to assess the value of consequences in terms of the amount of happiness or well-being caused?

As a result, we recommend that you find a middle ground and consider all ethical issues throughout the course of your research. It is important that you are responsive to the impact of your research on those who are involved in your study. The conduct of your research is likely to be guided by codes and regulations within your institution or university. Ethical approval is likely to be obtained before research is conducted. This will be discussed in more detail in Section 5.6.

5.3 Why ethics matter in research

In the earlier section, we had provided a more holistic definition of research ethics and its philosophical standpoints. However, why do we need to adhere to established norms and principles in research in the first place? Case 5.1. is an example of an ethical dilemma which shows why ethics matter.

Case 5.1   Deception

Charles is a research student who intends to examine the impact of advertising on customer retention within the supermarket industry. He is an employee of one of the big supermarket chains and intends to use his organisation as the context for his study. Rather than obtaining permission from the gatekeepers within the organisation before conducting his study, he goes around the supermarket distributing questionnaires to employees and customers. He was spotted by the store manager when doing this and faced disciplinary action for not obtaining consent. He finally was dismissed from his role after six months.

 * This is a fictional case. Names, characters, places and incidents either are products of the author's imagination or are used fictitiously. Any resemblance to actual persons, living or dead, or actual events is purely coincidental.

Looking at the case of Charles where he loses his job, many a time not adhering to the ethical guidelines might have significant repercussions to researchers and participants. However, following ethical principles also has its benefits. Resnick (2015) provides some cogent reasons for research ethics (see in Box 5.1)

First, the principles promote the general purpose of the study. Through ethics you can expand knowledge and avoid bias or error. For example, principles against misrepresenting and falsifying research data will promote truth and minimise error (Resnick, 2015).

Second, ethics helps build public support and credibility. The perception of the public and the acceptance of your results largely depends on the **authenticity** of the process. If the process is authentic and credible, people are more likely to fund the research project. In addition, providing such funding ensures that the researchers are accountable to the public for their actions.

Third, ethics promotes important moral and social values such as social responsibility, public health and safety. Ethical lapses in research can cause significant harm and distress to human participants and society in general. One of the most popular examples of how a lapse in ethics can affect human life is the case of Paolo Macchiarini, the Italian surgeon who was found guilty of scientific fraud and medical misconduct. He used synthetic scaffolds seeded with the patients' stem cells to create trachea transplants which was very promising for regenerative medicine. Unfortunately, it was later discovered that his experiments on human participants had questionable preclinical research trials. Seven of the nine patients who had received the treatment died. Further investigation showed that Macchiarini had manipulated some of the data in his publications, omitting and sometimes fabricating research to make his treatment efficacious. The scandal has led to the dismissal of Macchiarini and the resignation of several individuals from his previous employer: Karolinska Institute in Stockholm, Sweden.

Finally, research most times is a team effort and ethics is important in promoting values that are key to successful collaboration such as respect, trust, fairness and accountability. For example, ethical norms such as copyright and patents are designed to protect intellectual property while encouraging collaboration. In general, research ethics matter for integrity, accountability, human rights and collaboration. If good ethical practice is followed, there is a better chance of providing more credible and high-quality research.

Box 5.1   Importance of ethics in research

1. It promotes the aims of research, such as knowledge, truth and avoidance of error.
2. It supports the values that are essential for collaborative work, such as trust, mutual respect, accountability and fairness.
3. It ensures that researchers can be held accountable to the public for their actions.
4. It helps to build the public support for research. For people to support and fund research, they have to be confident in it.
5. It promotes a variety of other important social and moral values.

Source: Resnick, D.B. (2015) *What is Ethics in Research and Why is it Important?*

5.4 Ethical codes and principles

Over the years, different people have set down ethical codes and principles for researchers. One influential example in health sciences is the Belmont Report in 1979 which describes the basic ethical principles for research on human participants. However, beyond the Belmont Report, there have been various codes in the health sciences proposing several ethical principles (e.g. *Code of Ethics (American Society for Clinical Laboratory Science), American Psychological Association, Ethical Principles of Psychologists and Code of Conduct, Nuremberg Code, World Medical Association's Declaration of Helsinki*).

Table 5.1   Organisations and internet addresses for codes of ethics

Academy of Management (2021) *Code of Ethics.*
https://aom.org/about-aom/governance/ethics/code-of-ethics

Association of Social Anthropologists of the UK and Commonwealth (1999) *Ethical Guidelines for Good Research Practice.*
http://www.theasa.org/downloads/ethics/Ethical_guidelines.pdf

British Psychological Society (2021) *Code of Ethics and Conduct.*
https://cms.bps.org.uk/sites/default/files/2022-06/BPS%20Code%20of%20Ethics%20and%20Conduct.pdf

British Sociological Association (2017) *BSA Statement of Ethical Practice.*
https://www.britsoc.co.uk/media/24310/bsa_statement_of_ethical_practice.pdf

CABS/BAM/HEA Ethics guide (2015) *Ethics Guide 2015: Advice and Guidance* https://charteredabs.org/wp-content/uploads/2015/06/Ethics-Guide-2015-Advice-and-Guidance.pdf

Economic and Social Research Council (2022) *Framework for Research Ethics.*
https://www.ukri.org/councils/esrc/guidance-for-applicants/research-ethics-guidance/

Social Research Association. (2021) *Research Ethical Guidelines*
https://the-sra.org.uk/common/Uploaded%20files/Resources/SRA%20Research%20Ethics%20guidance%202021.pdf

UK Research and Innovation (2022) *Policy on the Governance of Good Research Practice*
https://www.ukri.org/wp-content/uploads/2022/03/UKRI-310322-GRP-Policy2022.pdf

Within business and management research, several learned organisations have put forward ethical codes and principles for their members. Table 5.1 sets out the internet addresses where the codes and principles for organisations aligned to business and management research can be found.

However, though the ethical practice of business research involving human participants is a complex and demanding responsibility for any researcher, it is widely acknowledged as important and the basis of moral reasoning. Within our book and other scholarly work, there are four basic ethical principles that every researcher must bear in mind namely, beneficence and non-maleficence, autonomy, justice and confidentiality and anonymity.

Beneficence and non-maleficence

Beneficence is the commitment to maximise possible benefits and minimise harm. The term is often understood to cover acts of kindness which involves ensuring the well-being of the participants. This principle obliges the researcher to assist the human participants to pursue their interest. However, beneficence goes beyond individual researchers and respondents to society at large. It is important that in carrying out research you consider how you could maximise the benefits and reduce harm during the study. As a researcher, you must consider all possible sources of harm to the participants. But what does harm mean in research? Harm may come in different forms. It may be psychological harm where sensitive questions during research may trigger negative emotions. It could be social harm where participation can lead to social issues and embarrassment. It could be physical harm in the form of pain or injury that your research can cause. Legal harm is another form where the study could lead to infringement of privacy and other legal risks. Finally, research could lead to financial harm when the participants involved in your research incur significant expenses to be involved or their engagement may affect their earnings.

Therefore, it is important that harm is avoided, and this is known as non-maleficence. It is the basis of most ethical issues that occur, which will be discussed later in the chapter. For example, the way you maintain confidentiality and anonymity and obtain consent could cause harm to the participants. While in some situations, there is clear guidance and widespread awareness about how to avoid harm, in others, the circumstances are not as clear and researchers need to make subjective judgements about risks (SRA, 2021).

In avoiding harm, it is important that you consider the participants, groups that are involved directly or indirectly in the study and the researchers. By considering these three perspectives you can make a balanced judgement about the acceptable risks for everyone involved. The case study below provides an example of a potential harm that research can bring and how it can be addressed.

Autonomy

Autonomy demands that individuals participate voluntarily, after having been told both what the research entails and its consequences (King and Horrocks, 2012).

Case 5.2   Potential for harm

The pandemic was a challenging time and a global crisis. Effective leadership was pertinent to succeed during this this period. In a study on leadership attributes during the time of crisis, semi-structured interviews were conducted with the employees of the business to examine how their employer led them during the pandemic.

Ethical issues

Some of the questions may lead to the employees providing negative qualities of their employer. It could be sensitive and adversely affect the emotional well-being of the interviewees leading to psychological harm. Finally, if the employer knows that some participants spoke negatively about him or her, their jobs could be at risk which could lead to financial harm.

Solutions

- Sensitive questions which could adversely affect the emotional well-being as well as the cohesion of the group should be excluded.
- The participants should be informed that it is not compulsory to provide answers to all questions.
- The employees do not need to be prompted to give their opinions about the negative qualities of their employers.
- Confidentiality and anonymity of the respondents should be ensured.
- Sufficient information and assurances about taking part should be provided to allow individuals to understand the implications of participation and to reach a fully informed decision about whether they should take part in the study.

It means that all individuals are free to choose to participate without any pressure, coercion or undue influence and their rights are respected. Respect for the rights of a person is a vital ethical principle across geographical boundaries and various disciplines beyond business and management. It recognises the inherent worth of all human beings regardless of perceived or real differences in social status, ethnic origin, gender, capacity or any other group-based characteristics (BPS, 2021).

The Belmont report proposed that respect for people should be divided into two separate moral requirements; the requirement to acknowledge autonomy and the requirement to protect those with diminished autonomy. An autonomous person is an individual capable of deliberating about personal goals and acting under the direction of such deliberation (Belmont Report, 1979). We take a simpler view by proposing that an autonomous person is independent and has the ability to make decisions based on their values and interest.

As a researcher, it is important that you respect autonomy and refrain from obstructing your potential participants' actions unless it is detrimental to others. All participants should be able to withdraw from the study at any point without feeling obliged to continue. Your participants do not need to provide a reason for leaving or opting out of the study. It is important that it is made clear to participants that they are not obliged to participate, and you have to respect their decisions even if they change their minds during the course of the research.

By contrast, when a potential research participant lacks the ability to make autonomous decisions, you are expected to protect them against harm. Some individuals are not able to make autonomous decisions due to illness or circumstances that affect their ability. Their participation in the study needs to be evaluated and if necessary, they might have to be excluded to protect them from harm. For example, a study which involves vulnerable groups such as children will need constant evaluation as the project is conducted. The children may want to decline participation after the study has commenced but may find it difficult to do so. In summary, the responsibility of the researcher is to understand the participants' capabilities and viewpoints and their right to make choices about whether they will take part in the study. Participants must be treated in a way that will ensure autonomy.

Justice

The concept of justice in a research project involves treating the participants fairly and equally. It requires that all respondents be provided with the same information by the researcher, and that there is a fair distribution of both the benefits and burden of the study. This is the principle which emphasises that each person must be treated morally rightly and properly. It is concerned with providing equal opportunity for all. It is linked to the earlier principle, autonomy, which focuses on respect for persons. However, the core principle of justice stresses that research participants must be given equal treatment. There needs to be fairness in conducting your study and in the distribution of the benefits and burden.

Injustice occurs when some benefit to which a person is entitled is denied without good reason or when some burden is imposed unduly on them (Belmont Report, 1979). As a result, it is important that researchers give thorough attention in their selection of participants and the benefits and burdens arising from it. For example, the selection of research participants needs to be examined in order to determine whether those selected were chosen justly and not for reasons which do not relate to the problem being studied. Sometimes research participants are chosen based on ease of exploitation. Taking such an approach is an injustice and does not help the proposed beneficiaries of the research. Case study 5.3. provides an example of how justice can be applied within a research project.

Case 5.3   Justice

In a study on entrepreneurial leadership skill development, entrepreneurs and their employees were selected as the participants of the study. The intent of the study was to explore how entrepreneurial leadership skills are developed by the entrepreneurs. A dual perspective was sought from both the entrepreneurs and their employees to understand the concept better. Semi-structured interviews with the entrepreneurs and employees of small to medium enterprises were conducted.

Ethical issues

Ensuring that all the entrepreneurs and employees involved in the study were treated fairly.

Solutions

- Ensuring that all respondents are treated equally and that no particular entrepreneur is assumed to be more successful or possessed greater entrepreneurial leadership skills (based on the size of their business or the revenue it generated).
- All participants should be asked similar questions during the interview and should also be briefed on the impact of their interview on the study.
- Ensuring that there is no bias in handling interviews with the employees, compared to those of their employers.
- Entrepreneurs and their employees should be treated equally, with the same level of consideration and commitment given to each group.

Confidentiality and anonymity

Confidentiality is an important ethical principle while conducting research especially in business and management. Confidentiality as the name implies means keeping secret one's identity. Within research it means that a research project is conducted without revealing the identity of the organisation or participants. As a researcher, you must be concerned about respecting the confidentiality of all parties in your study specifically the participants, the organisation and any third party that may be involved in the research.

The first group of people to consider are the participants especially in a qualitative study. Regardless of the nature of the study, you are obliged to ensure that all the information you collect remains confidential. The information and personal data provided should be respected. All participants have a right to privacy and it is important that you protect their personal data for as long as you store or use it.

In designing a research project, you must consider whether personal data or other forms of data such as interviews is to be stored. If this is the case, then informed consent (which is discussed later in the chapter) must be sought to ensure that the confidentiality of the participants is respected. Such data must also be stored securely in accordance with the relevant legislation and institution or organisation's policy. For example, it is a common policy among many institutions that data from which an individual is identifiable must be destroyed when no longer needed. This is also in line with the Data Protection Act 2018. In some cases, the researcher may need to retain such data beyond completion due to cogent reasons. But in such a situation, it must be clear why data has to be retained and written consent from the participants is required.

In keeping confidentiality, it is important that individuals cannot be identified from published results without their consent. In addition, such data should not be stored on computers or devices which unauthorised persons can access. A good way to store confidential information and personal data is in a locked file drawer and using passwords for the files. However not all research projects allow for confidentiality, hence it is important to inform participants of the risks involved. For example, in a focus group study on organisational culture within an organisation that involves seven participants, the identity of those involved is known by each of them as well as the information provided. Nevertheless, it is important that you stress while conducting the focus groups that everyone should keep what is discussed confidential and respect each other's privacy.

Anonymity on the other hand is very similar to the concept of confidentiality and most times used interchangeably. Anonymity means that no one can link the participant with the data collected. Many organisations wish to undertake research without revealing their identity. To ensure anonymity and confidentiality, a non-disclosure is usually signed. This is common when the data that is being sought may affect their competitive advantage or customer base. However, it is not every time that organisations or participants want to be anonymous. There might be times when they waive anonymity and want people to identify them in order to retain ownership of the content. As a result, it is not appropriate to assume anonymity and confidentiality is desired, but you need to consult research participants to make an informed choice about what they prefer.

Nevertheless, once assurance about confidentiality and anonymity has been given, it is paramount that you ensure that it is maintained. Box 5.2. provides practical ways to maintain confidentiality and anonymity while conducting a qualitative study.

Anonymising the data provided by participants requires researchers to remove personal details such as name, address etc. Sometimes other types of information could indirectly disclose identity such as employer, job title etc. As a result, it is important that data pseudonymisation is employed. This means the use of pseudonyms or fake identifiers to replace information about participants. This makes it difficult to link the participants to the personal information for the study. For example, in providing the demographic profile of your interviewees, the age, gender and ethnicity could be important to show the credibility and diversity of your sample but in order to protect their identity you could use random numbers or fake identifiers (Interviewee A, B, C).

However, there are limitations in maintaining confidentiality and anonymity in both qualitative and quantitative research. In qualitative research, it may be possible to identify an individual or organisation through the interview quotes even though they have been anonymised. As a result, it is important that you try to ensure that the interview quotes provided do not mistakenly reveal the identity of the participants or organisation; for example, an interview where the participant speaks about the organisation located in a specific district which is clearly stated. Within the interview quote, the interviewee describes a fire outbreak which occurred and was covered in the mainstream media. Such content will make it easy to identify the organisation, especially if it was well published and such an outbreak was unique to that organisation. In such cases, if anonymity and confidentiality has been assured, it is important that these quotes are not used within the research project.

Furthermore, as Bryman and Bell (2011) put forward the use of Internet and virtual platforms in collecting data may also lead to issues with confidentiality and anonymity. For example, it would be technically possible to forward the views of one research participant to another in order to ask the second person to comment on the issues being raised. Such action would infringe on the ethos of confidentiality and anonymity and may cause harm. This should be avoided. Although the use of the Internet especially through virtual interviews allows researchers to correspond with participants in distant location and has other benefits, it also has its ethical challenges. It could be intrusive and demanding for participants especially if discussion or chat forums are used. It should be looked at carefully to ensure credibility of the data.

Box 5.2   Protecting privacy, ensuring confidentiality and maintaining anonymity

Members of the business school community have a responsibility to:

a. Respect individual and collective rights to privacy in compliance with UK and European Union law and relevant regulations in other countries as appropriate. Criminal Records Bureau checks must be carried out when working with children and vulnerable people.

(Continued)

b. Ensure that administrative processes are designed to preserve the privacy of personal data, for example in the consideration of mitigating circumstances for student assessments.

c. Carefully consider the importance of confidentiality and anonymity to potential participants in research and scholarship and ensure the confidentiality and anonymity of participants is maintained where a prior commitment to do so has been made.

d. Consider the implications of using participant pseudonyms rather than real names to ensure anonymity. In some cases, it may be appropriate to use real names, for example when the revealing of identities does not pose a significant risk to participants, or when participants express a preference for the use of real names.

e. Recognise that there is no need to ensure confidentiality or anonymity where participants have agreed to their identities being made public, provided that informed consent procedures have been duly followed.

f. Make any provision of confidentiality or anonymity clear and, preferably, agree it in writing prior to data collection.

g. Take care when using online media as a data source. Ethical standards relating to the use of the Internet – for instance as a source of data – are not yet well developed and so there is a need to ensure continuing familiarity with current debates. Be aware of the potential abuse of online media in communicating with others and refrain from any such abuse.

Source: CABS/BAM/HEA Ethics guide (2015) *Ethics Guide 2015: Advice and Guidance*

The full document is available here: https://charteredabs.org/wp-content/uploads/2015/06/Ethics-Guide-2015-Advice-and-Guidance.pdf

5.5 General ethical issues

The earlier section provided an elaborate examination of the ethical codes and principles. However, in addition to those ethical codes and principles, there are other ethical issues that need to be considered in conducting research. A number of important ethical issues arise across the different stages of a research project and you need to pay attention to them as they may overlap with each other. They include:

- voluntary participation
- informed consent
- privacy of the participants
- data management
- intellectual property
- integrity

Voluntary participation

Voluntary participation is an important ethical consideration in every research project. It means that all research participants are free to be involved without any undue influence, pressure and coercion. Undue influence may occur when an unwarranted or inappropriate offer and reward is given to encourage participation. For example, it has become common practice to offer rewards or vouchers to respondents to complete surveys or participate in interviews. However, this may raise ethical issues if the reward is the major reason the individual decides to participate even if they do not really want to be involved.

Pressure usually occurs when persons in a position of authority urge a course of action for the respondents (Belmont Report, 1979). For example, an employee in an organisation is told by the manager to participate in a focus group examining customer satisfaction. The employee does not want to be part of the focus group but decides to do this because of the fear of possible sanctions if they fail to take part. Finally, coercion goes beyond pressure but is a deliberate threat of harm which is made to ensure compliance. For example, an employee is told that if he or she is not involved in the focus group, they would be made redundant. Failure to engage in the study will cause financial harm to the participant.

It is important ethically that participants can withdraw from or leave the study at any point in time without feeling an obligation to continue. They do not need to provide the reasons for leaving the study and should also not be asked. Before embarking on the study, it is important that it is made very clear to respondents that there are no negative consequences if they refuse to participate or withdraw after the project has commenced.

Informed consent

Similar to voluntary participation, informed consent is an important ethical consideration in a research project. Informed consent is obtained when the potential participants are provided with sufficient information in a comprehensible manner to allow them to decide. To ensure voluntary participation, it is important that the potential respondents understand the purpose of the research and what their participation entails. Based on the information provided, they are now able to decide whether they want to partake in the study.

The information required to obtain consent usually involves:

- the purpose of the study
- the research procedure
- the risks and anticipated benefits
- the person conducting the research
- how long the study will take
- who will use the data and its purpose?
- limits of confidentiality and anonymity

- their right to refuse to participate or withdraw from the study at any time
- statement offering the participants the opportunity to ask questions.

This is usually provided in a participant information sheet and accompanied by an **informed consent form**. An exemplar of a participant information sheet and informed consent form is provided in Box 5.3. and 5.4. below

---

Box 5.3   Example of a participant information sheet

Participant information sheet

Introduction

You are invited to participate in a research project, which is exploring the impact of financial education on students' entrepreneurial intention. Your participation in this research will generate rich insights. Participants may also find this research informative and interesting. This information sheet aims to communicate the purpose of this research and the role of participants. Further information is also available from the principal investigator.

What is the purpose of this research?

This research is exploring the impact of financial education on students' entrepreneurial intention.

Who is conducting this study?

This project will be conducted in Scotland. It will involve Dr Christian Harrison, within the School of Business and Creative Industries of the University of the West of Scotland.

What is your role in the research?

You have been invited to participate in this study due to your role as a student. Your involvement will include:

- completion of a 15-minute survey
- your contribution included in the final output and potentially other publications, of which you would be informed.

How will your contribution be used?

Your contribution will be considered data collected within the study. This data will be analysed statistically to address the research hypotheses of the study.

How will your anonymity and confidentiality be maintained?

A key consideration of this research is to ensure that both participants and their contributions are handled ethically and with care. Therefore, the researcher is committed to ensuring the anonymity of participants and their confidentiality is maintained. This will be ensured through:

- names of participants will not be included in any publications
- access to these files will be restricted to the members of the research team conducting the analysis with no copies being made or sent electronically.

Are you obliged to participate, or continue participation, in this study?

There is no obligation to participate in this study. If you do choose to participate in this study, you retain the right to withdraw both your participation and any contribution you have made at any point. To withdraw your participation and any contribution made you should contact the principal investigator.

What's next?

If you are interested in participating in this research, then please complete the Participant Consent Form and respond to the survey link which will be sent to you via email.

For further enquiries, please contact the principal investigator, Prof Christian Harrison: c.harrison2@bolton.ac.uk

---

Box 5.4   Example of an informed consent form

Consent form

Please read the following statements which outline participant involvement in this research. Check the statements to indicate your understanding and agreement.

I have read and understood the participant information sheet ☐

I have addressed any outstanding queries with the researcher ☐

I voluntarily agree to participate in this research ☐

(Continued)

I understand that I can withdraw my consent at any time, without reason or question	☐
I understand that my anonymity and confidentiality is guaranteed	☐
I understand that my anonymous contribution to this research may be published	☐
I consider my consent to participate as informed	☐

| **Participant Name** | **Signature** | **Date** |

| **Researcher Name** | **Signature** | **Date** |

However, not everyone can give informed consent. For example, minors (i.e., infants or young children under 16) or those with mental disabilities. For minors, you must obtain consent from their parents or legal guardians. The age of consent of a child may vary in different countries and regions; hence it is important that you confirm this prior to the conducting the research project with such a focus. For those with mental disabilities, you will need to refer to the Mental Capacity Act 2005. According to the Act, no one gives consent on behalf of a person lacking mental capacity. Instead, the researcher is required to seek advice from a consultee on what the feelings and wishes of the person might be and whether they would want to take part (SRA Research Ethics Guidelines, 2021).

It is important that all information is provided in a comprehensible manner to allow the potential participants to make an informed choice. For example, a participant who is not proficient in English language is not able to consent if the information is provided in English verbally or in written form. To ensure that an informed choice can be made in this case, the researcher would have to ensure that the information is translated into their language and an interpreter is used to provide the information in their language.

Consent is usually obtained verbally and in written form. Although for some studies, verbal consent is sufficient, we advise that written consent is also obtained as shown in the informed consent form. This is very important especially in studies that have a high risk of ethical challenge and discomfort associated with participation. However, sometimes giving written consent makes people feel less able to withdraw from the study. To ensure that this is not the case, it is the role of the researcher to keep reminding the participants throughout the process that they are free to withdraw at any time regardless of what they have signed.

As stated earlier (see 'Voluntary participation'), paying participants in the form of vouchers or cash has become commonplace in research, which may raise ethical issues. However, there are some benefits and justification of its use. It serves as a means of appreciation of your participants' time and effort they devoted to the research project. It could also support respondent groups who would not have been able to partake in the study. Therefore, when incentives are to be used, it is important that participants are reminded before and during the study that despite the remuneration they are not obliged to answer all questions and are free to withdraw at any time.

Though we have proposed that informed consent is important, it still remains a controversial and debated topic. For example, for most studies that adopt covert observation, informed consent is not usually sought. The participants are not given the opportunity to refuse to cooperate and are involved whether they like it or not (Bryman and Bell, 2011). This is common in community research involving observation of human behaviour and when informing the participants before the work is carried out may affect the credibility of the findings. In such cases, it is the role of the researcher to provide convincing reasons why such research should proceed without obtaining informed consent. As the CABS/BAM/HEA Ethics guide suggests:

> Appreciate that in exceptional circumstances, the requirements for prior informed consent may be set aside if it is neither feasible nor desirable to obtain this consent and if a strong public interest case can be made for undertaking the research without such consent. In such situations researchers should follow additional procedures and safeguards mandated by their institutional ethics committee.

In general, consent is a continuous process and requires considerable care and attention to detail. It is usually one of the crucial focal points of ethical review committees and approval which will be discussed later in the chapter.

Privacy of the participants

The right to privacy is an important ethical consideration in research. It goes beyond confidentiality which was discussed earlier. A right to privacy means that an individual has the right to refuse to be involved or provide any information in a research project. The privacy tenet is important in protecting the participants. This is why you would notice that in many telephone directories, the list of numbers is often incomplete because people have requested that their numbers are not listed. Individuals also have the right to engage in private behaviour in private places without fear of observation (Bryman and Bell, 2011). As a result, covert observation is often seen as a violation of the privacy principle as the participants are not given the opportunity to refuse invasion of privacy. Nevertheless, there remains a place for covert research as discussed earlier in business and management.

Privacy laws vary from country to country, and it is taken very seriously especially in the western nations. As the CABS/BAM/HEA Ethics guide states clearly:

> Members of the business school community have a responsibility to respect individual and collective rights to privacy in compliance with UK and European Union law and relevant regulations in other countries as appropriate. Criminal Records Bureau checks must be carried out when working with children and vulnerable people.

To address the right to privacy, researchers need to obtain informed consent. Participants should be informed of their right to withdraw at any time from the study. Most importantly, permission needs to be obtained before collecting sensitive information. Personal information concerning research participants should be kept confidential except where the participants are happy to waive confidentiality and anonymity.

Data management

Data management is a very important ethical consideration in conducting research as such projects deal with personal data. Personal data can be defined as any information that can be used to identify an individual. When this type of data is used in your study, it is usually subject to data protection legislation. Data protection legislations and acts are available in every country. In the UK, data protection is guided by the UK General Data Protection Regulation (UK GDPR) and the Data Protection Act 1998, 2018.

Some of the key recommendations of the Data Protection Act 1998 are stated below.

1. Personal data shall be processed fairly and lawfully.
2. Personal data shall be obtained only for one or more specified and lawful purposes and shall not be further processed in any manner incompatible with that purpose or those purposes.
3. Personal data shall be adequate, relevant, and not excessive in relation to the purpose or purposes for which they are processed.
4. Personal data shall be accurate and, where necessary, kept up to date.
5. Personal data processed for any purpose or purposes shall not be kept for longer than is necessary.

6. Personal data shall be processed in accordance with the rights of data subjects under this Act:

   ○ To have access to one's own personal data.
   ○ To prevent processing likely to cause damage or distress.
   ○ To prevent processing for the purposes of direct marketing.
   ○ To prevent decisions from being made based on the automatic processing of personal data.

7. Measures shall be taken to prevent unauthorised or unlawful processing of personal data and against accidental loss or destruction of, or damage to, personal data.

8. Personal data shall not be transferred to a country or territory outside the European Economic Area unless that country or territory ensures an adequate level of protection for the rights and freedoms of data subjects in relation to the processing of personal data.

In general, data should not be stored on devices to which unauthorised persons may have access. Once the research has been conducted, confidential data regarding the respondents should usually be destroyed. However, in some cases, this data may be kept for a longer period if necessary. Approval and convincing reasons are usually required for this. In addition, there is another form of personal data known as sensitive personal data. This form of personal data includes information such as racial or ethnic origin, sexual orientation, political opinions, religious beliefs and so on. This type of data due to its sensitive nature is usually more meticulously processed and there is more emphasis to obtain consent from the participants for this type of data. However, the Act does provide exemptions in the use of personal data for research purposes. If the data does not cause harm or distress, it might be processed at a later stage for other purposes. Additionally, if the results of the research are published in such a way that the participants cannot be identified, then the respondents do not have right of access to the data.

Intellectual property

Intellectual property is the product of a scholarly undertaking which can be identified. A common type of intellectual property in business and management research is copyright. Copyright is an intellectual property that protects the owner from illegal duplication. It is important that every researcher respect copyrights and always acknowledge the contribution of other researchers. As the CABS/BAM/HEA Ethics guide states clearly:

> Members of the business school community have a responsibility to acknowledge all substantive and identifiable contributions to work undertaken, and to be clear about and respect intellectual property.

It is the norm that the employer of the researcher usually has the copyright of the research data and publications. However, it is now common that universities waive this right to research data and publications and give it to the researcher. In addition, when publications emerge from the study that may involve more than one author, it is important that the order of authors reflects their input. It is not good practice to list as an author an individual who has not contributed substantively to the work.

Integrity

Integrity is an important component of every research project. It means designing and conducting your research honestly. Every research should be designed to ensure integrity is met and credibility and transparency are assured. There should be honesty in reporting the methods applied, data collected, findings and dissemination. It is not acceptable to falsify data or engage in inappropriate behaviour that may affect the credibility of your findings. It is important that you are sincere. There have been cases where researchers falsify participant consent or use without acknowledgement or permission. This does not show integrity but portrays research misconduct.

It is also important that every conflict of interest is made explicit. A conflict of interest may occur when a researcher is not able to conduct research independently. This may be because of members of family, personal relationships emerging during the study, personal gains or other situations that may affect the independence of the researcher. In some cases, the potential conflicts may not be actual conflicts of interest. Nevertheless, it is important that all potential conflicts of interest are declared.

5.6 Ethical approval

We have outlined the ethical codes, principles and issues in the field of business and management. However, it is important to note that in many universities before you embark on a research project, you need to obtain approval from a research ethics committee. A research ethics committee is a group of people appointed to review research proposals to ensure that they conform to the ethical standards of the institution. The ethical considerations of the project are meticulously scrutinised by the committee to ensure that it meets all the ethical codes of conduct.

In many universities, it involves more than one person to ensure that there is consistency in approach. A checklist of the common questions that can be found in an ethics application is provided in Box 5.5. below.

Box 5.5 Example of an ethics approval application form

Pre-screening questions:

Does your work involve human participants? Choose an item.

Does your work involve the use of personal data? Choose an item.

Does your work involve the use of animals? Choose an item.

Does your work involve risk to the investigator that is not adequately mitigated by proper application of the University's health and safety policies and procedures? Choose an item.

If you have answered **YES** to <u>any</u> of the above questions you should complete the remainder of this form and submit it to your school ethics committee for approval <u>PRIOR</u> to commencing any work on your project.

1. **Name of Principal Investigator:** Click here to enter text.
2. **School:** Choose an item.
    a. If you answered "other" above please provide details below:

3. **Position of Principal Investigator:** Choose an item.
4. **Name and contact details of collaborators**: Click here to enter text.
5. **Name of Supervisor:** Click here to enter text.
    a. **Position of Supervisor:** Click here to enter text.
    b. **School of Supervisor:** Choose an item.

6. **Title of the study:** Click here to enter text.
7. **Primary purpose of the study:** Choose an item.

If you answered "other" to this question, please provide details below:

8. **Has the proposed study been considered by any other ethics committee?** Choose an item.

If the study has been considered by another ethics committee, please provide details below:

9. **Please give a full summary of the purpose, justification, design and methodology of the planned study:**

(Continued)

10. **How has the scientific quality of the proposed research project been assessed?**

Independent external review   ☐

Review within a company   ☐

Review within a multi-centre research group   ☐

Review within the principal investigator's institution   ☐

Review within the research team   ☐

Review by supervisor/director of studies   ☐

Other   ☐

If you answered "other" above, please provide details below:

11. **Please explain/justify your intended sample size:**

12. **Please explain how you will analyse, present/disseminate the data you intend to collect:**

13. **Does the proposed research involve the use of individual/group interviews or questionnaires?** Choose an item.

    a. Will proposed interviews or questionnaires discuss topics that might be sensitive, embarrassing or upsetting for participants or is it possible that criminal or other disclosures requiring action could occur during the study? Choose an item.

*If you have answered **YES** to the question above please provide details below and how you propose to deal with such issues:*

14. **Is the study likely to cause any discomfort or distress, either physical or psychological?** Choose an item.

*If you have answered **YES** to the question above, please provide details below and how you propose to deal with this:*

15. **Does the proposed research involve any physically invasive procedures?** Choose an item.

    a. If physically invasive procedures are to be used what hazards are associated with them?

16. **Please identify any other ethical considerations with the proposed study.**

17. **Does the proposed research involve deception regarding aims, objectives or the identity of the investigator?** Choose an item.

If you have answered **YES** *to the above question, please provide an explanation/justification of this deception:*

18. **Will research participants be debriefed after their participation?** Choose an item.

If you have answered **YES** *to the above question, please provide details of when this* **debriefing** *will take place, who will do it and how it will be done:*

19. **What is the expected duration of participation in the study for each participant?**

20. **Please provide details of how you will recruit participants to your study:**

(you should include details of how potential participants will be identified, approached and finally recruited)

21. **What measures will you put in place to ensure the confidentiality of personal data gathered during your study?**

22. **Who will have access to the data collected during the study and how will you keep it confidential?**

23. **Will informed consent be obtained from study participants?** Choose an item.

If you have answered **YES** *to the above question, please provide details of how you will obtain this consent and the information you will provide to potential participants to allow them to make an informed choice about whether or not to participate in your research.*

If you have answered **NO** *to the above question, please justify your decision not to obtain consent from your participants.*

24. **How long will potential participants have to decide whether or not to take part in the study?**

(Continued)

25. **Will participants be informed that they can withdraw from the study at any time?** Choose an item.

26. **Will participants be from any of the following groups?**

    Children under 16   ☐

    Adults with learning disabilities   ☐

    Adults who are unconscious or severely ill   ☐

    Adults with a terminal illness   ☐

    Adults in emergency situations   ☐

    Adults with mental illness

    (particularly if detained under the Mental Health Act 2007)   ☐

    Adults with dementia   ☐

    Adults in Scotland who are unable to consent for themselves   ☐

    Those who could be considered to have a particularly dependent
    relationship with the investigator   ☐

    Other   ☐

    None of the above   ☐

*If you answered "**other**" above please provide details:*

If you intend to include participants from any of the above groups please outline how you will mitigate the risks involved:

27. **Are there any special pressures which would make it difficult for potential participants to refuse to take part in your study?**
    (e.g., relationship to the investigator)

28. **Will study participants be paid to take part?** Choose an item.
    *If you have answered **YES** to the above question, please provide details of the payments involved:*

29. **Where will the proposed research take place?**

30. **How will the costs of the study be met?**

31. **Please indicate which supporting documents you are submitting with this application:**

    Participant information sheet (PIS)   ☐
    Consent form   ☐
    Copy of the protocol   ☐
    Letters to participants   ☐
    Letters to parent/guardians/gatekeepers etc.   ☐
    Letter or ethical committee approval or other approvals   ☐
    Risk assessments   ☐
    Other relevant materials (please specify below)   ☐

The information supplied above is, to the best of my knowledge and belief, accurate. I have read the university ethics guidelines and clearly understand my obligations and the rights of study participants, particularly in relation to obtaining valid consent.

Signature of the principal investigator(s):

Date: Click here to enter a date.

Signature of the supervisor:

(if applicable)

Date: Click here to enter a date.

Source: UWS Ethics Committee Guidelines (2021)

Research proposal layout

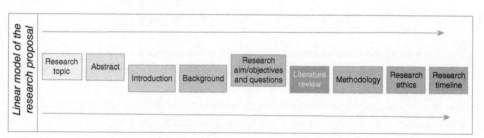

5.7 Summary

- Research ethics are the moral principles that guide how researchers should carry out their study. It involves the application of fundamental ethical principles to guide how research is designed and conducted.
- There are four basic ethical principles that every researcher must bear in mind namely, beneficence and non-maleficence, autonomy, justice and confidentiality and anonymity.
- There are a number of important ethical issues that arise across the different stages of a research project and you need to pay attention to them as they may overlap each other. They include voluntary participation, informed consent, privacy of the participants, data management, intellectual property and integrity.
- It is important to note that in many universities before you embark on a research project, you need to obtain approval from a research ethics committee. The ethical considerations of the project are meticulously scrutinised by the committee to ensure that it meets all the ethical codes of conduct.

Self-check questions

1. What is research ethics?
2. What are the two main philosophical standpoints of ethics in business and management research?
3. Why does ethics matter in research?
4. What are the basic ethical principles that every researcher must bear in mind while conducting research?
5. What is informed consent?
6. What information is usually required to obtain informed consent?
7. What are the ethical issues you will need to consider while conducting business and management research?

Questions for review and discussion

1. Think about the research project that you would like to embark on and discuss how you would obtain ethical approval from your institution bearing in mind the ethical principles and issues to be considered in your project.
2. How would you manage the data that you obtain from your chosen research topic?

Self-check answers

1. Research ethics are the moral principles that guide how researchers should carry out their study. It involves the application of fundamental ethical principles to guide how research is designed and conducted.

2. There are two established philosophical standpoints namely, deontology and teleology. In deontology ethics emphasis is placed on the principles of the decision or action itself and not on the outcome or consequence. In contrast, teleology focuses on the end rather than the action. If the outcome of an action gives rise to benefits, then that action is said to be morally right.

3. Ethics matter for the following reasons

   o The principles promote the general purpose of the study.
   o Ethics helps build public support and credibility.
   o Ethics promotes important moral and social values such as social responsibility, public health and safety.
   o Research most times is a team effort and ethics is important in promoting values that are key to successful collaboration.

4. There are four basic ethical principles that every researcher must bear in mind namely, beneficence and non-maleficence, autonomy, justice and confidentiality and anonymity.

5. Informed consent is obtained when the potential participants are provided with sufficient information in a comprehensible manner to allow them to make a decision.

6. The information required to obtain consent usually involves

   o The purpose of the study
   o The research procedure
   o The risks and anticipated benefits
   o The person conducting the research
   o How long the study will take
   o Who will use the data and its purpose?
   o Limits of confidentiality and anonymity
   o Their right to refuse to participate or withdraw from the study at any time
   o Statement offering the participants the opportunity to ask questions.

7. There are several important ethical issues that you need to pay attention to while conducting your research project. They include voluntary participation, informed consent, privacy of the participants, data management, intellectual property and integrity.

Further reading

Belmont Report (1979) *The Belmont Report: Ethical principles and guidelines for the protection of human subjects of research* Retrieved January 12, 2023, from http://ohsr.od.nih.gov/guidelines/belmont.html

Bryman, A. and Bell, E. (2011) *Business Research Methods.* 3rd ed. Oxford, England: Oxford University Press.

CABS/BAM/HEA Ethics guide (2015) *Ethics Guide 2015: Advice and Guidance* https://charteredabs.org/wp-content/uploads/2015/06/Ethics-Guide-2015-Advice-and-Guidance.pdf

Social Research Association. SRA (2021) *Research Ethical Guidelines* https://the-sra.org.uk/common/Uploaded%20files/Resources/SRA%20Research%20Ethics%20guidance%202021.pdf

6

Negotiating Access to Research Sites and Participants

Learning outcomes

By the end of this chapter, you should be able to:

- understand the problems associated with gaining access to research settings
- identify and determine a range of action plans needed to gain research access
- demonstrate knowledge of the role of gatekeepers and potential informants.

6.1 Introduction

In the previous chapter, we extensively covered the significance of research ethics in the research process. However, even before addressing ethical considerations, gaining access to the participants and organisations involved in your research is a crucial step that often gets overlooked by students and researchers eager to commence their projects.

Access holds the key to successfully collecting data for your research, and without it, your project may remain unrealised, regardless of its potential. In this chapter, we will probe the complexities of **gaining research access**. We will explore the different types and levels of access that researchers encounter and address the associated challenges. Moreover, we will present effective strategies and plans to assist you in securing access to the participants and organisations essential for your research endeavour.

6.2 Issues associated with gaining access

Most business and management research usually involve human participants, so it is not surprising that negotiating access is important. However, whether the data sought is primary or secondary, gaining access is key. Access entails a means of contacting key people in institutions; negotiating with them, being invited to obtain data, achieving formal permission, and constructing relationships with the participants (De la Cuesta Benjumea, 2014). It is the process by which a researcher and the sites and/or individuals he or she studies relate to each other, through which the research in question is enabled (Riese, 2019). Access to data has to be negotiated and trust established in relationships with study participants before data can be obtained.

We define access as the relational and dynamic process by which a researcher is able to approach and establish a relationship with participants and or institutions to enable that data is collected in a credible way to address the aim of the study. It is an ongoing and dynamic process and has to be negotiated and renegotiated.

Gaining access to participants and to information are crucial issues in qualitative research. It is necessary to obtain permission to contact the potential participants, find them, and build the type of relationship that would ensure that data can be collected. Most importantly, these need to be done in an ethical way. Please refer to Chapter 5 on ethics. According to Saunders et al. (2012), there are three types of access. The first type is the traditional access which is common, and it involves face to face interactions, telephone conversations, correspondence and data archives. The second type is the internet-mediated access which involves the use of information technology to gain virtual access and the last type is the hybrid access which combines both traditional and internet-mediated access. You will need to know the type of access you are contemplating when embarking on your research project. Traditional access is more commonly sought. However, gaining virtual access to deliver questionnaires or conduct interviews is now getting popular with more improvement in technology.

In considering access, it is essential to be aware of the level of access required for your research. The depth of access needed will vary depending on whether you are collecting data from an organisation or its participants, making physical access a crucial aspect. However, obtaining physical access can often present challenges. First, organisations are typically inundated with numerous requests for research access, and they may be hesitant to participate in studies they perceive as not adding sufficient value to their operations. Limited time and resources may also discourage their involvement unless they see clear benefits from your research.

Second, gatekeepers within organisations may restrict access to protect potential informants from potential harm or due to concerns about confidentiality. This can impede researchers' efforts to collect the necessary data. Third, bureaucratic structures within organisations can pose barriers to gaining access. Requests for research access may not reach the authorised personnel if the project is not deemed interesting or relevant to the organisation.

Moreover, past negative experiences with research projects can influence how organisations respond to future requests for access. If previous interactions resulted in adverse effects, the organisation might be wary of cooperating, regardless of the potential merits of your current project. Last, personal or egoistic reasons could also influence an organisation's decision regarding research access. Individual stakeholders may prioritise their own interests over participating in external research.

Though physical access is important, it is not the only level of access to be considered. Most of the time you also need to have cognitive access. Cognitive access is the ability to select a representative sample of participants or secondary data to answer your research questions and meet your objectives in an unbiased way (Saunders et al., 2012). Access is likely to be a continuous process and so it could be problematic. It is important that you consider the scope of access you would require to meet your research questions and objectives. The feasibility of your research is dependent on having the ideal participants or secondary data that would answer your research questions and address the purpose of your study.

The duration of the research will also play a key role in the ability of the gatekeeper to provide access. In longitudinal studies, it might be more difficult as the organisation would have to provide access for a sustained period compared to cross sectional research. However, this would not necessarily be an unsurmountable issue, if the organisation is comfortable with the study, its benefits and perceives the researcher to be credible. The onus rests on you as the researcher to create a positive perception to the participants and the organisation. The strategies and plans that we advise that you employ to negotiate access are discussed in section 6.3.

When negotiating access in qualitative research, researchers often find themselves taking on either an external or an internal role. An external role is assumed when the researcher has no prior affiliation or existing relationship with the organisation under study. This is commonly encountered by full-time students who do not have access to a workplace and need to approach organisations that align with their research topic and study objectives. In such cases, gaining access relies heavily on the organisation's willingness to participate and the researcher's ability to convince gatekeepers of the project's value.

However, being an external researcher poses several challenges. One major obstacle is that the organisation may not be familiar with the researcher, leading to a lack of trust or credibility. Building rapport and earning the organisation's confidence becomes crucial in this situation. Demonstrating competence and showcasing the research's potential value can help gain the organisation's cooperation. Case 6.1 provides an illustrative example of the role of an external researcher in the context of access negotiation.

On the other hand, an internal role is assumed when the researcher has an existing affiliation or connection with the organisation being studied. This may occur when researchers have worked in the organisation or have established relationships with key personnel. An internal role can offer advantages in terms of easier access and pre-existing trust. However, it is essential for researchers to maintain objectivity and avoid bias in their research, given their insider status.

Case 6.1   Challenges of an external researcher

George, a full-time research student, aims to investigate the influence of advertising on customer retention within the supermarket industry. His chosen study location is the largest supermarket in the region, aligning with his research questions and sampling strategy. However, George has no prior work experience in this supermarket and is not acquainted with the management team. Securing permission from the gatekeepers and authorised individuals for research is essential before he can proceed with his study. With a strict six-month timeline, time is of the essence for George to gain access and commence his research.

Questions

- What challenges would George have to consider in negotiating access?
- Based on the specificity of the research purpose, which level of access do you envisage would be appropriate for his study?

This is a fictional case. Names, characters, places and incidents either are products of the author's imagination or are used fictitiously. Any resemblance to actual persons, living or dead, or actual events is purely coincidental.

The other role as an internal researcher is adopted when you are working within the organisation. This is common for part-time students who have an affiliation with the establishment. You are less likely to face more problems compared to the external researcher as you have some knowledge about the workings of the organisation. You know the relevant gatekeeper to meet for permission and are more likely to achieve cognitive access as you can identify the participants that meet the criteria for your study easily. However, at times this could also be a challenge. The management might perceive your role in the research to be covert and suspicious about the intent of your study. They might not be keen on providing access to the sensitive information of other employees as you work with them. For the participants involved in the study there could also be some trust issues. A research participant may not trust the internal researcher if they gained access via a gatekeeper who is higher up in the hierarchy than them.

Finally, beyond the traditional access that we have focused on there are also issues with the internet-mediated access. With the rise of the Internet, many modes of data collection can be delivered online. Interviews are conducted via Zoom, Microsoft Teams and Skype. Questionnaires can be sent via email. Nevertheless, these internet-mediated methods face the same issues we highlighted for traditional access. You will still need to obtain permission from the gatekeeper to gain access to participants in the organisation to collect data virtually via interviews or questionnaires.

Scholars such as Saunders et al. (2012) propose that traditional access may be more appropriate than internet-mediated access to collect data. The challenges of access such as creating trust and demonstrating competence can be easily addressed when this is done in person rather than virtually. However, internet-mediated access is beneficial as you can reach out to your participants from any location and at their convenience. As a result, we advise that a hybrid access strategy is employed which combines both and is arguably a good way of getting the best of both worlds.

6.3 Strategic action/plans for gaining research access

As qualitative researchers, we always seek the best strategy for empirical inquiry. The path taken by qualitative scholars intersects more frequently than those dedicated to quantitative studies. For qualitative research, the common currency for research inquiry recognises that credible approaches should involve making connections among social and cultural structures. Yet, gaining access to these structures continues to be an ongoing limitation for many researchers. A more formally acceptable justification lies in the lack of adequate knowledge needed to access such structures. The distinction is that gaining research access comprises possessing the assumptions, skills and approaches needed to collect empirical data. As a matter of fact, the best strategies would easily connect researchers to specific approaches and practices to gaining access. To put this into motion, we turn now to an overview of our preferred approaches.

Warming up to gain access

A difficult part of any research project is the initial process of gaining access, identifying what to do and approaching the right contacts. To gain access, the first decision has to do with preparation. Morse (1999) advocates that researchers may find that practising explaining their study via role plays can help mitigate anxiety barriers. This will include the research questions you seek to address, the nature of the research and with whom. While preparations and adequate planning are needed when one seeks to gain physical access, it may not be less applicable when relying on postal services or internet-based questionnaires. Because qualitative research can be unstructured, the warming up stage requires allocating the right choices needed to gain research access. A helpful tactic relates to planning, which includes identifying the research site, refining the research purpose, obtaining ethical institutional ethical approvals, and locating possible participants. Good qualitative researchers are detailed, meticulous with excellent organisational skills. They ensure they have investigated the organisation, gatekeepers and potential participants. This ensures that they are familiar with the context and ensures success. Acknowledging this much, we believe that the following basic question to inform one's ability to gain access should include the following:

1	What is the purpose of my study and why does it matter?
2	What do I want to know in this study?
3	How do I overcome the barriers of access?
4	Do I have any contacts any contacts there?
5	How do I convince gatekeepers to listen to me?
6	How do I establish credibility?

In terms of the above items, it is important to emphasise at the outset that gaining research access involves developing passage and contacts within a given research setting, such that it is possible for the research to gather data. Once these questions have been answered, the next step will be to select the appropriate approach.

Making the introductory contact

In scenarios where researchers conduct their research in unfamiliar settings, which is often a prevalent scenario in various research projects, they are faced with limited informants. They will have to resort to contacting potential interviewees directly via mail to request an interview. A well-crafted introductory mail for this purpose should clearly communicate the research's purpose, the significance of the study, the expected interview duration, and most importantly, the researcher's credibility. If necessary, a letter of introduction from the researcher's institution can be included to enhance credibility. However, it is essential to acknowledge that waiting for replies to interview or access requests may be time-consuming. In such cases, making polite telephone calls can be an effective solution to request access and discuss the research intent directly. On the other hand, researchers may also initiate contact through a telephone call and follow up with an official letter addressed to the appropriate contact. This approach allows the researcher to communicate their intention clearly and professionally.

It is essential to avoid conducting research in settings where the researcher is employed, as it may lead to conflicts of interest and potential workplace tensions. The role of the researcher and that of an employee are incompatible, and undertaking research in such settings may compromise confidentiality and anonymity, both of which are critical principles in the research process.

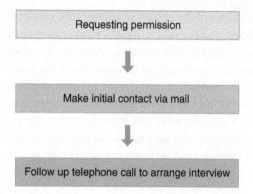

Figure 6.1   Negotiating initial contact

Entering the research setting

Identifying an appropriate setting is an important part of the research process. Familiarity with the organisation, the nature of its business and the group to be studied reduces the likelihood of an unduly lengthened research process. Note that gaining access to research sites requires the approval of gatekeepers. More precisely, such difficulty is prevalent accessing larger organisations, where the approval of several gatekeepers is needed. But the trite question here is who are the gatekeepers? The role of the gatekeeper as a propelling factor in gaining access cannot be over-emphasised. They are individuals who provide access or authority to the way information is disseminated. As a result, they possess the power to control whether the researcher can access the data they seek. In other words, their role involves providing permission to access data. As a matter of fact, express permission from a central authority, for example the CEO, can facilitate contact with participants across the various departments. Initial conversations with these gatekeepers would demand that you highlight the credibility and purpose of your intention. You will need to demonstrate that you will abide by ethical principles guiding your research (see more on ethics in Chapter 5). At this stage, it will be useful to provide copies of your likely questions, a consent form, your letter of introduction from your university, a document stating the purpose of your research and how it will be disseminated.

Locating informants or insiders

Accordingly, the process of gaining access involves developing relationships which will be conducive to the execution of the study. In this process, the researcher must understand that access typically involves understanding the language; the expectations; the rules, norms and boundaries of the research setting (Schensul et al., 1999). Consequently, it is convenient to identify and locate contacts who may provide relevant information pertaining to the study setting. For instance, the use of informants is evidently one approach that, in principle, is congenial to researchers because it is practical and cost effective. The fact of the matter is that the term informant can be ascribed to a person who has knowledge about an organisation, culture or membership of a given group.

We refer to them as people who can contribute to the investigation of the unit of analysis. The emphasis on the technique of relying on informants must contend with several different considerations, the most important of which stresses that in the early stages of the research, the informant should be seen to access information, gain access and receive ongoing feedback during the data collection process. There are also other important reasons but, so far, informants are recognised as reliable because they possess knowledge about what the participants may think, believe and feel. They are noted to be gatekeepers and insiders within the research setting. Indeed, an important decision implies that the logic behind selecting informants is that they must be information rich. The central point here is that to achieve the best explanations of a phenomenon, informants must be determined according to the needs of the study. The suggested explanation is that seeking out exceptionally knowledgeable and reliable informants can be an arduous task.

One issue concerns bias. However, we acknowledge that bias in such cases can be mitigated by relying on multiple informants. Elsewhere, Omeihe (2019) has advanced the thesis that espouses this discourse. In his study of West African entrepreneurs, he reports that the position of the key informants and their status within the community underscores their roles as gatekeepers. His interactions with key informants facilitated access to a sufficiently vast range of research participants. Of the possible ways of achieving this, his ability to develop trust and rapport with these informants is one which probably enables the opportunity to meet with key actors. As Omeihe, for one, has pointed out, more often than not, informants who are identified for their particular knowledge and position can provide insights to the richness and breadth of the data to be obtained.

Obtaining trust during research

Good qualitative researchers must understand the art of being trusted in the research setting. The need for trust is seen to arise from the existence of curiosity generated on the part of the gatekeeper or the doubts on the part of participants. Given such constraints, trust as a lubricating mechanism is required to make the interaction appear to work in a well-defined ethical manner. Thus, the real challenge for researchers is ensuring that they can obtain trust, first from the gatekeepers and second, from the participants. Yet, there is no way to overcome this constraint without being open and truthful in your dealings. If on the other hand, your motives appear unclear and unconvincing, you will meet with stiff resistance and possibly be refused access. Hence, once the gatekeeper has expressed some initial interest, the next step in the process would be developing the relationship. This often takes time. However, for the research to take place, trust can be obtained by building a good rapport. This would involve being honest, true to yourself, patient and pleasant. Others may include general conversations around the organisation and perhaps areas where you believe you both share mutual interests. This said, there is clearly a need to ensure such conversations are held in a setting where discussions can be open and natural. Another, more realistic issue is that the use of audio recorders during initial conversations can lead to anxiety on the part of the gatekeeper or participant. As noted by Easterby-Smith et al. (2008), anxiety can be mitigated by handing over the audio recorder such that it can be turned on and off when they don't want parts of the conversation to be recorded, can be a means of obtaining trust. One thing is clear, anxiety leads to more scrutiny which inhibits the potential for continued progress.

Table 6.1   Strategic actions for gaining research access

Decisions	Description
Warming up access	This stage involves preparing and adequate planning before approaching the research setting. This includes making the right choices needed to gain research access.
Making the introductory contact	This is a golden opportunity to communicate your intention. It involves making initial contact through telephone calls and following up with an official letter addressed to the right contact (or the other way round).
Entering the research setting	This stage involves gaining the approval of gatekeepers. Initial conversations with these gatekeepers would demand that you highlight the credibility and purpose of your intention.
Locating informants	This involves identifying and locating insiders who may provide relevant information pertaining to the study setting.
Obtaining trust during research	Trust can be obtained by building a good rapport. This would involve being honest, true to yourself, patient and pleasant during conversations.

6.4 Summary

- Access entails a means of contacting key people in institutions; negotiating with them, being invited to obtain data, achieving formal permission, and constructing relationships.
- Cognitive access is the ability to select a representative sample of participants or secondary data to answer your research questions and meet your objectives in an unbiased way.

- Traditional access may be more appropriate than internet-mediated access for collecting data.
- As qualitative researchers, we always seek the best strategy for empirical inquiry.
- A helpful tactic for gaining access relates to planning, which includes identifying the research site, refining the research purpose, obtaining institutional ethical approvals and locating possible participants.
- Gatekeepers are individuals who provide access or authority to the way information is disseminated.

Case study   gaining research access

I embarked on a four-hour road journey, and upon arrival, I met with my guide and informant, Maxwell, who had been eagerly waiting for me. Maxwell is deeply knowledgeable about the local commerce in the market and holds a prominent position within the community as an active farmer. Having him as my guide proved immensely beneficial, as it provided me access to a diverse group of local entrepreneurs. Our strong rapport and relationship paved the way for a positive perception of me among the community members. To blend in and avoid standing out as an outsider, I dressed in the traditional northern kaftan, complete with a matching hat, similar to Maxwell's attire. I was also cautious about the sensitive environment, considering past cases of ethnic clashes and attacks in the region.

The trust and cooperation I received from the interview participants were largely based on the trust they had in Maxwell, and subsequently, the rapport I built with them. Initially, some of the traders were intrigued by my audio-recorder, mistaking me for a journalist. However, they became even more excited to share their experiences with a foreign researcher.

Class Questions:

Who is Maxwell, and what role did he play in the passage?

How would the researcher's access have been difficult without Maxwell's assistance?

Why is obtaining trust essential during the research process?

Discuss the significance of anonymity in research and why it is crucial.

What could have fascinated the participants about the audio recorder during the interviews?

Source: Excerpts from Omeihe's (2019) reflexivity journal

Self-check questions

1. What is access?
2. What are the three types of access?
3. What are the reasons that may prevent gatekeepers from providing access?
4. Provide a list of strategic action/plans for gaining research access?

Questions for review and discussion

1. Think about the research project that you would like to conduct within a chosen organisation and discuss how you would negotiate access into the organisation as an external researcher.
2. As an internal researcher who intends to conduct research within your workplace, consider a list of possible barriers to your gaining access and how these might be overcome.

Self-check answers

1. Access is the relational and dynamic process by which a researcher is able to approach and establish a relationship with participants and/or institutions to enable data to be collected in a credible way to address the aim of the study. It is an ongoing and dynamic process and has to be negotiated and renegotiated.
2. There are three types of access. The first type is the traditional access which involves face to face interactions, telephone conversations, correspondence and data archives. The second type is internet-mediated access which involves the use of information technology to gain virtual access and the last type is hybrid access which combines both traditional and internet-mediated access.
3. There are several reasons that may prevent gatekeepers from providing access namely:

   o Organisations are usually inundated with many requests for research access and are usually not keen to embark on studies that they perceive not to add value to their organisation.
   o Their time is limited and supporting research is mostly out of good will if they cannot see the advantage from your study.

(Continued)

- o Gatekeepers may restrict researchers' access because they fear that potential informants will be harmed by the research.
- o The information that you may be requesting could be confidential and they are not open to divulging such information.
- o Many organisations have a bureaucratic structure and your request for research access may not get to the gatekeeper or authorised person especially if the project is not interesting to the organisation.
- o Prior experience with research projects could also determine how organisations react to a request for research access. If they have been negatively affected in the past, they might not be keen on cooperating regardless of how good your project seems.
- o It could also be for egoistic reasons.

Further reading

Easterby-Smith, M., Thorpe, R. and Lowe, A. (2008) *Management Research.* 3rd ed. London: Sage.

Morse, J.M. (1999) Qualitative methods: The state of the art. *Qualitative Health Research,* 9(3), 393–406.

Saunders, M., Lewis, P. and Thornhill, A. (2012) *Research Methods for Business Students.* 6th ed. Edinburgh Gate, Harlow, Essex, England: Pearson Education Limited.

7

Sampling

Learning outcomes

After completing this chapter, you will be able to achieve the following objectives:

- understand key sampling assumptions and defend the chosen selections
- examine the issues associated with making sampling decisions
- identify the connections between the primary types of probability and non-probability sampling
- recognise the different types of non-probability sampling, including quota sampling
- justify the participant selection process to provide comprehensive, in-depth, and relevant data for reporting and authentic analysis
- demonstrate your knowledge by applying the information gained in this chapter to your research project.

By achieving these objectives, you will develop a strong understanding of sampling for qualitative research and be able to apply this knowlesdge to ensure that your research design is sound and that your data collection process is robust.

7.1 Introduction

This chapter looks into the topic of sampling for qualitative research. Our aim is to explore various sampling techniques and address the inherent pitfalls in the process. The chapter will primarily focus on the selection of sample types, which has long been a well-researched aspect of the research process. To obtain an information-rich sample, we acknowledge that researchers need to select informants logically. Therefore, we argue that sample determination should align with the study's needs to provide the best explanation of the phenomenon under investigation. This is because reporting and authentic analysis will be based on comprehensive, in-depth and relevant data. Hence, it is crucial to justify the participant selection process.

Furthermore, we will demonstrate how sampling aligns with the research question, the study's objectives, and the overall research design. A robust sampling process enhances the credibility and rigour of the research findings, such that the data analysed is representative and reflective of the study population. As you know, conducting interviews or surveys with the whole population is often not feasible. We will conclude by drawing attention to how several sampling techniques enable researchers to capture data from specific sub-groups rather than the entire population.

7.2 Sampling: significance for research

Chapter 6 examined the subject of negotiating access, outlining the process of obtaining permission to access data by reaching out to influential figures within institutions, engaging in negotiations, securing invitations, obtaining formal clearance, and building relationships with participants. The chapter underscored the importance of establishing trust with study participants before data can be collected, emphasising the pivotal role of participant selection based on specific criteria. For readers who are students or researchers, sampling can emerge at different points of the research process. This is consistent with Flick (2020) who notes that sampling decisions occur at three stages in the research process. For example, as qualitative researchers, sampling considerations would naturally arise with decisions relating to the interviews-data collection process (*data collection stage*). It can also emerge during the interpretation of the findings (*interpretation stage*) and when presenting your findings (*presentation of findings stage*). In this vein, the key questions to be asked include determining which portion of the data corpus should be interpreted and identifying the most effective way to present the findings.

Table 7.1   **Research stages and sampling approaches**

Research Stages	Sampling Approaches
Sampling during the data collection stage	Sampling via interviews, observation or case
Sampling during the interpretation stage	Sampling within the data corpus
Sampling during the findings stage	Sampling during the research presentation

Sampling is a crucial component of the research process. The term originated from quantitative research, where researchers sought to identify participants drawn from a larger population sample. It is a systematic approach to identifying cases that can help address the purpose of the study. This involves selecting a subset of the population for data collection, and the data obtained from this subset can then be used to make inferences about the wider population. Understanding the principles that govern sampling is essential for selecting a representative sample. As a matter of fact, sampling reduces the amount of data to be considered, as it is often impractical to collect data from an entire population due to budget constraints, time limitations and other factors. In our conversations with students, we often mention that the choice of sampling method is important regardless of the data collection technique employed, whether it be interviews, questionnaires, observation or another method. For example, researchers may only be able to obtain permission to collect data from a limited number of organisations. Similarly, testing an entire population of products for certain characteristics may be impractical for manufacturers. Moving ahead, the next section will focus on exploring two key methods for exploring qualitative research.

Exploring sampling techniques: an overview of two main sampling types

Deciding which technique to adopt during a given study is crucial for any research study. The best form of research has been found to select the most appropriate sampling technique to ensure that the right results are achieved. When used appropriately, sampling techniques are useful for obtaining valid and very reliable results that can accurately capture the populations of interest. In simple terms, the term sampling can be defined as the process of selecting parts of a population to collect data, with the goal of drawing findings from parts of an entire group. Sampling techniques can be categorised into two types: probability and non-probability sampling. We locate these two sampling techniques at the extreme of two poles – with the first focusing on abstract criteria while the other focuses on a concrete set of criteria.

Probability is associated with quantitative research and is often associated with the use of experimentation and surveys. With probability sampling, there is indeed an equal chance of being selected from the population. This implies that one can almost accurately estimate the characteristics of a population by relying on the findings from a given sample. As a sampling technique, its focus involves the random selection of participants from a given population. By doing so, the goal is to ensure that every member of the population has an equal opportunity of being selected. This then increases the likelihood of achieving accurate results, thereby reducing the risk of bias. The logic of probability sampling involves studying samples according to certain criteria such as demographic criteria or perhaps samples that capture the representation of such criteria within a given population.

Obtaining a probabilistic sampling methodology in the field can be very challenging, particularly for hard-to-reach or hidden populations. However, this is often not a primary concern in field studies since they tend to be oriented towards exploring theoretical insights and in-depth research questions rather than statistical generalisability. As a result, a non-probability sampling (or non-random sampling) approach is generally considered the most practical option as it allows for an information-rich study that can provide valuable insights.

Underscoring the above, the alternative approach to probability sampling is the technique of non-probability sampling. For non-probability on the other hand involves selecting participants based on a set of predetermined criteria. This technique is most productive when studying smaller or specific sub-groups within a given population. Given this case, sampling here is often limited in criteria: for instance, sampling a given culture, student experience, region, and specific cases to mention a few. To achieve progress, selections of the population that do not meet the criteria will be excluded in advance. What this implies is that the researcher would have to make sampling decisions and devise structures aimed at selecting the relevant groups or cases.

Nonetheless, it is important to recognise that non-probability sampling may lead to biased results as some of the participants within the population will have a higher opportunity of being selected than other members. It is important to note that for non-probability sampling, samples do not have an equal chance of being selected as in probability sampling. A researcher who considers the non-probability technique would find it impossible to address research questions that involve making numerical or statistical assumptions about the attributes of a given population. While there exists the chance of making generalisations, these generalisations are not grounded on statistical interpretations. From this perspective, it is why probability sampling is commonly used in quantitative studies, whereas non-probability sampling is more prevalent in qualitative research. For instance, when collecting data through interviews, the number of samples selected is driven by the need to comprehend the local actors' real-world experiences. However, non-probability sampling for qualitative research is influenced by factors such as access, resources and time, rather than statistical constraints. As a result, non-probability sampling techniques are often valuable in qualitative research.

Given that this text is largely devoted to qualitative research, our goal here will be to examine the types of non-probability sampling with a view to understanding its relevance for data collection and analysis.

7.3 Non-probability sampling types

In the earlier discussions, we have come to understand that there are primarily two types of sampling – probability and non-probability. However, in the context of this section and by extension this book, we will devote our learning to understanding the types of non-probability sampling. As discussed, in non-probability sampling, the

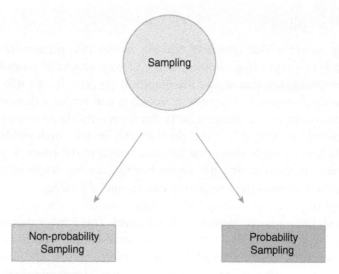

Figure 7.1   **Sampling techniques**

likelihood of each entity in a population entity being considered cannot be known. This is because it is difficult to ascertain the probability of any of the selected members within the population being selected. That is why for non-probability sampling, it is often difficult for a researcher to report that the findings generated from a particular sample may be applicable to the larger populations from which the samples were selected.

Another striking feature of non-probability sampling is that it provides a series of alternative means to capture subjective judgements in the research selection process. And in this vein, by undertaking qualitative research, non-probability sampling is always considered the most appropriate approach as it provides the opportunity to yield a more robust understanding of the selected samples. It is also very useful in providing information-rich findings and theoretical insights that explore research questions in-depth. Consequently, good researchers always determine non-probability sampling via the proposed research strategy – this will involve a consideration of the research objectives and questions. There is admittedly the fact that in-depth studies that examine certain research phenomena would adopt a non-probability sampling technique. Such an approach allows the researcher to uncover valuable and information-rich results that explore the given research questions. In qualitative parlance, non-probability sampling can also be useful in situations where it is difficult to define the sample frame or in other instances, where there may be a scarcity of resources. In this light, one or more non-probability sampling techniques can be considered. As a result, the next section is devoted to examining the types of non-probability sampling as well as presenting new evidence for their interpretations.

Purposive sampling

A noteworthy aspect is that sampling typically serves two primary objectives. The first objective is to ensure that samples fulfil either an empirical purpose or a theoretical purpose. Sampling that serves the empirical purpose is valuable in providing answers to research inquiries. Conversely, sampling that serves a theoretical purpose is employed to construct or enhance a particular theory. By aligning this better, purposive or purposeful sampling is best described as a technique employed by researchers to deliberately select sample cases that are most suited to the research purpose. This unique sampling method allows the researcher to exercise discernment and select cases that can best address the research questions and objectives.

The concept of **purposive sampling** revolves around the selection of samples that are aligned with the research question and objectives. This implies that as a technique it can be particularly relevant in situations where small sample sizes are required, such as in case studies. However, a set of inclusion criteria is typically needed to guide the selection process, whereby entities are screened to determine their eligibility for inclusion in the sample. Once the selected entities meet the inclusion criteria, they are included in the sample. As a result, the utility of purposive sampling lies in its ability to aid researchers in selecting sample cases that align with the research objectives.

Although purposive sampling is a valuable research method, we acknowledge that it has the potential to exclude certain participant samples, leading to bias. In such cases, the researcher may overlook other potentially relevant samples that could have contributed valuable insights to the research findings. Reasons for such exclusions may include suspicion about the researcher's intentions or the role of gatekeepers and perhaps, risks to the participants, as well as the fact that these samples may be unknown to both the researcher and the informant.

Types of purposive sampling

It is important to emphasise that there are various types of purposive sampling that a researcher can utilise, and this has direct relevance to our understanding of sampling. As previously mentioned, purposive sampling is a non-probability sampling method that involves the identification and selection of participants based on a specific objective, as opposed to random selection.

Moving forward, we will explore the different types of purposive sampling techniques that researchers can employ. These include:

> *Extreme Case Sampling:* This form of purposive sampling entails choosing participants who are considered unusual or exceptional within a particular population of interest. The objective is to enable the researcher to obtain a better understanding of the experiences of the selected participants. This means that

by selecting extreme participants, or what is commonly known as outliers, the researcher can unearth the various aspects and boundaries of a given phenomenon and, in turn, identify the factors that influence these extreme outcomes.

Critical Case Sampling: This form of purposive sampling entails the identification and selection of samples that are anticipated to be crucial and highly valuable to the specific study. The approach seeks out participants who are not only essential in addressing the research question but are also capable of providing profound insights into the phenomenon under investigation. This technique is typically employed when a researcher endeavours to pinpoint participants who can offer a wealth of information for a given study. This becomes particularly vital when the population of interest appears to be vast or diverse.

Heterogeneous or Maximum Variation Sampling: In this sampling method, the researcher aims to include participants who possess a range of varied characteristics that are pertinent to the research inquiry. The objective is to guarantee that the sample selection encompasses individuals from various age groups, genders, backgrounds, socioeconomic statuses and other relevant factors. This enables the researcher to obtain a comprehensive range of insights regarding the experiences and viewpoints of the population sample. Although it may seem slightly confusing, utilising the heterogeneous sampling technique yields numerous advantages since the diverse characteristics of the participants can facilitate the identification of valuable and intriguing findings.

Homogenous sampling: As a purposive sampling method, it involves selecting participants who possess similar characteristics or experiences that are pertinent to the research question. This technique is commonly applied when the researcher intends to examine a specific aspect of the population, such as a particular sub-group or experience. Unlike the heterogenous sampling approach, the objective of homogeneous sampling is to identify participants who share significant characteristics that are relevant to the research question. For instance, if a researcher seeks to investigate the experiences of Covid-19 patients, they may utilise homogeneous sampling to select participants who have all undergone symptoms. By selecting participants who have this shared characteristic, the researcher can explore the common experiences, challenges and coping mechanisms that are specific to this sub-group.

Another benefit of homogeneous sampling is that it can generate detailed and comprehensive data that is specific to a particular sub-group. Nevertheless, it is important to note that this technique may limit the generalisability of the findings to the larger population. Furthermore, we recommend that the researcher must carefully consider the criteria for selecting participants, to ensure that they are pertinent to the research question.

Typical Case Sampling: This method involves selecting participants who are considered typical or representative of the larger population being studied. The aim is to choose cases that embody the most common or standard characteristics or experiences within the population. By selecting participants who are representative of the population of interest, the researcher is able to gain insights into the most widespread experiences, perspectives and behavioural patterns within the population.

In acknowledging the various types of purposive sampling, we do state that each of these types of purposive sampling techniques has its strengths and limitations. However, it is important to note that the choice of sampling technique should be guided by the research question, the characteristics of the population of interest, and the resources available to the researcher. Figure 7.2 captures the types of purposive sampling.

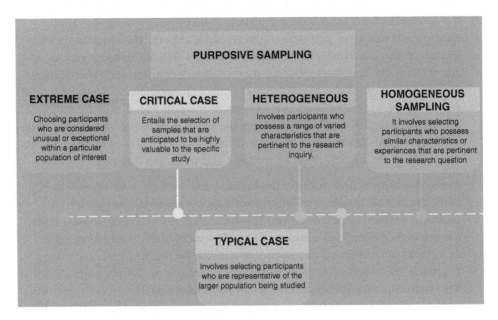

Figure 7.2 **Types of purposive sampling techniques**

Quota sampling

Quota sampling is a popular method used in non-probability sampling for interview surveys. This technique involves dividing a population into specific units and setting quotas for each unit based on relevant information. Researchers then collect data from each quota group and combine them to obtain a more comprehensive sample result. Compared to probability sampling methods, quota sampling is often preferred due to its cost-effectiveness and simplicity, particularly for data collection that does not require a sample frame. Quota sampling is also useful for market research and gathering opinions on demographic characteristics such as age, gender and class. However, quota sampling has its limitations. The selection process may introduce biases if researchers select respondents based on ease of access or willingness, which could lead to participants not meeting the quota criteria. To minimise these biases, protocols should be in place to ensure the proper selection of participants.

Convenience sampling

Convenience sampling involves selecting participants or samples based on their accessibility. For instance, a researcher may distribute a questionnaire on bank loan savings to fellow executive MBA students who are also bankers. However, because this approach involves selecting participants based on ease of selection, there is a high likelihood of bias and uncontrolled influences. It is essential to note that the findings from convenience sampling cannot be easily generalised due to uncertainty about the representativeness of the selected sample. Nevertheless, convenience sampling is a valuable tool for conducting pilot studies that can inform future research that employs more rigorous sampling techniques.

Snowball sampling

Snowball sampling has garnered increasing attention among both novice and experienced researchers due to its efficacy and resemblance to convenience sampling. This sampling method entails initially contacting a small group of individuals pertinent to the research focus and subsequently utilisng their networks to identify additional relevant participants. The goal will be to leverage their networks to identify other participants who will be relevant to the research. For instance, Omeihe's (2019) study on trust among Nigerian entrepreneurs employed snowball sampling by leveraging the support of informants and the head of a trade association to gain access to several indigenous traders. These traders facilitated introductions to other relevant traders, thereby enhancing the informativeness of the interviews and providing an accurate representation of the process of building and repairing trust.

The snowball sampling method involves initially targeting a group of individuals who can provide links to other potential participants, as seen in the case of Omeihe (2019). This process continues until the researcher reaches a point where no further participants are needed for the study. While snowball sampling shares the limitation of other sampling methods in that it may not provide a representative sample of the entire population, its strength lies in the fact that it is typically used when accessing the appropriate sample participants is challenging.

As snowballing progresses, it introduces more bias challenges, increasing the likelihood that researchers will be partial towards certain sample networks. This, in turn, may restrict the potential for discovering comprehensive and reliable results in the study. To address this issue, researchers should be attentive and incorporate a varied range of sample participants based on their understanding of the population within the sample size.

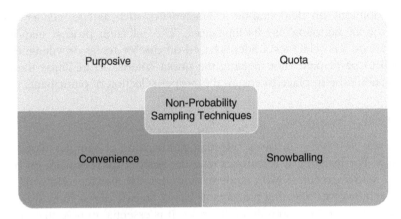

Figure 7.3   **Types of non-probability sampling**

Other sampling approaches

Although there are four primary non-probability sampling methods, it's important to acknowledge that there are additional approaches for selecting samples from a larger population corpus. This section aims to explore some of these alternative methods and broaden our understanding of contemporary sampling concepts. After reviewing Salmons's (2022) work, we have presented the information in a tabular format to make it easier to comprehend and learn. We have also summarised some of the concepts discussed above in the table below.

7.4 Benefits of non-probability sampling in qualitative research

In this section, we will discuss the advantages of using non-probability sampling in qualitative research. While we have previously discussed the types of non-probability sampling and their limitations, non-probability sampling offers several benefits.

First, non-probability sampling enables researchers to gain a more in-depth understanding of the phenomenon being studied. By collecting relatively small data, researchers can immerse themselves in the world of the actors and gain insights into the research question. Non-probability sampling also provides flexibility, allowing researchers to adjust their techniques based on the data collected, and refine their research objectives and questions. Another benefit of non-probability sampling is that it allows for subjectivity in decision-making. This is because qualitative research is interested in the subjective nature of human interactions and experiences. Thus, adopting a non-probabilistic sampling approach enables researchers to capture the lived experiences, perceptions, attitudes and opinions of the selected participants, leading to a more robust understanding of the phenomenon being studied.

Table 7.2 Qualitative sampling approaches and concepts

Type	Description of Approach	Benefit
Convenience sampling	This involves the selection of participants based on their availability and ease of access.	Though it is recognised for having the lowest credibility due to its ability to produce information-weak samples and findings, it is helpful in saving time, money and research effort.
Critical case sampling	In this approach, the researcher identifies samples which are critical to the understanding of the phenomenon being investigated.	It is useful in making generalisations about other parts of the population. This implies that what holds for the critical cases, may apply to other sample cases.
Emergent sampling	This sampling approach involves selecting participants as they emerge in the research process.	It is very useful during fieldwork, especially in cases where there is no prior sample specification.
Heterogeneous samples	This can be defined as a strategy to capture participants with different experiences of the phenomena being investigated. This may include samples deliberately drawn from a wide range of individuals, cases or events.	The goal is to enable the researcher to identify distinct but diverse themes and patterns that may not be evident in a homogenous sample.
Homogenous samples	These refer to samples that share similar traits or characteristics that are relevant to the phenomenon being studied.	It focuses on common traits and as a result, reduces the variation. They are also useful for increasing the internal validity of a study. However, it limits the generalisability of the findings to other populations with different characteristics.
Deviant or extreme cases	This is a sampling technique where the researcher intentionally selects sample participants who are atypical or extreme in some way. This approach to sampling is useful when the researcher is very interested in studying groups or individuals who fall outside of the norm.	This technique is useful as researchers can learn highly unusual manifestations of interests such as outstanding success, the effects of body stress, investigating soldiers who have survived combat in wars, notable failures or the number of dropouts.
Theoretical sampling	This involves the selection of participants based on the emerging theories and concepts being developed during the research process. In this technique, the researcher selects samples based on the insights gained during the data collection and analysis phases of the research, rather than selecting participants in advance based on preconceived notions.	It is useful as it can lead to the emergence of rich insights into complex phenomena.
Volunteer sampling	This is a type of sampling where participants are selected based on their willingness to participate in the research. Here, participants would usually respond to invitations seeking research participants. It is also referred to as a self-selection sampling technique. It is very useful for online research where participants can easily respond to an invitation to participate in the research.	It is useful as participants can easily respond to an invitation to engage in a given research. Furthermore, it stands out in situations where participant recruitment may be challenging or in cases where the population to be studied is difficult to reach. For example, investigating people with rare diseases.
Typical case sampling	This is a type of purposive sampling where participants are selected because they appear to be representative of the larger population under study. In such an instance, the researcher selects participants based on the notion that they exhibit typical or the most characteristics of the population being studied.	An important benefit of a typical case sampling is that it allows the researcher to identify and select participants who can provide in-depth and rich information that represents the population under study.

Particularly worth stressing is the fact that non-probability sampling recognises diversity as a benefit. In this vein, researchers can collect data from participants with different cultural, ethnic and background experiences, adding credibility and richness to the findings. Additionally, contextualisation is a crucial benefit of non-probability sampling. By investigating how participants perceive and make sense of their experiences within specific contexts, researchers can develop a more holistic understanding of the research topic.

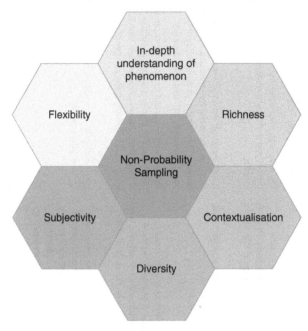

Figure 7.4   **Benefits of sampling in qualitative research**

7.5 Summary

The chapter focuses on the importance of sampling in the research process.

- First, understanding the principles that govern sampling is crucial for selecting a representative sample.
- Sampling decisions occur at three stages in the research process: during the data collection process, interpretation of findings, and systematic identification of cases.
- Sampling reduces the amount of data to be considered and is often necessary due to budget constraints, time limitations and other factors.
- Sampling techniques can be categorised into two types: probability and non-probability sampling.
- Probability sampling involves the random selection of participants from a given population.
- In contrast, non-probability sampling involves selecting participants based on a set of predetermined criteria. While probability sampling ensures an equal

chance of being selected from the population, non-probability sampling allows for subjectivity and flexibility in the selection process.

- Sampling is an essential component of the research process and requires careful consideration and decision-making. The selection of a representative sample through probability or non-probability sampling techniques is necessary to achieve the purpose of the study.
- The chapter emphasises the potential bias that may result from non-probability sampling, as some participants may have a higher chance of being selected than others.
- Purposive sampling is described as a technique used by researchers to deliberately select sample cases that are most suitable for the research purpose.
- Quota sampling involves dividing a population into specific units and setting quotas for each unit based on relevant information.
- Convenience sampling involves selecting participants or samples based on their accessibility.
- Snowball sampling entails initially contacting a small group of individuals relevant to the research focus and utilising their networks to identify additional participants, making it useful for hard-to-reach populations.
- In summary, purposive, quota, convenience and snowball sampling are alternative techniques that researchers may employ to achieve their research objectives.

Self-check questions

1. What is non-probability sampling, and how does it differ from probability sampling?
2. What are some common types of non-probability sampling, and how do they differ from each other?
3. What are the advantages and disadvantages of using non-probability sampling techniques in research?
4. What are some potential sources of bias in non-probability sampling, and how can researchers address them?
5. When might researchers choose to use non-probability sampling techniques over probability sampling techniques?
6. What are some common criteria used to select participants in non-probability sampling, and why are they important?
7. How might researchers ensure that their non-probability sample is representative of the larger population?
8. How can researchers increase the reliability and validity of findings obtained through non-probability sampling?
9. In what circumstances might non-probability sampling not be appropriate for a research study?
10. What is purposive sampling and what are the types of purposive sampling?
11. How does quota sampling differ from convenience sampling?

Self-check answers

1.   Non-probability sampling involves selecting participants based on a set of predetermined criteria, whilst probability sampling ensures an equal chance of being selected from the population, non-probability sampling allows for subjectivity and flexibility in the selection process.

2.   Convenience Sampling: This involves selecting participants who are easiest to access. Judgmental or Purposive Sampling: This involves selecting participants based on their knowledge or experience related to the research topic. Snowball Sampling: Here, participants recruit other participants from their network. Quota Sampling: This involves ensuring that the sample reflects certain characteristics of the population in specific proportions.

3.   For advantages: It is easier and quicker to organise, cost-effective, and suitable for exploratory research or when probability sampling is impractical. For disadvantages: There is a higher risk of sampling bias, limited generalisability, and challenges in inferring population-level conclusions from the sample.

4.   A range of potential biases include self-selection bias, over-representation of particular groups, and under-representation of others. In such cases, researchers can address them by being transparent about the sampling limitations and carefully justifying the choice of sampling method relative to the research objectives.

5.   When the research is exploratory or descriptive, when the population is hard to define, when time and resources are limited, or when the study focuses on a specific case or phenomenon rather than aiming for broad generalizability.

6.   Some of the relevant criteria might include specific demographic characteristics, experience, knowledge, or proximity to the research topic. These criteria are important to ensure that the sample adequately represents the population or phenomenon of interest, enhancing the relevance and utility of the research findings.

7.   While true representativeness is challenging with non-probability samples, researchers can strive for it by carefully defining sampling criteria and providing a thorough, transparent account of the sampling process and its limitations.

8.   Researchers can achieve reliability and validity of their findings by ensuring the research design is robust, validating findings through participant feedback, and being transparent about the study's limitations.

9.   When the aim is to make generalisable inferences about a population where statistical representativeness and the ability to calculate error margins are crucial.

10.   Purposive sampling involves selecting participants based on specific characteristics or qualities. Types include expert sampling, critical case sampling, homogeneous sampling etc, each should be tailored to the particular research needs and questions.

11.   Quota sampling involves identifying specific characteristics that the sample must reflect and then selecting participants until these quotas are met. This implies ensuring some level of representativeness. Convenience sampling, however, involves selecting participants based on their ease of access, with no regard for how well they represent the broader population.

Case study   Non-probability sampling in action

Title

Trade Associations and Trust in Weak Institutional Contexts: *Exploring SME Relationships in Nigeria.*

Introduction

Many scholars have criticised the adoption of quantitative analysis in interpreting social behaviour and entrepreneurial experience, arguing that such processes are difficult to capture through surveys and statistical analysis. Therefore, qualitative methodological analysis has been suggested as a suitable approach to allow for the emergence of new knowledge found within socioeconomic relations not previously identified in the literature. The purpose of this study is to explore trade associations and trust in Nigerian SMEs through a qualitative multiple-case study approach.

Methodology

Following Yin (2014), this study adopts a qualitative exploratory approach, leading to multiple case studies that allow respondents to recount their unique narratives. A purposive sampling technique was adopted, with 14 traders operating within Northern and Southern Nigerian markets being selected. The selection criteria involved specific characteristics, including a range of SMEs deeply involved in the manufacturing and agricultural sectors. Diversity was ensured in the selection, with even spread across gender, age, sector, education level, nature of trade and history of trading activity. The sample size of 14 SMEs was justified by the expert advice of Guest et al. (2006) that a sample selection of 12 is adequate if the goal is to illuminate the shared endeavour, beliefs, and perceptions of a homogenous group.

Results

The multiple case studies conducted through **in-depth interviews** with the selected respondents revealed insights into trade associations and trust in Nigerian SMEs. The data collected allowed for the inclusion of a range of interview foci within our database. The selected respondents shared their experiences and perspectives, shedding light on the workings of trade associations in their respective markets. The results also showed that trust is crucial for the success of trade associations and SMEs in Nigeria.

(Continued)

Conclusion

The qualitative multiple case study approach used in this research allowed for the exploration of trade associations and trust in Nigerian SMEs, providing new knowledge not previously identified in the literature. The purposive sampling technique adopted ensured the selection of participants with specific characteristics, enhancing the diversity and richness of the data collected. The results of this study have important implications for the development of trade associations and the promotion of trust in Nigerian SMEs.

Case study questions

1. How was the purposive sampling technique used in this study to select participants?
2. What specific characteristics were used to select the 14 traders operating across the markets?
3. How was diversity ensured in the selection of participants for this study?
4. What is the justification for using a sample size of 14 SMEs in this study?
5. How did the use of non-probability sampling affect the results of this study?
6. In what ways did the selected participants shed light on the workings of trade associations in their respective markets?
7. How did the study show that trust is crucial for the success of trade associations and SMEs in Nigeria?

Further reading

Bryman, A. (2016) *Social Research Methods*. 5th ed. London: Oxford University Press.

Bryman, A. and Bell, E. (2015) *Business Research Methods*. 4th ed. Oxford: Oxford University Press.

Creswell, J.W. (2014) *Research Design: Qualitative, Quantitative and Mixed Methods Approaches*. Los Angeles: Sage.

Denzin, N.K. and Lincoln, Y.S. (2020). *The SAGE Handbook of Qualitative Research*.

Merriam, S.B. and Tisdell, E.J. (2015). *Qualitative Research: A Guide to Design and Implementation*. Sage.

Miles, M.B., Huberman, A.M and Saldaña, J. (2013). *Qualitative Data Analysis: A Methods Sourcebook*.Sage.

8

Qualitative Data Collection Part I

Learning outcomes

By the end of this chapter, you should be able to:

- explain the different forms of observation in business and management research
- apply ethnography within qualitative research
- conceptualise the process of diary studies
- employ visual methods in business and management research
- elucidate the concept of archival research.

8.1 Introduction

Collecting data is very important in qualitative research and in this chapter, we explore some of the modes of data collection. Observation methods, relying substantially on 'structured' and 'participant observation,' have differing origins and applications. Although they have been employed by scholars across a variety of disciplines, both have been found to be particularly influential in the areas of business and management research. Since qualitative researchers are mostly interested in understanding social meanings, this chapter will focus on participant observation – particularly through ethnographic approaches. Participant observation draws its roots from anthropological research, where research is involved in the customs and societies of a given group of people. It is useful for uncovering the meanings and interpretations people attach to their social reality. An understanding of participant observation and its role as a data collection method is therefore very useful for qualitative researchers.

Within this chapter, a diary study (a research method used to collect qualitative data about user behaviours, activities, and experiences over a longitudinal period) will be examined. When is the right time to conduct a diary study and how you can ensure it is done appropriately, will be analysed in this chapter. Visual research methods, which are a new and novel approach to qualitative research derived from traditional ethnography methods used in anthropology and sociology, will be explained. Finally, we examine archival research that involves searching for and extracting information and evidence from original archives.

8.2 Observation

Observation is an exciting means of gathering data. As the name implies, it is a way of collecting data through observing. It is particularly useful for understanding how or why something occurs within a natural or controlled setting. *We define observation as a method of collecting data through watching people in their natural or controlled environment.* Such a form of data collection helps us see how people interact in different situations and which environmental factors influence their behaviour.

The choice of observation as a mode of data collection is dependent on your research aim, questions, and objectives. If the purpose of your study is about what people do, then observation is a good fit for conducting your research. Though observation could be fun, it needs to be systematically planned and executed to provide a credible account of what happened and justify its use as a scientific enquiry. The advantages and limitations of using observation as a mode of data collection can be seen in Box 8.1

Box 8.1   Observation

Advantages of observation

1. Observation could be less demanding compared to other forms of data collection and participants may respond better.
2. Observation is a suitable method of obtaining information from respondents who cannot adequately articulate themselves such as young children or people with severe mental disability.
3. Observation can capture the event and behaviour as it occurs and if properly conducted, reduces bias.
4. It could provide information about difficult topics in a cost-effective manner.

Disadvantages of observation

1. Though it may be low cost at times, there is a potential for it to be a slow and expensive process especially when many human observers must be recruited and costly surveillance equipment purchased.

2. There is also a high risk of observer bias. If the researcher becomes too involved, they may lose objectivity and become biased about the outcome and reporting.

3. It is not suitable for a wide variety of topics. For example, it is difficult to obtain information about intentions or opinions via observation.

4. Observation is only as reliable as the competence of the researcher. The researcher has to be trained and competent in recognising aspects of a situation or behaviour to ensure that the findings are credible.

There are many types of observation, and it can be challenging to differentiate them. In this book, we will be focusing on **structured observation**, participant observation, ethnography, diary study, visual method and archival research.

8.3 Structured observation

Structured observation is a method of systematically observing the behaviour of individuals using a predetermined schedule. It is also referred to as systematic observation. It involves utilising a coding schedule to observe participants to count how often a particular phenomenon occurs. It provides quantitative information about behaviour. It tells you how often things happen rather than why they happen (Saunders et al., 2012). For example, the number of times students contribute in the classroom is a form of structured observation.

It has been proposed as one of the solutions to the shortcomings of survey research. One of the major advantages is that it allows behaviour to be observed directly, unlike in survey research which only allows behaviour to be inferred (Bryman and Bell, 2011). As a result, there has been an increased interest in the use of structured observation in business and management as it provides a richer insight into what managers do. Integral to any structured observation is an observation schedule or coding scheme. The observation schedule specifies what the observer should be looking for and how the behaviour should be recorded. It is quite similar to a structured interview guide which will be discussed in Chapter 9. The researcher systematically classifies the behaviour they observe into distinct categories. The categories on the schedule are coded so that the data collected can be easily counted and turned into statistics.

One of the best-known studies to have used structured observation is the work of Mintzberg (1973) in examining senior managers. Mintzberg observed five chief executives for one week as they went about their daily routine. The observational schedule was based on scheduled meetings, unscheduled meetings, desk work, telephone calls and tours. Time and activities were coded separately so that the distribution of the management overlaps an activity or vice versa. From his observation, he was able to change the popular notion of managerial work at that time which suggested that it was planned and rational. His findings showed that managerial work is highly fragmented.

A key consideration in conducting structured observation is whether you intend to use an established coding schedule or design your own. An example of an observation schedule is seen in Case 8.1.

Case 8.1   Structured observation on the high street

A researcher used an observation schedule to study how people on the street responded to marketers when approached. The observation schedule was formulated to observe five behaviours namely, smiling, proximity, maintaining contact, avoidance of proximity and resistance to contact. The observer recorded the behaviour displayed during a 30-second interval and scored the intensity of behaviour on a scale of 1 to 5.

Intensity	Smiling	Proximity	Maintaining Contact	Avoidance of Proximity	Resistance to Contact
1					
2					
3					
4					
5					

This structured observation can be replicated by other researchers in the high street by using the same observation schedule and the information obtained is numerical.

Every observation schedule must provide a clear statement and focus. It needs to be explicit about who and what behaviours are to be observed. The structured observation can easily be replicated by other researchers by using the same observation schedule. The data obtained is numerical. However, if you decide to create your schedule, then you have to ensure that there is a clear focus and the recording system is easy to operate. It should be clear to the observer what is to be observed. Furthermore, observing large numbers of behaviour adds to its complexity and may affect reliability.

8.4 Participant observation

In the previous section, we examined structured observations, which is more quantitative in nature. Participant observation is a different approach that originated from anthropology and sociology. This is where the researcher attempts to be involved in the world by using research to understand it. Unlike structured observations where the observer is not a participant, in this approach, the researcher becomes a member of the group, organisation, community or society. For example, spending a few months working in an organisation to understand the culture of the place.

Participant observation is quite popular among interpretivists and social constructivists as their assumption of the world is of social construction by individuals and a subjective nature. Such a worldview requires that the researcher becomes a part of the participant's world and immerse themselves in their world over a period to understand and give meaning to it. The main benefit of participant observation is that the researcher is in a much better position to understand the viewpoint and experiences of the people they are studying when they are part of the study group.

However, its limitation is that the presence of the observer could affect the behaviour of the people being observed. A popular example is the Hawthorne study which was conducted in 1958 by Henry Landsberger. During the study, it was noted that the participants altered their behaviour in response to their awareness of being observed. There was an increase in the performance of individuals when watched and paid attention to by their supervisors. Another limitation stressed by quantitative scholars is that the researcher becomes too involved which may lead to bias and loss of objectivity. There is a danger that you see what you want to see. However, the nature of participant observation ensures that what is observed is recorded to ensure credibility.

Although participant observation is very popular in sociology and anthropology, it is gradually being used within management and business research, especially by qualitative researchers. A typical example would be a student working in a retail shop for six months as an employee. He wants to understand how the customer service provided could improve sales performance. Another example is a student who is examining the culture of an organisation, she decides to work in the organisation for a year to decipher the underlying culture of the organisation and not just the visible artefacts. These are common examples of students that align with participant observation. However, the focus of the study would also determine the role the participant can adopt and this is discussed in the next section.

Researcher roles within participant observation

We have explained participant observation in detail but what is even more important is how this is conducted. What are the roles which the researcher would have to adopt while carrying out participant observation? Raymond Gold, a well-known sociologist in 1958 proposed a schematic classification of participant observation roles. These are the four roles.

Complete observer

In this role, the observer is totally detached and not seen or noticed by the participants. It is not obtrusive, and it helps minimise the Hawthorne effect where participants act differently when they know that they are being observed. However, it raises some ethical questions about asking for permission to observe people, hence it is usually applied in public places. An example is a researcher watching people on the high street or train station.

Observer as participant

Here the researcher is known and recognised by the participants. The researcher is more of an interviewer. The participants know the research agenda of the observer but the interaction with them is limited. Watching how an employee uses the computer to support sales at work and helping with the computer when the shop floor is busy is a good example of this role.

Participant as observer

Here the researcher is fully engaged with the participants and the members of the social setting are aware of the intent of the researcher. The researcher is engaged regularly with the participants and open about their research. This would be valuable in gaining the trust of the participants. An example is taking up employment in an organisation to observe the work practices and the entire organisation is aware of your role.

Complete participant

In this role, you are a full functioning member of the social setting, but your true identity is not known to the members. Most people take up this role based on the argument that if the purpose is revealed to the participants, it would affect the outcome of the study. For example, you may be interested in knowing more about gang culture, so you become a member of the gang. If you had explained your research objectives to them, it would be unlikely that they would cooperate with you or give you access. However, this raises questions of ethics similar to what we said in the complete observer role. As a covert observer, you are a spy and could lose trust if caught. Many of the participants have shared their life stories and would not if they had known your research agenda. As a result, it is not the most encouraged approach to take in participant observation.

Data collection and analysis within participant observation

The type of data collected is dependent on your research objectives and the focus of your observation. The roles of the participant observation that we have discussed earlier would also determine the nature of the data collected. According to Robson (2002), data obtained from participant observation can be categorised as descriptive observation and narrative account. The descriptive observation involves observing the participants, the physical setting, the activities and behaviours which serve as the bed-rock for providing a narrative account. There is a consensus view that all field notes must take place at the point of observation to ensure that such data is not missed out (Saunders et al., 2012).

Due to the imperfections of human memory, it is critical that you take notes while making observations. These are usually referred to as field notes. These are summaries of the activities, events, behaviour, emotions and your reflections on them. While doing this, you need to ensure that the notes are written immediately or before the end of the day. The notes must be clear, stating the location and time, and digital recorders could also be used to support note taking.

The data collection from participant observation is usually analysed through different methods of qualitative data analysis which is discussed in Chapter 10. However, you should note that in participant observation, data collection and analysis can be carried out concurrently. This would help the researcher to note what can be followed up in further participant observation.

8.5 Ethnography

Though participant observation has been the common approach in business research and examined in detail within this chapter, there has been an increased emphasis on ethnography. For many scholars and researchers, participant observation is similar to ethnography and is just a change in nomenclature in recent times. However, many like us have argued otherwise about such a view. We agree that ethnography is a more holistic approach in which participant observation is a research method. In clearer terms, all ethnographers are participant observers but not all participant observers are ethnographers!

Ethnography is derived from a prefix, 'ethno' which means culture and a suffix, 'graphy' which means the practice of writing. It is more focused on the culture of a people or organisation, hence ethnographers take a more immersive approach. Ethnography has been defined in various forms. Bryman and Bell (2011) defined ethnography as a process of joining a group, watching what goes on, making sense about it and finally writing it up. We define ethnography as a type of qualitative research that provides a deeper understanding of the culture and dynamics of a group. It involves immersing yourself in a particular social setting to observe their behaviours, attitudes and emotions so as to produce a written report afterwards. A good example is a researcher living in a particular society for a period to understand the culture of the group.

A typical ethnographic approach involves intense involvement by the researcher and when such involvement is done within an organisation, it is referred to as organisational ethnography. Organisational ethnographers immerse themselves within the organisation so that they can understand other people's realities and conduct field-work within the organisation. Similar to participant observation, the main advantage of ethnography is the in-depth understanding of the culture and behaviour of the people. By immersing yourself in their social setting, you can obtain genuine and authentic information about the culture.

The disadvantage of ethnography as we have discussed earlier within participant observation is in terms of observer bias and ethical considerations within the study. Another issue with ethnography is the time commitment required to conduct it. You may have to spend months or even years when conducting ethnography. This may not be the best choice for an undergraduate dissertation that has to be completed within three months. So, the choice of ethnography is dependent on the time required to conduct your research. In addition, before choosing to employ ethnography we advise that you also consider access to the respondents and the ethical considerations as dis-cussed within participant observation.

Writing ethnography

After observations have been conducted, the next step in ethnography is the writing up or reporting. The report should provide a clear account of the behaviours, attitude and emotions observed. Its structure could come in various forms such as a thesis and an article. Regardless of the form it takes, it is expected that a rich and reflective account of the study is provided within the body of the report with a clear introduc-tion and conclusion.

8.6 Diary method

In the earlier section, we discussed qualitative data collection via ethnography and participant observation. There is another type of research method quite similar to both which involves collecting qualitative data in the form of behaviours, activities and experience using logs, journals or diaries. This is called diary method or studies.

It is not as popular as the participant observation in business and management research but has been used extensively in other fields especially in the health and medical sciences. It is used for recording experiences of participants suffering from chronic pain and research in aging and well-being (Unterhitzenberger and Lawrence, 2022). However, there has been a clarion call for its use in management research and some scholars have used it to explore employee well-being and work/life balance (Radcliffe, 2013).

Diary method is a research method which is used to collect qualitative data about people's behaviour, activities and experience over time. Such data is usually self-reported and it involves participants recording entries about their experience in a log, diary or journal. It usually takes a longitudinal approach and the participants record their experiences for several weeks, months or even longer. During the study period, the participants are asked to log to their diaries at a specified time to enter the information needed for the study. They are expected to report repeatedly over days or weeks. The data is recorded by the participants and not the researcher and it could be handwritten or typed. Online diaries have also become popular, which involves the use of visuals in the form of photographs, audios and video recordings. A well-known diary study was conducted by Beckers and colleagues (2016) in a university to evaluate how learning spaces affect student learning activities. Fifty-two students kept records of the learning activities they worked on, where they worked and why they worked there for a week. Through evaluating the diary entries of this study, the researchers found a significant correlation between the spaces in which the students chose to work and their learning activities.

The diary method has several advantages. First, it offers the researchers the opportunity to capture first-person experience of participants since they are the ones keeping the record and providing their perception of the event. It also helps to reduce recollection errors since it is logged in close to when the event occurs. Such recollection errors and post rationalisation are usually common with other modes of qualitative data collection. In addition, it is useful in collecting longitudinal data and provides a clear picture of attitudes, motivations, changes in behaviour and perception. For example, a diary study can be conducted on users engaged with a particular product. The study could be designed to examine what time they engage with the product, what motivates them to use it and how loyal are they to its use. The focus of a diary method can be very broad or narrow depending on the topic being examined.

Nevertheless, there are limitations to the diary method. First, there is a high tendency for bias since the data is recorded by the diarist. The diarist's motivation and recording skills could affect the accuracy of the process. People may be more apt in the use of diaries and have good diary recording skills while others could be new to it, hence some level of support and training is required to help them. Another limitation is the diarist remembering to record their experiences in the diary. There is an assumption that the participants will comply with the instructions and record the event or phenomena of interest to the researcher. However, this is not usually the case and most of the time, the researcher needs to prompt the diarist to ensure compliance.

Collecting and analysing qualitative data using diaries

A diary method is typically composed of five phases.

1. ***Preparation phase:*** In this phase, the focus of the study is defined. You would also need to define the timeline, specify the tools to be used for the participants to report data, recruit participants and prepare the support materials.

2. ***Pre-study phase:*** In this phase, you have to get the participants ready to log the data in their diary. There need to be meetings with each participant to discuss the details of the study, the time schedule and expectations. In this phase, you would discuss any issues that the diarist may have to ensure that the process is seamless.

3. ***The logging phase:*** This is an important phase, and it involves logging of the data into diaries. A framework and template should be provided. Within the framework, you need to specify what information you want the participants to log. The logging process may take several forms. It could be done in predetermined intervals. For example, participants can take note every six hours through the day. Such an approach is suited for behaviours that are not situation dependent. The second approach is in-situation logging. This reporting occurs immediately the event occurs. For example, when the participant observes a particular activity, it is immediately recorded.

4. ***Post-study phase:*** After the logging process, it is important that all the information provided by each participant is evaluated. A follow-up meeting is scheduled to discuss the information in the diary. Within this phase, questions are asked to probe more on the information provided and to obtain their feedback about their experience.

5. ***Data analysis:*** The qualitative data analysis techniques discussed in Chapter 10 such as thematic analysis and grounded theory are all methods of analysis which can be used to analyse diary data. Since diary methods are longitudinal in nature then a large amount of qualitative data is generated. When analysing the data, it is important that you review the research questions and the rich insights collected.

Though the diary method is a distinct data collection technique, researchers tend to support it with other data collection techniques. One common method is the use of interviews. Many researchers tend to commence with diaries and then follow up with interviews or vice versa. Interviews are useful in building relationships between researchers and participants. They are also effective in addressing the limitations of diary and follow-up events.

8.7 Visual methods

Visual method is a novel approach to qualitative research derived from ethnography. Some scholars refer to it as visual ethnography (Bryman and Bell, 2011). Similar to ethnography, it has its roots in anthropology and sociology and is now widely used in social science and health research. As the name implies, it involves making sense of visual data to produce knowledge. It is used to understand and interpret images and it includes photography, film, video, collage, maps, diagrams, selfies and other artistic mediums. Such artistic mediums are valuable as they provide insights into the everyday life of the participants and capture rich multidimensional data.

Visual methods are used to elicit discussion and experiences that might not be easy to do because of language problems and often used in settings where language may constitute a barrier between participant and researcher. For example, visual methods have been applied in studies that address issues of social exclusion and hard to reach groups (Delgado, 2015). Though visual methods are novel and relatively new, they are now becoming more popular in business and management as an effective method for qualitative research. The advantages and disadvantages of visual methods are discussed in Box 8.2

Box 8.2   Visual methods

Advantages of visual methods

1. Visual methods are valuable for respondents who may find it difficult to communicate because of language barriers, disability or lack of education. For example, the homeless can be easily studied using this method to gain a detailed picture of their unique experience.
2. As a research method, it allows the researcher to understand the study from the participants' perspective. Through creating visual images, they can explain and show the researcher their experience.
3. Visual methods have been found to give richer insights compared to other qualitative methods of data collection such as interviews (Glaw et al., 2017). They add richness and depth by revealing more than what more traditional methods would if they were the only ones conducted.

Disadvantages of visual methods

1. There are ethical issues that emerge with visual methods around ownership and consent. For example, who owns the copyright of the images in cases where pseudonyms are used to protect the anonymity of the participants? To avoid potential copyright issues, it is advised that the researchers obtain permission from the participants to use the photographs they take. Although it is ideal, obtaining written consent from those appearing in the images may be difficult.
2. The cost of visual methods could be exorbitant. Cameras and other sophisticated visual equipment are usually required to successfully conduct the study and this can be problematic if there are limited funds available for the research.

There are three common visual methods used:

- **Auto photography** involves the use of photographs to create an environment where the researcher and the reader can see the world through the participants' eyes (Glaw et al., 2017). Photographs are taken by the participants and provide depth that cannot be conveyed through words. They enables participants, especially marginalised groups that are not fluent in the required language, to express themselves via images. For example, a participant might want to discuss the loneliness involved in their journey and would provide a photograph to depict this. Figure 8.1 is a photograph showing this view

Figure 8.1   Loneliness

Source: https://unsplash.com/s/photos/lonely

- **Photovoice** was conceptualised by Caroline Wang and Mary Burris. Similar to autophotography, it employs the use of photography. However, for photovoice, there is a focus on a larger community of members using photographs to identify and represent their community. Stories are told through the photographs thereby giving voices to the group.
- **Photo elicitation** involves the use of photographs to generate verbal discussion. The visual images can be produced by either the participant or the researcher. It has been shown to be more effective than conventional traditional interviews (Bigante, 2010; Glaw et al., 2017). In photo elicitation interviewing, the photographs are usually the focus of the interaction. The photographs when taken by the informant before the interview help them to be more relaxed and conversant with what is to be discussed. During the interview, the researcher observes the participant emotions as they discuss the meaning of the photographs. This allows the participant to provide deep and interesting conversation that is not clear from the photographs.

Analysis

Similar to **participant observation** and ethnography, visual data can be analysed by several qualitative data analysis techniques such as content analysis, discourse analysis, grounded theory and thematic analysis. These are discussed elaborately in Chapter 10.

8.8 Archival research

Archival research is a type of research which involves searching for and extracting information from archival records and other repositories. Archives are usually organised collections of records and documents of government agencies, research organisations, business, industry and other relevant institutions. Archival data refers to information that already exists. It has already been collected for reporting or research purposes and kept for legal requirements. Many scholars tend to use archival data and secondary data interchangeably. Nevertheless, both forms of data are obtained by others and not originally by the researcher.

Many scholars argue that original data is important, and you need to control the data collected. On the other hand, there are several reasons why archival data is important. First, it is easy and less time-consuming. When data has already been collected by someone else, you are able to save yourself time. This is even more beneficial when you intend to obtain a large amount of information. A good example is the GLOBE studies where more than 200 researchers from 62 countries studying more than 17,000 managers were part of the project examining leadership behaviours across cultures. Several studies examining leadership have drawn from the extensive archival data of the GLOBE project.

Archival data may provide information that you would not have been able to gather if you did it yourself. Previous researchers may examine a particular area or focus that you would have missed if you did it yourself. It also eliminates the problems of sampling, observer bias and other methodological limitations that may occur with primary data collection. It is cost-effective and makes it possible to conduct large-scale research with limited funds.

Similar to other methodological approaches, the choice of archival research depends on your research aim and question. The archival data sought must provide answers to your research question. If the data already exists, then you must ask yourself how relevant the data will be in addressing your research questions. If the focus of your research is on historical data, then archival research would be apt for your study. It is also important that you consider the time and resources available to collect data yourself. If time is of the essence especially in cross sectional projects, then archival data may be the best path to take.

Though archival research has its benefits, it also has some limitations. A significant issue in archival research is construct validity and reliability of the data for research purposes. Since the data has been collected by someone else it might not be appropriate for your study. Archives are subject to gaps and incompleteness that makes it difficult to determine whether the data obtained represents the population that you want to study.

Archival data are not only available onsite but are now more accessible offsite. The rise of the Internet has made it easier to access archival data. Most public documents are now available on the websites of the relevant organisation. Many government agencies, businesses and industry stakeholders have their data on the website.

Finally, when the archival data has been collected, it is important that you analyse it appropriately. The analysis could either be quantitative or qualitative. If the intent of your study is to obtain rich insights, then a qualitative method of analysis as discussed in Chapter 10 should be employed. However, many researchers take a quantitative approach to archival data and use statistical analysis especially when a large population is to be evaluated.

8.9 Summary

- The choice of observation as a mode of data collection is dependent on your research aim, questions and objectives. If the purpose of your study is about what people do, then observation is a good fit for conducting your research.
- Structured observation is a method of systematically observing the behaviour of individuals using a predetermined schedule. It is also referred to as systematic observation. It involves utilising a coding schedule to observe participants in order to count how often a particular phenomenon occurs.
- Participant observation is quite popular among interpretivists and social constructivists as their assumption of the world is of social construction by individuals and a subjective nature. Such a worldview requires that the researcher becomes a part of the participant's world and immerses themselves in their world over a period of time to understand and give meaning to it.
- Ethnography is derived from two parts of words, 'ethno' which means culture and 'graphy' which means the practice of writing. It is more focused on the culture of a people or organisation, hence ethnographers take a more immersive approach.
- The diary method is a research method which is used to collect qualitative data about people's behaviour, activities and experience over time. Such data is usually self-reported and it involves participants recording entries about their experience in a log, diary or journal.

- The visual method involves making sense of visual data to produce knowledge. It is used to understand and interpret images and it includes photography, film, video, collage, maps, diagrams, selfies and other artistic mediums.
- Archival research is a type of research which involves searching for and extracting information from archival records and other repositories. Archives are usually organised collections of records and documents of government agencies, research organisations, business, industry and other relevant institutions.

Self-check questions

1. What does observation mean?
2. What are the pros and cons of adopting observation as a research method?
3. What are the key requirements of an observation schedule in structured observation?
4. What are the roles which the researcher would have to adopt while carrying out participant observation?
5. What is ethnography?
6. What are the phases employed in the diary method?
7. What are the three common visual methods applied?
8. When is archival data appropriate for your study?

Questions for review and discussion

1. Discuss how you would collect and analyse data obtained from participant observation and critically reflect on one of the four roles namely, Complete Observer, Observer as Participant, Participant as Observer and Complete Participant that you would adopt?
2. Devise an observation schedule of your own for observing an area of social interaction in which you are regularly involved.
3. Think about a research topic that you would like to undertake and reflect on what archival data would be required.

Self-check answers

1. Observation is a method of collecting data through watching people in their natural or controlled environment. Such a form of data collection helps us see how people interact in different situations and which environmental factors influence their behaviour.

(Continued)

2. Observation is a suitable method of obtaining information from respondents that cannot adequately articulate themselves such as young children or people with severe mental disability. However, there is also a high risk of observer's bias. If the researcher becomes too involved, they may lose objectivity and become biased about the outcome and reporting.

3. Every observation schedule must provide a clear statement and focus. It needs to be explicit about whose and what behaviours are to be observed.

4. These are the four roles namely, Complete observer; in this role, the observer is totally detached and not seen or noticed by the participants. Observer as participant; the participants know the research agenda of the observer but the interaction with them is limited. Participant as observer; here the researcher is fully engaged with the participants and the members of the social setting are aware of the intent of the researcher. Complete participant; in this role, you are a fully functioning member of the social setting but your true identity is not known to the members.

5. Ethnography is a type of qualitative research that provides a deeper understanding of the culture and dynamics of a group. It involves immersing yourself in a particular social setting to observe their behaviours, attitudes and emotions so as to produce a written report afterwards.

6. A diary method is typically composed of five phases namely; Preparation phase, Pre-study phase, Logging phase, Post-study phase and Data analysis

7. The three common visual methods used are Autophotography, Photovoice and Photo elicitation.

8. If the focus of your research is on historical data, then archival research would be apt for your study. It is also important that you consider the time and resources available to collect data yourself. If time is of the essence especially in cross sectional projects, then archival data may be the best path to take.

Further reading

Glaw, X., Inder, K., Kable, A. and Hazelton, M. (2017) Visual methodologies in qualitative research: Autophotography and photo elicitation applied to mental health research. *International Journal of Qualitative Methods*, 16(1).

Mintzberg, H. (1973) *The Nature of Managerial Work*. New York: Harper & Row

Robson, C. (2002) *Real World Research*. 2nd ed. Oxford: Blackwell.

Unterhitzenberger, C. and Lawrence, K. (2022) Diary method in project studies. *Project Leadership and Society*, 3.

9

Qualitative Data Collection Part II

Learning outcomes

By the end of this chapter, you should be able to:

- explain the different forms of interviews and how to conduct them in business and management research
- apply focus groups in business and management research
- conceptualise the process of the Delphi method
- employ surveys within qualitative research
- adopt critical incident technique in qualitative research
- elucidate the concept of the case study method
- apply action research within business and management research.

9.1 Introduction

In the earlier chapter, we discussed some modes of data collection namely: structured observation, participant observation, ethnography, diary method/studies, visual method and archival research. This first phase of qualitative data collection provided insight to methods that uncover the meaning and interpretations people attach to their social reality.

In the second part, we go deeper into more modes of data collection that provide a clear picture of people's experiences as socially constructed by them. **Interviews** are probably the most widely employed method in qualitative research. It is recognised as the gold standard of qualitative research. In the previous chapter, we saw how interviews are combined with other modes of data collection such as visual method and diary studies to enhance their credibility. Interviews are core to qualitative research and when complex issues are to be uncovered, they remain one of the best means of collecting data. In this chapter, we will be examining the different types of research interviews and how to apply them in qualitative data collection. The chapter will also examine the strategies, competencies and skills required in conducting qualitative interviews.

Focus groups play a crucial role in qualitative research. They are interviews which involve several people on a specific topic or issue. Within this chapter, we will explore the importance of focus groups and how they should be conducted. When the view of subject experts is important in answering your research question, then the Delphi technique is the most suited. This chapter will examine how the Delphi method is applied within business and management research. Its strengths and weaknesses will also be identified.

The critical incident technique is a widely recognised qualitative research method used for obtaining recalled observations about significant events from observers with first-hand experience. In section 9.6, we explore the application of critical incident techniques in qualitative studies.

Case study as an established research design is used not only in business and management but in a wide variety of disciplines. It provides an in-depth understanding of a complex issue using several modes of qualitative data collection. Within this chapter, we will be exploring the role and application of case study methodology within business and management research. Finally, action research, an interactive research method which aims to concurrently investigate and solve an issue is examined in section 9.8.

9.2 Interviews

Interviews are the most widely used method in qualitative research especially in the form of one-to-one interviews. They are used broadly across several disciplines as a gold standard in qualitative research. Interviews have been defined in several ways by scholars. According to Saunders et al. (2012, p. 372), a research interview 'is a purposeful conversation between two or more people, requiring the interviewer to establish rapport, to ask concise and unambiguous questions, to which the interviewee is willing to respond and to listen attentively.' We define interviews as a research method that involves a conversation between two or more people which relies on asking questions to obtain rich insights about a phenomenon. It is valuable in gathering credible data that are relevant to your research aim and objectives.

Interviews are suited to qualitative research when the aim is to study people's experience as seen from their points of view or the social construction of knowledge concerning the chosen topic (Eriksson and Kovalainen, 2011). This method is the most conducive in understanding uncountable, process data peculiar to individuals (Galloway and Kelly, 2009). When complex issues are to be covered, an interview is the best or only means of collecting data. For example, in examining the impact of entrepreneurial leadership in a business, interviews would be more appropriate. Studies have shown that entrepreneurs are often keen to share their experiences and enjoy telling stories (Gray, 2009; Harrison et al., 2018; McKenzie, 2007); hence, the use of interviews, which provides this opportunity, can be an effective approach to capture rich data.

Types of interviews

There are three recognised types of interviews based on the level of structure namely, structured, semi-structured and unstructured interviews.

Structured interviews

The structured interview favours the positivist philosophy and a quantitative methodology, whereby data is collected systematically and put into numerical form (Johnstone, 2007). They have predetermined questions in a set order. These questions are often closed-ended or multiple-choice. While open-ended structured interviews exist, they are much less common. Structured interviews are useful if the intent of your study is to describe or explain. For example, you want to investigate the impact of branding in consumer purchase. In a structured interview, you would ask the respondents to rate their level of agreement with statements such as, 'The brand – influences my purchase' on a Likert scale, you would ask how many times they buy the product and so on. Data analysis is more straightforward because the researcher can compare different answers given to the same questions. This helps to mitigate bias and increase reliability.

However, structured interviews are not often used in qualitative research because of their limited scope and flexibility. Most qualitative research is exploratory in nature with an intent to obtain rich descriptions and meaning rather than numerical data which structured interviews provide.

Box 9.1. shows the difference between structured, semi-structured and unstructured interviews.

Box 9.1   Difference between structured, semi-structured and unstructured interviews

	Structured	Semi Structured	Unstructured
Purpose of Study	Explanatory or Descriptive	Explanatory or Exploratory	Exploratory
Instrument	Predetermined questions in form of a questionnaire	Interview guide	Single questions which lead to other follow-up questions
Format	Fixed	Flexible	Very flexible

Semi-structured interviews

These are more commonly used in qualitative research and in addition to unstructured interviews are usually referred to as qualitative interviews. They are a blend of structured and unstructured interviews. The researcher has a list of questions on a particular issue which the interviewee would respond to known as an interview guide or protocol. In providing responses to these questions, it also permits the interviewer to follow on earlier responses through probing. Probing techniques are used to induce more information and questions do not need to follow the exact format in the schedule as seen in structured interviews. They are often open-ended and flexible but also show a degree of structure, hence could be considered as the best of both worlds.

Semi-structured interviews are used in studies that are exploratory or explanatory. The use of semi-structured interviews often leads to discussion in areas that had not been previously considered, but which may be of significance to the understanding of the subject area, and also valuable in addressing the research questions and objectives (Saunders et al., 2012). This is achieved by the researcher probing for more detailed responses by asking the respondent to provide clearer answers to the issues discussed (Gray, 2009). As stated by Blumberg et al. (2011, p. 258), semi-structured interviews have two main objectives: 'On one hand, the researcher wants to know the informant's perspective on the issue; on the other, they also want to know whether the informant can confirm insights and information the researcher already holds.' Semi-structured interviews also tend to the interpretivist philosophy discussed in Chapter 4 where the social world is constructed and given meaning by people. For example, a study on the entrepreneurial skills required to succeed in a crisis can be investigated aptly using semi-structured interviews. Through the semi-structured interviewing format, it captures the perspective of the entrepreneur on the issue.

It should be noted, however, that semi-structured interviews are not without their limitations. One major limitation to their use is the issue of reliability as similar information is expected to be revealed by alternative researchers. It is usually challenging to compare the findings between participants as they don't have to follow a fixed format. Another limitation is the issue of bias of the interviewee or interviewer. The interviewer can demonstrate bias in the way he or she interprets responses, and the interviewee may also introduce bias by withholding relevant information on the topic of interest. However, many researchers have argued that findings derived from semi-structured interviews are not meant to be repeatable, since they reflect the reality at the point in time that they were collected; hence, the situation could be subject to change (Bryman and Bell, 2011; Saunders et al., 2012). Although interviewer and interviewee bias is a recognised limitation, it can be mitigated by an interviewer's situational competence (Flick, 2011). This can be addressed by developing appropriate interview themes and an interview guide.

Preparing an interview guide

Developing an interview guide is an important part of the semi-structured interview. An example of an interview guide is provided in Box 9.2. Since they are often open-ended, it can be challenging to develop questions that can provide the information required without bias. In preparing an interview guide, we suggest that you consider the following questions.

- What topic will be you focusing on during the interview? This will help you draft questions that provide the information you seek and ensure focus all through the process.
- Are the questions clear and comprehensible? It is usually better to use language that is clear to ensure that the respondents understand what you are asking. You can start with simpler questions before moving to more complex issues. The use of jargon should be avoided if is not essential to the study.
- Are the questions too specific? Although focus is required, you also do not want to prevent rich insights from the interviewer. You need to prevent overt restriction and allow ample time to reflect on the questions.
- Are the questions leading? To mitigate bias, it is best practice to avoid leading or suggestive questions.

Interview guides in general have a wide range of questions. According to Kvale (1996), nine different types of questions should be provided in the interview guide namely, introductory questions, follow-up questions, probing questions, specifying questions, direct questions, indirect questions, structuring questions, silence and interpreting questions. The impact of such questions is dependent on the competence and strategy of the interviewer discussed in the latter section.

Box 9.2   Interview guide for study investigating entrepreneurial challenges

Section 1

Introduction and explanation of research - expand on previous email correspondence - provide additional background information
Underline the anonymity of interviewees will be maintained.

Section 2

Ask the Employers about their background, and how, when and why they established the business and the challenges faced.

Unstructured interviews

At the opposite end of the continuum is the unstructured interview, which is non-standardised and informal. It is the most flexible type of interview. In this form of interview, there is no predetermined list of questions, and the interviewee is allowed to talk freely about events and behaviour in the topic area. They mostly start with the respondent's narrative and the questions and order in which they are asked are not set. The open-ended nature and flexibility are usually suitable for studies that are exploratory. It helps the respondents to frame the study based on their social constructive view of the world and not limited to a structured questionnaire. Rich insights that were not envisaged before the interview are elicited. Such an approach helps form a deep connection with your respondents, encouraging them to feel comfortable revealing their opinions.

However, it has its limitations. It is usually suitable if adopted by an experienced researcher who has a strong background in the research topic. You need to have good communication skills to keep the conversation going and also know the nature of follow-up questions to ask. The process could be very time-consuming. Since there are no pre-set questions, there is a high tendency to get so much data and this leads to more time spent transcribing and analysing. In addition, some of the data obtained may be irrelevant to the study.

The open-ended or unstructured interview, although flexible and of great importance in exploratory studies, does not provide a concise view of the topic area. According to Easterby-Smith et al. (2008, pp. 143–4), an unstructured approach is more likely 'to produce no clear picture in the mind of the interviewee of what questions or issues the interviewer is interested in, and in the mind of the interviewer of what question the interviewee is answering.' This also exacerbates the danger of the 'interviewer effect' (Gray, 2009, p. 217), where the interviewer may influence the course of the interview. Such interviews are also difficult to analyse since different questions may be asked of different interviewees, with the result that there is no emergent pattern. Due to the limitations of unstructured interviews, many scholars propose semi-structured interviews depending on the nature of the study and the level of experience of the researcher.

Interview strategies, competencies and skills

With all modes of data collection, the key to successful interviews is thorough preparation. The following strategies, competencies and skills should be considered when conducting interviews.

Location

You need to consider the location where the interviews will be conducted. Interviews are traditionally conducted in-person or by telephone. Sometimes the location could determine the credibility of the interviews. The location should not cause harm to the participant as discussed in Chapter 5 about ethics. For example, when conducting an interview with employees about their employer, it would be best to do this in a location where such sensitive information can be shared without fear of victimisation. In addition, the location should allow for easy recording and be free from noise and other distractions. In recent times, interviews are now conducted virtually using platforms such as Zoom, Microsoft Teams, Skype and so on. Such platforms have made the interviewing process easier and accessible. Nevertheless, it is important that any location whether virtual, telephone or face to face is convenient for the respondent.

Information recording

Many interviews produce a large amount of information, especially qualitative interviews. As a result, it is more convenient to record the interviews conducted. The advantage of recording the interview is that it gives you the opportunity to listen again and reduces the chance of missing out rich information. It makes the **transcription** process easier especially if the intent is to transcribe **verbatim** for coding. However, you should bear in mind that not all respondents might want to be recorded. Some people might feel uncomfortable and it could influence their behaviour. In all situations, it is important that you obtain consent before recording commences. Virtual interviews are easier because they tend to have automatic recording options and you don't need to use tape recorders. It also makes transcription easier as some of the platforms can generate transcripts.

Commencing the interview

How the interview commences is critical to its outcome. You need to shape the start of the interview to put the respondents at ease. You must explain your research to the participants and gain their consent. It is also important that you are friendly and the interviewee feels comfortable. One of the ways to do this is by ensuring that you let the respondents know that information detrimental to them is not being sought and all information will remain anonymous.

Dealing with difficult participants

During interviews, you might meet some people who are difficult to interview. It is important that you know how to address such challenges. For example, some people tend to digress from the question and tell stories that are not relevant to the study. For those respondents, you will need to subtly refer them back to the original question and focus of the study. Some might be at the other end of the continuum and won't provide rich answers to the questions asked. For those respondents, you would probe more skilfully and rephrase the questions to elicit more answers.

9.3 Focus groups

The interviews we discussed earlier involved just the interviewer and one interviewee. However, if the intent is to have rich insights from more than one person at the same time, then another technique is employed which is referred to as a group interview. Group interviews are non-standardised interviews conducted with two or more people (Saunders et al., 2012), while focus groups refer to group interviews where the topic is clearly defined and the interaction between the participants is important. Both terms are used interchangeably in many books and can be differentiated based on efficiency reasons (i.e. group interviews are more cost effective). In this chapter, we would be concentrating on focus groups as it is a universally accepted method of group interviewing.

We define focus groups as qualitative interviews which involve a panel of people that focus on a particular topic to provide perspectives and enable interaction between the participants. The number of people in a focus group should be about 6 to 12. However, the precise number would depend on the topic, the nature of the participants and the skill of the moderator. For very sensitive topics, it is expected that the number would be lower to encourage engagement. It is usually led by a moderator or facilitator, and it could take up to one or two hours. The role of the moderator is to guide the group and ensure that there is sufficient interaction on the specific topic.

As with other modes of qualitative data collection discussed in Chapters 8 and 9, the choice of a focus group is dependent on the nature of the study. It is employed for exploratory and explanatory studies and provides rich insights into the socially constructed perspective and worldview of the respondents. The focus group approach offers the opportunity for people to probe each other's perspective for holding a certain view. Through this, it helps to elicit a wide variety of views on a certain issue. They are often used in market research and consumer buying decisions, for example, a focus group organised to investigate the consumer perception of a particular product. Six people who have used the product are selected and interviewed together to ascertain their views.

Through focus groups you can develop an understanding about why people feel the way they do compared to individual interviewing. During the focus groups, individuals could argue with each other and challenge their views. It also allows the participants to listen to other answers through which they may recall previous experiences and modify the answers earlier provided. They could also voice agreement with the views of others.

However, there are limitations to the use of focus groups. The efficacy of focus groups is dependent on the skills of the moderator or facilitator. A well trained and experienced moderator is required to guide the discussion and process to elicit the relevant information sought. Within focus groups, you might have individuals who dominate the conversation. The intent of the focus group is to have the issue discussed by all participants, so it is important that everyone is allowed to contribute their views. Finally, as is common with group activities, some people might be reluctant to talk or express their true feelings because of the group composition, so the information provided might not always be a true reflection of their views.

Conducting focus groups

There are a few key considerations to make while conducting a focus group. These are discussed below.

Participant selection

The type of participants required in a focus group depends on the topic to be considered. It is important to think of the relevant stakeholders to the issue being considered and invite them to participate in the study. As stated earlier, 6 to 12 people is ideal but could be less if sensitive issues are discussed. People could be selected randomly or through a non-probability sampling strategy. One of the key considerations in the sample is its homogeneity or heterogeneity. Homogenous groups consist of people who know each other and share similar attributes while heterogenous groups are usually more different. The rule of thumb is to use homogenous groups when the objective is to promote more intense discussion. If the intent is to explore shared meanings held within a work group, then this is easily achieved by homogenous grouping (Bryman and Bell, 2011). On the other hand, heterogenous groups are used when the objective is to provide more argumentative interactions. If the intent is to reduce groupthink and elicit taken for granted assumptions, then heterogenous groups would be ideal. Selected participants should receive an invitation stating the purpose of the session, time, date and location. Incentives in the form of gifts could also be provided to support more engagement by the participants.

Asking questions

Critical to the success of the focus group are the questions asked and the moderator's involvement. Like semi-structured interviews which have an interview guide, a script has to be developed for a focus group. The script should have an introduction, opening question, discussion topics and conclusion. Before the commencement of the session, the moderator is supposed to introduce the participants to each other, explain the purpose of the study and lay out the ground rules for the session. As stated earlier, it is important that the moderator is very skilled to ensure that every participant is involved and prevent domination of the process by one or two individuals.

Recording and transcription

Like qualitative interviews, the focus groups work best if the session is recorded and transcribed. Unlike qualitative interviews, transcription of focus groups could be more complex as more people are talking and it could be difficult to distinguish voices. As a result, it is important that you use good digital recorders to ensure that you can easily distinguish between respondents.

Virtual focus groups

As we saw earlier with interviews, recent developments in technology have also made it possible to conduct focus groups virtually. Virtual platforms such as Microsoft Teams, Zoom and Skype are used to host focus groups. Such focus groups can be conducted either synchronously where all participants meet at the same time or asynchronously where they don't meet at the same time but are able to respond or contribute to each other's comments.

The advantage of virtual focus groups is the ease of accessing people despite their location and the decreased cost. However, it also means that everyone must have access to the Internet which is not always the case.

9.4 Delphi method

When the opinion of experts is key to your study, then the best technique to employ is the Delphi method. The Delphi method is a systematic process of forecasting which relies on a panel of experts. It is a structured technique to modulate a group communication process and allows a group of experts to deal with a complex problem (Nasa et al., 2021). It was first developed in the 1950s by Norman Dalkey and Olaf Helner to achieve reliable expert consensus. It was derived from the Greek oracle of Delphi which could predict the future and provided anonymity. As a result, the Delphi technique is built on the anonymity of the participants to ensure honest results.

The Delphi technique has been extensively used in health sciences and business forecasting, but it has also become increasingly popular in finance and economics. Though it was initially developed for business forecasting, it is now increasingly used to obtain consensus with collective intelligence of the experts.

Conducting a Delphi study

As with all modes of data collection, the Delphi technique has evolved since it was first put forward. The overarching approach is based on a series of rounds. It is important to decide the number of rounds and the time frame of the study. In general, if the intent of your study is exploratory, then three or more rounds are preferable. On the other hand, if the Delphi technique is more explanatory then fewer rounds are required.

The panelists required for the Delphi study are experts and you need to define what expertise means while selecting them. It is expected that the panelists should have sufficient knowledge of the area and a track record in the field. In addition, the number of panelists should not be too few or too many to ensure consensus can be reached and analysis not cumbersome. We advise a panel number between 7 and 50.

Questionnaire

Open-ended questions are used since the intent of the Delphi method is to generate rich ideas. The questionnaire is created based on the purpose of the study and the panelists can populate the questionnaire across a series of rounds. The questionnaires can be distributed physically or online. However, online methods via systems such as Qualtrics, Google forms and so on are more popular due to their ease of access and analysis.

The experts are asked their opinions about a particular issue and questions for each round are based on the findings of the previous round. In the first round, the contributions from the experts are collected in the form of answers to the questions. For example, Massiah et al. (2017) employed Delphi techniques in investigating Humanitarian Disaster Management. Using the experts within the field, they were able to determine the best approach to managing crisis.

After round 1, the findings obtained are analysed using qualitative and quantitative data analysis and used to inform the development of the questionnaires for round 2. The findings from the next round would lead to the development of another questionnaire. The intent of the next round of questionnaire is to invite the panelists to consider their initial response compared to the group and change any of their responses. The experts are allowed to see the results and reflect on the views of others and alter their responses if needed. Once this has been circulated, you check whether changes have been made and a consensus reached. Finally, you disseminate your findings among the participants. Common and conflicting views are identified and if a consensus is not reached the process of rounds would continue until one is attained. Then the framework of the expert opinion is built on all the rounds showing how consensus was reached in answering the research question.

However, although the Delphi method offers a flexible approach to building a consensus using experts, it is not without its limitations. One key limitation is that it could be time-consuming and complex. The need for multiple rounds to reach a consensus could also lead to a high dropout rate. Finally, the efficacy of the Delphi method is based on the research question to be addressed. Not all research questions can be answered based on an expert consensus and there is a high chance of bias as many of the experts may go for the majority view.

9.5 Critical Incident Technique

Qualitative researchers increasingly recognise the value of the critical incident technique for uncovering comprehensive and in-depth aspects of research. But what is the critical incident technique all about? Many of the students that we have come across tend to avoid this approach in their data collection, while others claim they are unfamiliar with it. In simple terms, a critical incident is an event or an occurrence that results in evident consequences, leaving the local actors with an understanding of its distinct impact.

Thus, drawing from its original conceptualisation, the critical incident technique (CIT) consists of:

> a set of procedures for collecting direct observations of human behaviour in such a way as to facilitate their potential usefulness in solving practical problems and developing broad psychological principles.

> (Flanagan, 1954, pp. 327–58)

As a technique, it was first adopted and applied to understand the reasons why candidates were unable to pass flying tests. Flanagan's (1954) study sought to define how effective or ineffective flying techniques could be established. This was done such that explicit standard of effective standards could be achieved with given criteria. The technique was useful in making several adjustments to the panel and cockpit designs within aircraft. While subsequent studies since Flanagan's study have followed by aligning CIT to quantitative approaches, scholars such Chell (1998) have advocated that narrative data via qualitative studies are very appropriate.

Following Chell and Pittaway (1998), we define CIT as a qualitative interview data collection approach, which enables a researcher to explore significant events or incidents through the lens of the interviewee, together with how they were handled and their perceived impacts. With this technique, the aim is to comprehend the incident from the individual's viewpoint, considering the emotional dimensions of the narrative.

Viewed from this perspective, a critical incident technique can be best defined as a method that derives its uniqueness from drawing questions about the significant experiences of research participants. As a data collection method, it is particularly advantageous for its ability to gather specific information on a crucial or significant incident or situation. Here, the researchers would invite the participants to provide a detailed account of one or several incidents which they have experienced relating to the research question. Usually, these incidents refer to situations or activities that have occurred but have clear consequences. In this way, the participants can relate and provide their interpretations of the events. As a point to note, the researcher is expected to have a sound understanding of the theoretical issues involved with the study, such that they can determine areas requiring further probing, giving them the opportunity to adapt questions to particular respondents (Chell and Pittaway, 1998).

Typically, the technique relies very much on structured interviews, which are commonly employed with the critical incident technique. Participants are probed to recall or narrate their experience or observation of a particular event (critical incidents) and the outcomes. During the inquiry stage, it is recommended that participants are probed clearly based on their real experiences, rather than on vague or abstract concepts. Thus, by exploring the incident's contributing factors, the researcher aims to identify recurrent themes and patterns towards gaining a more profound understanding of the incident. As a qualitative data collection method, the critical incident techniques typically involve the following approaches. We have captured these four steps below:

Table 9.1   The Four Steps Critical Incident Technique (CIT)

Steps	Description
Identifying and locating the incident	In this process, the researcher focuses on the distinct and significant occurrence of events that align with the research question. Here, the researcher invites the participant to narrate or recall their relevant experiences.
Collecting data	The next stage involves the interview process. In this stage, the researcher collects data probing the participants to give a detailed account of this incident. The narration usually encompasses the series of incidents, the actors involved, where it happened, why it happened, and how they felt.
Analysing the data	The process involves the scrutiny of the data collected from the recollections with a view to identifying patterns or themes related to the incident. In most cases, this would normally involve assigning codes to the data and categorising the responses. Some other scholars may choose to adopt other qualitative analysis approaches.
Drawing conclusions	With the use of data analysis, the researcher then arrives at a conclusion that captures the causes of the incident as well as likely solutions or remedies.

While the critical incident technique can be a powerful tool to gain insights into the experiences of incidents within distinct contexts, it is important to note that the findings from such experiences may not be generalisable across contexts to other populations.

Box 9.3   Case study

Critical Incident Technique (CIT) in Action

In this project, the critical incident technique was utilised to analyse entrepreneurial behaviours within the restaurant and café industry. The **research population** consisted of 204 locally based business owners in Newcastle City Council's administrative area. A telephone interview was conducted with all business owners to gather information about their operations, including the number of employees and period of operation. A sample frame was

(Continued)

constructed based on businesses operating for more than three years and employing fewer than 50 people, and a random sample of 42 business owners was selected for interviews using the CIT technique.

A total of 126 critical incidents were collected and analysed according to the CIT type, business growth type, and demographic profile of the owner. The sample included 30 per cent expanding businesses, 10 per cent rejuvenating businesses, 42 per cent plateauing businesses, and 18 per cent declining businesses. The CIT approach encouraged business owners to think retrospectively about their business development and also revealed that owners may view their businesses as an extension of their personality. The CIT proved to be a versatile and useful tool for gathering primary data of a subjective nature, and it provided both quantifiable data and qualitative descriptions. The approach also enhanced reliability through cross-checking with other field observers and sources of data. Furthermore, the incidents studied could be replicated in other businesses as a pattern of related activities.

Source: Chell and Pittaway (1998). A study of entrepreneurship in the restaurant and café industry: exploratory work using the critical incident technique as a methodology. *Hospitality Management* 17 (1998) 23–32.

9.6 Case study strategy

The case study is a qualitative data collection method that is often referred to as a strategy due to its systematic approach to investigating phenomena. By examining one or more cases, it is used to gain a deeper understanding of the factors that impact outcomes in real-world situations. Its uniqueness lies in the fact that it provides valuable insights for researchers, educators and practitioners who seek to better understand the complexities of a given context. Yin (2018) describes case studies as the preferred strategy when addressing the 'what,' 'how' and 'why' questions, especially those that the researcher has little control over.

The case study strategy is commonly used to address research questions that aim to uncover hidden dynamics within research settings. As an empirical inquiry, it is recognised for its ability to 'investigate a contemporary phenomenon within its real-life contexts, particularly when the boundaries between the phenomenon and contexts are not clearly evident' (Yin, 1994, p. 13). In essence, it is a valuable tool for uncovering contextual conditions that are pertinent to a given study. This is because its unique aspect lies in its ability to provide insights into a set of decisions, their implementation, and their outcomes (Schramm, 1971; Yin, 2018). This enables one to illuminate factors that contribute to the success or failure of the decision-making process, which we argue is a critical aspect of research.

Stake (1994) does not consider case studies to be a methodological choice, rather he views case studies to be the choice of object to be studied. He points out that

Table 9.2   Sample excerpt of a case study protocol

Case Study Protocol

Section A

Case study and purpose of the protocol

This provides an important way of improving the reliability of the case study by guiding the investigator through procedures and general rules on how to carry out the data collection.

No	Case Study Questions
RQ1:	What are the institutions that influence small business relationships?
RQ2:	How is trust developed in these small business relationships?
RQ4:	How does distrust affect small business relationships?
RQ5	How is trust repaired in small business relationships?

No	The theoretical frameworks adopted in the study
1.	Embeddedness theory
2.	Institutional theory

Role of Protocol

No	Role of Protocol
1.	Give an overview of the case study projects, highlighting the main questions that are being investigated.
2.	Provide clear guidelines for writing the case study report to help the investigator stay on topic and avoid irrelevant information.
3.	Enhance the reliability of the case study by supporting the investigator in anticipating potential issues that may arise during the completion of the report.

Section B

Data Collection Procedures

Names of sites visited (including contacts)
Small Business Department:
Contact: Director of Trade
Market trade fairs
Contact: 12 Small business owner-managers

Events observed (2023)
Activities of Small businesses across seven markets

Data Collection Plan
Semi-structured interviews with 12 small business owners
Interviews with informants and policymakers
Supporting policy documents: World bank report, Central bank report, IMF report
Data analysis
Thematic analysis

Source: Adapted from Omeihe (2019)

the case study strategy also allows for a deeper exploration of phenomena which then inform broader theoretical and practical insights. This is why it is recognised as an effective way to generate knowledge that can be applied to strengthen decision-making and problem-solving interventions.

As a related but important note, case studies also offer a systematic and methodical approach to investigating a given phenomenon, providing valuable insights into the complexities of real-world situations. This is why it is employed by researchers, educators and practitioners when they seek to gain a deeper understanding of the contextual conditions that influence outcomes, leading to better decision-making processes. Yet, there is a widely held belief that case studies lack rigour due to the possibility of researchers failing to follow systematic procedures, resulting in equivocal bias that can impact research findings. To overcome this challenge, it is recommended to adopt multiple data collection methods and report evidence in a fair manner to prevent any form of bias throughout the study.

Another concern with case studies is that they lack the basis for scientific generalisations. However, the goal of case studies is to contextualise and perhaps expand theories, not to make statistical generalisations. Despite the perceived misconceptions, case studies provide richer insights than most data collection approaches. We point out that they are particularly appropriate for exploring new and unexplored topics. Another point worth noting is that the credibility of case studies relies on the researcher's ability and effort to design and develop a case study protocol.

A protocol provides a set of procedures and general rules that guide the data collection process. This would typically outline the case to be investigated, the research question, the methods of collecting data and how it will be analysed, including the expected study outcomes. This provides a roadmap that ensures transparency and consistency are applied in the process.

Exploring case study designs

Research designs are shaped by their general characteristics, and these serve as the background for identifying the specific designs for case studies. Yin (2014) distinguishes between four case study designs.

- Single-case and multiple-case designs
- Holistic and embedded-case designs.

These designs are used over time to generate comprehensive, detailed and robust data.

Single-case and multiple-case designs

These are used to investigate a particular case or entity to examine the intricate dynamics or relationships that exist within it. Single-case designs can be employed to verify the accuracy of a theory's proposition or to consider alternative explanations that may be pertinent. They have the potential to make a significant contribution to our knowledge and can guide subsequent research efforts in a particular field. Single cases are also suitable research designs for investigating exceptional or extraordinary phenomena. This is because they are characterised by their revelatory nature, which means that they can unveil concealed phenomena that may be inaccessible to other methods of inquiry.

On the other hand, the use of multiple cases has experienced a rise in qualitative studies. In contrast to single case studies, multiple case studies examine several cases to identify patterns or similarities that exist across them. As a matter of fact, the rationale behind multiple case designs is that the cases should be chosen with care to produce convincing findings. It is also important to note that multiple-case designs have distinct advantages and disadvantages compared to single-case designs. Here, evidence from multiple cases is more robust and persuasive, although this does not imply that single cases cannot produce compelling findings. As previously mentioned, the unique aspect of single cases lies in their revelatory potential and their use in exceptional or extraordinary situations. Notwithstanding, a major drawback of multiple-case designs is their need for extensive resources and time, which often goes beyond the means of the researcher.

Holistic versus embedded case designs

In certain instances, a case study may involve analysing more than one unit of analysis, also known as subunits. These subunits are referred to as embedded units and are

Table 9.3   Types of case study designs

	Single-case designs	Multiple-case designs
Holistic (single units of analysis)	Type One	Type Three
Embedded (multiple units of analysis)	Type Two	Type Four

Source: Adapted from Yin (2014)

typically chosen through a sampling process, resulting in an embedded case study design. Conversely, a holistic case study examines the study as a whole rather than its subunits. For example, if an organisation's global nature is being studied, a holistic design would likely be employed. This implies that holistic designs are appropriate when no subunits are identified or when the theory guiding the case study is holistic in nature.

9.7 Action research

As a data collection method, action research stands out from other types due to its focus on practical outcomes. It is a data collection approach that involves the participation and collaboration of researchers and practitioners to address, solve and analyse problems within a particular setting. Here, the researcher collaborates with a client(s) to diagnose problems to develop solutions based on the diagnosis. Another way of thinking about action research is as a collaborative effort that addresses issues that are of genuine interest (Bryman and Bell, 2015). According to Argyris et al. (1985), action

Table 9.4 Characteristics of Action Research

Characteristics	Description
Implications must go beyond the immediate purpose	Action research should have implications that go beyond its immediate purpose of informing action or generating knowledge in the specific domain of the project. The theories developed should be applicable to other situations, making it possible to discuss them in a broader context. This means that the results of the research should be capable of informing other contexts, at least by suggesting areas for further consideration.
Should demand explicit concern with theory	In addition to its practical applicability in daily life, action research requires a deliberate focus on theory. This theory is developed by characterising or conceptualising the specific experience in a manner that is intended to be comprehensible to others.
Must demonstrate the explicit basis of the design	Merely designing tools, techniques, models and methods to express the generalisations drawn from action research is insufficient. The rationale behind their design must be made explicit and demonstrated to be linked to the underlying theory.
The development of emergent theory	Action research should produce an emergent theory, which arises from synthesising the theory that emerges from the data with the theory that informs the intervention and research intent, as it is utilised in practice.
Incremental theory building	Through action research, theory building occurs incrementally, advancing from the specific to the general through small steps.
Clear expectations	Action researchers must have a clear understanding of what they intend for the audience to gain from it, and should present the research in a manner and style that aligns with this objective.
Organisation and orderliness	A significant level of method and organisation is necessary when reflecting on and retaining the emerging research content from each stage of involvement in the organisation.

Characteristics	Description
Replicability	In action research, the process of exploring data to identify emergent theories must be replicable or demonstrated through argument or analysis, rather than merely collecting data.
Procedural knowledge	Possessing the knowledge and skills necessary to employ appropriate methods and analysis procedures for collecting and exploring detailed data is indispensable
Contextual understanding	The historical and contextual background of the intervention must be considered crucial when interpreting the probable scope of validity and practicality of the outcomes.

research is a cyclical process that involves problem identification, planning, acting and evaluation. These are often done repeatedly and iteratively until an appropriate solution is found. As a point to note, within action research, the research subjects are often referred to as clients and their involvement in the research process leads to their empowerment and improved pattern of thinking and actions.

Surprisingly, unlike other data collection methods, the primary objective of action research is to enhance the interplay between theory and practice. This approach aims to provide valuable insights into real-world problems and improve practices and processes, which can have broader benefits across various industries and disciplines. Despite its ability to address significant organisational issues, it has been criticised for its lack of repeatability and rigour, as the interventions are often one-offs (Eden and Huxham, 1996). However, despite this criticism, action research can provide a level of richness and robustness of insights that other approaches may not be able to achieve.

In Table 9.4, we have captured the key characteristics of action research. Following the studies of Eden and Huxham (1996) we have captured features and characteristics of action research below (see Table 9.4).

9.8 Summary

- Interview is a purposeful conversation between two or more people. It requires the interviewer to establish rapport, ask concise and unambiguous questions, listen attentively, and encourage the interviewee to respond.
- There are three recognised types of interviews based on the level of structure: structured, semi-structured and unstructured.
- Semi-structured interviews are used in exploratory or explanatory studies. They allow for discussion in areas that had not been previously considered, which may be valuable in addressing research questions and objectives.
- In unstructured interviews, there is no predetermined list of questions. The interviewee is allowed to talk freely about events and behaviour related to the topic area.

- Focus groups are a type of qualitative interview that involves a panel of people focused on a particular topic to provide perspectives and enable interaction between participants. They allow participants to probe each other's perspectives and opinions.
- The focus group approach offers the opportunity for people to interact with and learn from each other's views on a particular topic.
- The Delphi method is a systematic forecasting process that relies on a panel of experts. It is a structured technique for group communication that allows a group of experts to deal with complex problems.
- The critical incident technique is a qualitative interview data collection approach. It enables a researcher to explore significant events or incidents through the lens of the interviewee, including how they were handled and their perceived impacts.
- Critical incident techniques involve four steps: identifying and locating the incident, collecting data, analysing the data and drawing conclusions.
- Case studies are an empirical inquiry that investigates a contemporary phenomenon within its real-life contexts. They are useful when boundaries between phenomena and contexts are not clearly evident.
- A case study protocol provides a set of procedures and general rules to guide the data collection process.
- Case study designs can be categorised into single-case and multiple-case designs, and holistic and embedded-case designs. They are used over time to generate comprehensive, detailed, and robust data.
- Action research is a cyclical process that involves problem identification, planning, acting and evaluation

Self-check questions

1. What are research interviews?
2. What are the different types of questions employed in an interview guide?
3. What are the strategies and competencies to be considered when conducting interviews?
4. What are focus groups?
5. What are the key considerations to be noted when employing focus groups as a mode of data collection?
6. When is the Delphi method appropriate?
7. What does critical incident technique mean?
8. What is action research?

Questions for review and discussion

1. Discuss how you would apply the Delphi method in your research.
2. Devise an interview guide that you could use to conduct semi-structured interviews for your chosen research.

Self-check answers

1. A research interview is a conversation between two or more people which relies on asking questions to obtain rich insights about a phenomenon. It is valuable in gathering credible data that are relevant to your research aim and objectives.
2. Nine different types of questions should be provided in the interview guide namely, introductory questions, follow-up questions, probing questions, specifying questions, direct questions, indirect questions, structuring questions, silence and interpreting questions.
3. The strategies or competencies to be considered when conducting interviews include location, information recording, commencing the interview and dealing with difficult participants.
4. Focus groups are qualitative interviews which involve a panel of people who focus on a particular topic to provide perspectives and enable interaction between the participants.
5. The key considerations to be noted when employing focus groups as a mode of data collection include participant selection, questions asked, and recording and transcription.
6. When the opinion of experts is key to your study, then the best technique to employ is the Delphi method. The Delphi method is a systematic process of forecasting which relies on a panel of experts.
7. Critical incident technique is a widely recognised qualitative research method used for obtaining recalled observations about significant events from observers with first-hand experience.
8. Action research is an interactive research method which aims to concurrently investigate and solve an issue.

Further reading

Bryman, A. and Bell, E. (2011) *Business Research Methods*. 3rd ed. Oxford, England: Oxford University Press.

Gray, D.E. (2009) *Doing Research in the Real World*. London: Sage.

Saunders, M., Lewis, P. and Thornhill, A. (2012) *Research Methods for Business Students*. 6th ed. Edinburgh Gate, Harlow, Essex: Pearson Education Limited.

Yin, R.K. (2014). *Case Study Research: Design and methods*. 5th ed. Los Angeles, CA: Sage

10

Qualitative Data Analysis

Learning outcomes

Upon completing this chapter on qualitative data analysis, you will be able to:

- recognise and prioritise essential considerations when preparing qualitative data for analysis, with a specific focus on leveraging computer-aided qualitative data analysis software
- demonstrate proficiency in transcribing audio-recorded interviews or interview notes and generating a data file suitable for computer-based analysis
- clearly articulate the rationale for using qualitative data as a viable method of analysis
- apply the acquired knowledge from this chapter by successfully integrating it into your own research project, thereby demonstrating its practical application.

It is expected that you will develop a robust understanding of qualitative data analysis, encompassing essential aspects such as data preparation and analytical approaches. This knowledge will empower you to ensure the integrity of your research design and the strength of your data collection process.

10.1 Introduction

In this chapter, we embark on an exciting exploration of data analysis for qualitative research. Our aim is to investigate a range of data analysis techniques while addressing the challenges inherent in this process. Our primary focus here is on the rationale of qualitative data analysis, where we examine the dimensions of preparation for data analysis. This includes identifying key considerations before commencing the analysis, specifically in relation to transcriptions and records. We will also explore the stark differences between qualitative and quantitative data analysis and conclude by highlighting some important functions of computer-aided qualitative data packages (CAQDAS).

Over the years, qualitative data analysis has garnered significant attention from researchers, marking a notable shift from the previous emphasis on quantitative research and its analysis. We enthusiastically embrace this paradigm shift and look forward to an auspicious future for students who seek to harness the potential of qualitative approaches in their data analysis projects. As a matter of fact, the analysis of data holds a significant position in scholarly literature and articles on methodology. However, we have identified a noticeable gap in the existing discourse, specifically in relation to the analysis of qualitative data. We firmly believe that it is crucial to provide comprehensive guidance to students and researchers on how to effectively analyse qualitative data. Therefore, the primary objective of this chapter is to address this gap by presenting a diverse range of qualitative data analysis approaches and methodologies.

Our aim here is to empower students and researchers with the necessary tools and knowledge to undertake qualitative data analysis in their research. Throughout this chapter, we will explore various approaches to qualitative data analysis and provide insights on overcoming the constraints and challenges that often arise during this process.

The goal is to contribute to the advancement of qualitative research practices and facilitate robust and insightful analysis of qualitative data. As a result, this chapter will serve as an essential resource for individuals seeking to enhance their understanding and proficiency in qualitative data analysis. We aspire to foster a greater appreciation for qualitative research by bridging this gap in the existing discourse.

10.2 Features of qualitative data analysis

Qualitative research is widely recognised for its potential to generate valuable insights. At the core of qualitative analysis lies the pursuit of rich and robust findings. While researchers may receive training in conducting qualitative analysis, it is crucial for them to develop a deep understanding and cultivate effective strategies. So far as we know, the essence of qualitative analysis revolves around exploring central themes and uncovering meaningful insights from the data. As a matter of fact, it goes beyond a mere surface-level examination and probes the nuances and complexities present within the research subject, such that when appropriate strategies and techniques are employed, researchers can extract valuable information and draw significant conclusions from their qualitative data.

However, it is important to acknowledge that qualitative analysis requires a certain level of skill and expertise. And it differs largely from how quantitative analysis is conducted. All this would mean that researchers must possess a nuanced understanding of various analytical approaches and be able to adapt them to their specific research context. Additionally, they should be mindful of potential biases and actively work towards maintaining rigour and objectivity throughout the analysis process.

This leads us to our initial inquiry: What sets qualitative data analysis apart from quantitative data analysis? First and foremost, it is crucial to grasp that qualitative data analysis revolves solely around the interpretation of meanings conveyed through words, rather than numerical data. This distinction emphasises the qualitative researcher's immersion in the linguistic and narrative aspects of the data.

Furthermore, a distinctive characteristic of qualitative data analysis is its affiliation with concepts derived from the richness of interpretations. This enables researchers to explore deeper into the phenomenon under investigation and gain a more comprehensive understanding of it. We know as a rule that through the exploration of multiple perspectives, contexts, and nuances embedded within qualitative data, researchers can uncover valuable insights that contribute to the richness of knowledge in their field. Of course, qualitative data analysis provides a framework for exploring the intricate layers of meaning conveyed through words, allowing researchers to grasp the essence of a phenomenon in a holistic and nuanced manner. It enables the focus on the interpretive nature of qualitative data, through which researchers can unlock a wealth of insights that may not be captured by quantitative approaches alone.

There is a valid claim to be made regarding the robustness and potential for more promising findings in qualitative data analysis compared to quantitative analysis. While we recognise the importance of quantitative data analysis, we contend that qualitative data analysis, despite being time-consuming and demanding, guarantees thoroughness and enhances the validity of the findings. The time-consuming nature of qualitative data analysis stems from its propensity to generate a substantial amount of data. This is primarily due to the inclusion of inputs such as interview transcripts, documentary evidence and fieldwork, which contribute to the volume of information to be analysed.

In contrast to quantitative analysis, qualitative data analysis encompasses a notable feature known as thematic analysis. The thematic analysis involves the systematic identification of meanings, patterns and trends within the data, aiming to uncover themes that emerge from the dataset. It is important to note that the exploration of themes is also embraced by other analytical approaches, including narrative analysis and grounded analysis, which play significant roles in the overall analytical process. These aspects have received extensive attention and scrutiny from numerous authors and texts, contributing to the existing body of knowledge. Building upon these foundations, our discussion will offer unique insights and interpretations, delving further into the topic of thematic analysis in the subsequent sections of this chapter. The table presented below outlines additional distinctions between qualitative and quantitative data analysis.

Table 10.1   **Features of Qualitative Data Analysis**

Features	Qualitative Data Analysis	Quantitative Data Analysis
Nature of data	Non-numerical, descriptive and subjective	Numerical, measurable and objective
Sample size	Smaller, often focuses on in-depth analysis of a few cases.	Larger, typically representative of a population
Data collection methods	Interviews, observations, focus groups	Surveys, experiments, measurements
Data analysis approaches	Inductive, interpretive and exploratory	Deductive, statistical and confirmatory
Data representation	Textual, narrative and visual depictions	Numerical tables, charts and graphs
Generalisability	Findings are context-specific, limited generalisability	Findings can be generalised to a larger population
Subjectivity	Relies on the researcher's interpretation and judgement	Strives for objectivity and minimising researcher bias
Time and resources	Time-consuming and resource intensive	Efficient and less resource demanding
Depth of understanding	Provides rich, in-depth insights and detailed explanations	Provides a broad overview and statistical patterns
Research questions	Typically, open-minded and exploratory	Typically, closed-ended and hypothesis-driven

10.3 Effective strategies for preparing and managing qualitative data

As previously mentioned, the approach to handling qualitative data is often tailored to the researcher's intended objectives. The entire process is carefully managed to ensure that the audit trail reflects the researcher's systematic approach, anticipating the desired outcomes from the data. The process of managing qualitative data typically begins with an initial step, often accompanied by the transcription phase frequently employed by qualitative researchers during interviews. Transcription entails documenting the interviewee's responses, ensuring that the audio recording accurately captures their answers. Although it is not uncommon for researchers to conduct interviews without audio recorders, this practice is typically reserved for specific situations, for example, when addressing sensitive topics where participants may feel uncomfortable being recorded, or in impromptu encounters. However, we assert that audio-recording interviews is generally preferable as it enables the precise capturing of participants' words and valuable information. Despite acknowledging that this approach can be time-consuming, it offers the advantage of capturing non-verbal cues and the conversational tone.

One significant advantage lies in the timely transcription of interviews immediately after they are conducted. This approach mitigates the risk of overlooking crucial elements, interpretations, and non-verbal cues present in the responses. Delaying the transcription process can lead to a backlog of pending transcriptions, which can become cumbersome and exhausting to manage. Therefore, prioritising timely transcription ensures greater efficiency, prevents the accumulation of unfinished tasks, and enhances the overall management of qualitative data.

It is important to acknowledge that transcription is an essential step in analysing the entire dataset. While it can be time-consuming, it offers the benefit of familiarising oneself with the data by converting recorded information into text. When transcribing, it is crucial to find the appropriate setting, ensuring quiet and privacy for attentive listening to the verbal recordings. Using technology, such as audio recorders, can result in high-quality recordings that can be conveniently transferred to a computer for transcription.

To support the audio recordings, documenting notes can be taken simultaneously, capturing any non-verbal behaviours or strong emotions that may convey important meanings. These notes can also be incorporated into computer-aided qualitative data analysis packages (CAQDAS), such as Nvivo Software, to facilitate the coding process. However, it is essential to recognise that transcriptions require a substantial investment of time and resources. Verbatim transcription is often preferred to ensure the capture of actual and salient narratives. For instance, when interviewees mispronounce words, it is recommended to transcribe them as pronounced. Therefore, diligent effort should be made to ensure that the transcript is clean of slangs, grammatical errors, or misconceptions.

Furthermore, in situations where pronunciations result in difficulties in comprehending the text, it is advisable to include the correct words in square brackets. This practice ensures clarity and improves understanding during the transcription process. Inserting the accurate words within square brackets ensures that one can easily grasp the intended meaning and avoid any potential confusion arising from unclear or mispronounced words. This approach enhances the overall quality and accuracy of the transcribed data, contributing to more robust qualitative analysis and interpretation.

Example 1

P: I only went to Islamia [/Islamic School/].

P: I will plead with the person so I can pay it small, small [/gradually/].

Example 2

P: Ehen [Yes] [Inaudible – 3 seconds of interview missing] I belong to the association.

In addition to the previous points, it is crucial to recognise and capture the use of filler words during the transcription process. Words such as 'hmmm,' 'ehem,' 'um,' yeah,' 'hunh,' 'oh,' and 'ah' should all be transcribed. Paying attention to these verbal expressions contributes to a comprehensive and accurate representation of the interviewee's speech patterns and nuances. When interviews are conducted in languages other than English, it is essential to translate them while ensuring that key information is not lost in translation. To ensure the highest level of accuracy, we recommend employing a three-step translation criterion process. First, the initial translation should be reviewed by an additional translator. Second, the researcher should independently review the translated text. Last, it is advisable to cross-check and verify the accuracy of the translation with the interviewee, ensuring that the intended meaning is captured effectively.

Ethical considerations should be carefully followed during the transcription process. This involves storing all transcriptions in protected files to maintain confidentiality and anonymity. These measures safeguard the privacy of the participants and uphold ethical standards in qualitative research. Once familiarised with the data, researchers can proceed to upload the transcriptions into computer-aided qualitative data analysis software (CAQDAS) such as QSR-NVivoTM. Prior to conducting fieldwork, it is highly recommended to attend training workshops to enhance proficiency in utilising the relevant software. This software is necessary for facilitating the coding process and effectively managing the entire dataset.

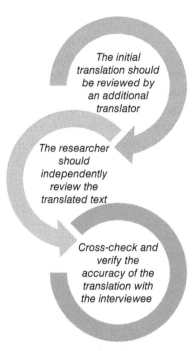

Figure 10.1   **The three-step translation criterion process**

Exercise 10.1 Interview transcription exercise

This workbook exercise is designed to provide practical experience in interview transcription, a fundamental skill in qualitative research. The exercise will familiarise you with the transcription process, including capturing key elements, managing translations, ensuring ethical considerations, and utilising computer-aided qualitative data analysis software. Follow the instructions provided and complete the exercise to enhance your proficiency in interview transcription.

Materials Needed:

A recorded interview (audio or video) with a duration of approximately 10–15 minutes
A computer with word processing software
Access to transcription software or a blank transcription template
Access to computer-aided qualitative data analysis software (CAQDAS), such as QSR-NVivoTM
Instructions:

Step 1: Preparing for Transcription

Select a recorded interview that aligns with your research interests or choose one provided by your instructor.
Familiarise yourself with the audio/video recording and ensure you have a clear understanding of the content.

Step 2: Transcription Process

Set up your transcription software or create a blank transcription template.
Start transcribing the interview and capturing the responses in text format.
Pay attention to verbal cues, non-verbal expressions, and filler words.
Include them in the transcription.
Ensure accuracy by transcribing words as pronounced, including any mispronunciations.
Use proper punctuation and formatting to enhance readability.
Save the transcription file with a suitable name and in a secure location, following ethical considerations for confidentiality and anonymity.

Step 3: Translation Process (if applicable)

If the interview is conducted in a language other than English, translate the transcription into English.

Employ the three-step translation criterion process:

a. Have the initial translation reviewed by another translator to ensure accuracy.
b. Independently review the translated text for clarity and meaning.
c. Cross-check and verify the accuracy of the translation with the interviewee, if possible.

(Continued)

Incorporate the translated text into the transcription document, clearly indicating the sections that have been translated.

Step 4: Utilising CAQDAS
Open the CAQDAS software (QSR-NVivoTM or any other relevant software).
Create a new project and import the transcribed interview.
Familiarise yourself with the software's features for coding and data analysis.
Utilise the software to code themes, identify patterns and analyse the data in the transcribed interview.
Explore the various functionalities offered by the software to manage and analyse qualitative data effectively.

Note

This workbook exercise is intended to provide you with hands-on experience in interview transcription, and translation (if applicable). Remember to practise regularly to further enhance your transcription abilities and familiarise yourself with different software tools.

10.4 The idea of coding

When it comes to data analysis, one key concept you need to familiarise yourself with is coding. At first, it may sound like a complex and technical term, but as you explore further, you'll realise it's not as daunting as it seems. In fact, coding is a straightforward and effective method to analyse qualitative data. In simple terms, coding can be defined as a concise word or phrase that captures the essence of a single sentence, paragraph, or even an excerpt from an interview. It serves as a summary or label that encapsulates the key idea or theme of the given text. There are several compelling reasons to emphasise the significance of coding as a crucial stage in the data analysis process. Understanding its essence is essential, and what sets it apart is the ability to assign labels or tags to information during analysis. In fact, whether consciously acknowledged or not, the truth is that once you begin assigning units of meaning to information during your analysis, you have already commenced the coding process.

When it comes to coding, there are two primary methods: manual coding and the systematic use of computer-aided qualitative data analysis software. Regardless of the approach taken, coding follows a straightforward process. To illustrate this process, let's focus on the straightforward approach. Coding begins by immersing oneself in qualitative data, which can be derived from sources like interview transcripts or textual documents. This immersion facilitates a thorough understanding of the content.

Immersion is crucial as it provides valuable insights into the analysed information and forms a strong foundation for subsequent coding steps. It emphasises the importance of attentive reading or listening, enabling researchers to identify significant patterns, recurring topics, and essential ideas embedded within the data.

However, achieving immersion is only possible after familiarising oneself with the data. Familiarisation involves carefully studying the data to gain a deeper grasp of its context and themes. It plays a vital role in enabling effective coding by helping researchers identify patterns. This, in turn, allows for informed coding decisions and a comprehensive understanding of the themes and nuances present. With this contextual knowledge, researchers can assign appropriate codes that accurately capture the main concepts or ideas expressed. The next stage of coding involves breaking down the data into smaller, manageable segments for effective analysis. These segments can vary from sentences and paragraphs to specific ideas found within the data. The identification of these meaningful units forms the basis for analysis and coding, creating the fundamental building blocks for further examination.

An essential aspect closely tied to this process is the assignment of relevant codes or labels to each unit during analysis. These codes should succinctly capture the main themes, concepts or ideas expressed in the data. It is crucial to ensure that these codes are concise yet meaningful, capturing the essence of each unit. This process entails recognising patterns, recurring topics or significant information within the data and assigning appropriate codes accordingly.

To maintain consistency and organisation throughout the coding process, it is crucial to establish a coding system or coding schedule that provides a comprehensive list of codes and their corresponding definitions. This can be achieved by utilising Nivio, which allows for the easy creation of a coding system as a reference guide, ensuring uniformity in code assignment and enhancing the reliability of the analysis. Alternatively, researchers who prefer manual methods can also develop their coding system. Once the coding system is in place, the next step is to systematically apply the assigned codes to each relevant unit of data. This can be accomplished through various techniques such as highlighting, underlining or using symbols to indicate the assigned codes. Consistently applying these codes creates a structured representation of the data, enabling easier analysis and interpretation.

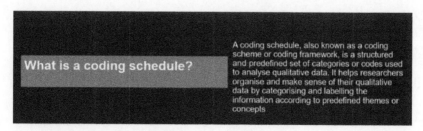

What is a coding schedule?

A coding schedule, also known as a coding scheme or coding framework, is a structured and predefined set of categories or codes used to analyse qualitative data. It helps researchers organise and make sense of their qualitative data by categorising and labelling the information according to predefined themes or concepts

Figure 10.2 **Coding schedule in a nutshell**

Table 10.2 **Sample manual coding schedule**

Category	Category	Definition
Trust	1	Trustworthiness – Instances reflecting perceived reliability or trust
Trust	2	Distrust – Instances indicating scepticism or lack of trust
Trust	3	Trust-building – Instances illustrating efforts to foster trust
SMEs	4	Expertise – Instances highlighting subject matter expertise
SMEs	5	Authority – Instances demonstrating recognised authority
SMEs	6	Credibility – Instances emphasising the credibility of SMEs
Institutions	7	Organisational culture – Instances discussing institutional values
Institutions	8	Governance – Instances pertaining to institutional decision-making
Institutions	9	Transparency – Instances involving openness and disclosure
Institutions	10	Legitimacy – Instances addressing the perceived legitimacy of institutions

The concluding phases involve the ongoing evaluation of the encoded data to uphold consistency and precision. It is crucial for researchers to emphasise the verification of potential disparities or incongruities in the assigned codes and implement essential enhancements. Neglecting this step frequently undermines the coding choices and the dependability of the analysis. Therefore, rectifying this issue presents an opportunity to recognise emerging patterns or insights that might necessitate modifications to the coding framework. Table 10.2 provides a sample manual coding schedule.

In this table, the coding schedule includes three categories: *Trust, SMEs, and Institutions*. Under each category, there are multiple codes that represent specific coding items or concepts.

For the Trust category, we have three codes:

- Code 1 represents instances reflecting **trustworthiness**
- Code 2 indicates instances of distrust
- Code 3 captures instances illustrating efforts to build trust.

Under the SMEs category, there are three codes as well:

- Code 4 represents instances highlighting subject matter expertise
- Code 5 indicates instances demonstrating recognised authority
- Code 6 captures instances emphasising the credibility of SMEs.

Last, the Institutions category includes five codes:

- Code 7 represents instances discussing organisational culture
- Code 8 pertains to instances related to institutional governance

- Code 9 captures instances of accountability
- Code 10 involves instances of transparency
- Code 11 addresses instances pertaining to the perceived legitimacy of institutions.

Manual Coding

> **What is Manual Coding?**
>
> Manual coding is a systematic approach to analysing qualitative data, and the manual coding schedule is a valuable tool for researchers. In the table below, we present a manual coding schedule that outlines categories, codes, and their definitions. Researchers can refer to this coding schedule as a reference guide throughout their analysis. This enables the researcher to create a structured representation of the data, that facilitates easier analysis and interpretation.

Spotlight on NVivo

NVivo is a powerful software tool for qualitative data analysis, and NVivo enables researchers to organise and analyse their data efficiently. It is a user-friendly computer software program designed to manage, analyse and visualise qualitative data and documents systematically and individually. It caters to researchers who are familiar with coding and qualitative data analysis strategies, offering an efficient tool for their work.

Table 10.3 presents an example of an NVivo coding schedule, consisting of categories, alphanumeric codes and their definitions.

Table 10.3   NVivo coding schedule

Category	Code	Code Definition
Emotions	EM1	Joy – Instances where the data expresses happiness
Emotions	EM2	Sadness – Instances where the data conveys sorrow
Emotions	EM3	Anger – Instances where the data reflects frustration
Skills	SK1	Leadership – Instances discussing leadership qualities
Skills	SK2	Teamwork – Instances highlighting the importance of teamwork

The NVivo coding employs alphanumeric codes to uniquely identify each category and code. In this example, under the Emotions category, codes EM1, EM2 and EM3 are used to tag data segments that exhibit joy, sadness and anger, respectively. Similarly, under the Themes category, codes TH1 and TH2 represent discussions on leadership qualities and the importance of teamwork.

The NVivo coding enhances the organisation and management of qualitative data analysis within the software. Researchers can refer to this coding schedule as a guide while coding and analysing their data in NVivo, ensuring consistency and facilitating a comprehensive analysis and interpretation.

10.5 Data analysis strategy: Thematic analysis

When it comes to selecting a data analysis strategy, it is advisable to choose a method that treats the evidence fairly, eliminates alternative interpretations, and produces compelling conclusions (Yin, 2014). Considering this, we assert that thematic analysis often proves to be the most fitting option due to its provision of a structured methodology for identifying key themes within a dataset, irrespective of the underlying epistemological stance (Boyatzis, 1998). It is noteworthy that thematic analysis not only serves the purpose of identifying, analysing and reporting patterns within the data but also ventures further to interpret diverse facets of the research topic.

For scholars and researchers aiming to present a comprehensive thematic analysis of their dataset, ensuring an accurate representation of the entire data is of paramount importance. In this regard, we note that they should actively seek out potential areas of interest and patterns of significance within the data. This process necessitates a constant iteration between the complete dataset, coded data extracts, and the analysed data.

The justification for thematic analysis holds a prominent position as a widely employed qualitative data analysis method, playing an indispensable role in unearthing patterns, meanings, and insights within a dataset. One of its main aspects is that it endows researchers with a systematic approach to identifying and interpreting emergent themes or patterns derived from the data, transcending mere summarisation to generate meaningful insights and foster a deeper comprehension of the research topic.

On our part, we define thematic analysis as a qualitative data analysis process encompassing the identification, analysis and interpretation of recurring patterns or themes within a dataset. Its purpose is to unveil underlying meanings and facilitate a comprehensive understanding of the research topic through a systematic and iterative process of coding and theme development.

So, what makes it unique?

Thematic analysis has demonstrated its resilience and versatility as a data analysis process, empowering researchers to extract valuable insights from datasets. Through a systematic process of identifying, analysing, and interpreting recurring patterns or themes within the data, thematic analysis facilitates a comprehensive understanding of the research topic. The meticulous and iterative nature of coding and theme development facilitates the exploration of connections, nuanced perspectives, and profound implications, thereby enriching the depth of the research findings. As a method for analysing data, it enables the researcher to move beyond basic observations to deeply understand the data, and thereby reveals the detailed and complex aspects of the subject being studied. The thematic analysis serves as a catalyst for the generation of novel knowledge and progress in the field.

Principles of thematic analysis

A notable distinction of thematic analysis lies in the requirement for researchers to engage in a systematic and iterative process when analysing data. It commences with the initial phase of preparing and familiarising themselves with the data, wherein they immerse themselves in its content through repeated readings. This process enables researchers to obtain a comprehensive understanding of the data's context and substance. Firstly, the researcher embarks on the coding phase, whereby they systematically identify and label specific segments of the data that align with relevant themes. These codes serve as the foundational elements for subsequent analysis and interpretation. Throughout the analytical process, the researcher continually reviews and refines the identified themes, meticulously examining their interrelationships, patterns and subtleties. This iterative approach ensures the accuracy, reliability and credibility of the analysis. Furthermore, thematic analysis demonstrates its flexibility as an approach that can be applied across diverse research disciplines and theoretical frameworks, thus providing immense value for qualitative researchers.

As previously captured, the central objective of thematic analysis lies in generating insights and contributing to theoretical advancement. By interpreting the themes that manifest within the data, researchers have the potential to make significant contributions to their respective fields of study. This enables it to equip researchers with a potent tool for uncovering latent meanings and generating profound insights from qualitative data.

Proficiency in the practice of thematic analysis empowers researchers with a valuable repertoire of skills, enabling them to unlock the complex narratives and profound meanings embedded within their qualitative data. In the context of this discourse, we have introduced a nomenclature to encapsulate this process – ADEPT Method – Analysis, Data Exploration, Pattern Identification, Theme Development, for thematic analysis. The ADEPT Method comprises four fundamental phases, each playing a crucial role in fostering a systematic and exhaustive approach:

Phase 1: Analysis

The first phase of the ADEPT Method involves a comprehensive analysis of the qualitative data. The researcher is immersed in the dataset, gaining a deep understanding of its content, context and nuances. The researcher conducts initial readings, noting important concepts, ideas and patterns that emerge from the data. This analysis sets the foundation for subsequent exploration.

Phase 2: Data exploration

In the second phase, the researcher engages in data exploration. The researcher systematically reviews and examines the dataset, identifying segments of data that are relevant to the research question or objective. The researcher organises and categorises the data based on themes, concepts, or patterns that they observe. This process allows for a thorough exploration of the dataset, ensuring that important information is not overlooked.

Phase 3: Pattern identification

Moving into the third phase, the researcher focuses on identifying patterns within the coded data. The researcher analyses the relationships, connections and variations between the data segments. Through a comparison of different instances, the researcher can recognise recurring patterns, variations and subtleties. This phase is crucial for uncovering the underlying themes and commonalities embedded within the dataset.

Phase 4: Theme development

In the final phase of the ADEPT Method, the researcher develops comprehensive themes based on the patterns identified in the previous phase. The researcher carefully analyses and interprets the data segments within each theme, considering their significance and theoretical implications. The researcher is then expected to refine, merge, or split themes as necessary to ensure they capture the complexity and richness of the data. This phase culminates in the development of well-defined and coherent themes that reflect the essence of the dataset. In the final stage, the researcher draws conclusions from the thematic analysis and reports the findings. The researcher

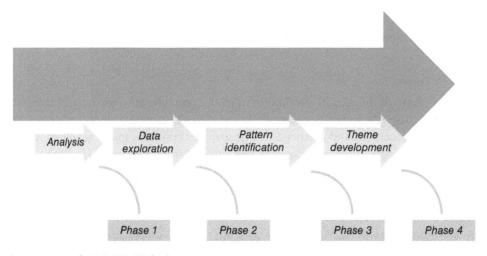

Figure 10.3   **The ADEPT Method**

Stage	Description	Key activities	Inputs	Outputs
Phase 1: Analysis	In this initial stage, researchers conduct a comprehensive analysis of the qualitative data. They immerse themselves in the dataset, gaining a deep understanding of its content, context and nuances. Initial readings are performed to identify important concepts, ideas and patterns emerging from the data.	Read and re-read the data multiple times to gain an in-depth understanding. – Make preliminary notes capturing observations and potential patterns.	Raw qualitative data	In-depth understanding of the dataset
Phase 2: Data Exploration	Researchers systematically review and examine the dataset, identifying relevant segments of data related to the research question or objective. The data is organised and categorised based on themes, concepts or patterns observed. This stage ensures a thorough exploration of the dataset, preventing the oversight of important information.	– Review the dataset and identify relevant segments of data. – Organise and categorise data based on emerging themes or patterns	Analysed dataset from Phase 1	Categorised dataset based on themes
Phase 3: Pattern Identification	In this stage, researchers analyse the relationships, connections, and variations between the coded data segments. By comparing different instances, recurring patterns, variations and subtleties are recognised. This phase is crucial for uncovering the underlying themes and commonalities within the dataset.	– Analyse relationships, connections and variations between data segments. – Recognise recurring patterns and variations.	Categorised dataset from Phase 2	Identified recurring patterns and variations.
Phase 4: Theme Development	Researchers focus on developing comprehensive themes based on the identified patterns. They carefully analyse and interpret the data segments within each theme, considering their significance and theoretical implications. Themes are refined, merged or split as necessary to accurately capture the complexity and richness of the data.	Develop comprehensive themes based on identified patterns. – Analyse and interpret data segments within each theme. – Refine, merge or split themes as necessary. Synthesise themes and draw conclusions. – Analyse the theoretical implications of the themes. – Present findings in a clear and organised manner.	Identified recurring patterns, variations and well-defined coherent themes from Phase 3	Well-defined and coherent themes. Including conclusions and findings report

will synthesise the themes, interpret their implications, and present the key findings in a clear and organised manner.

The ADEPT Method provides a systematic and rigorous approach to thematic analysis. It encompasses the essential phases of analysis, data exploration, pattern identification and theme development. We believe that through this four-phase process, researchers can effectively uncover, analyse and interpret the themes embedded within their qualitative data.

The ADEPT Method for thematic analysis can be easily understood by referring to the table above. This table introduces the method and provides a breakdown of the stages involved in conducting thematic analysis.

Each column in the table serves a specific purpose to aid readers in comprehending the process.

The table above provides a clear and comprehensive explanation of the ADEPT Method for thematic analysis. It guides researchers through the process, detailing the purpose, activities, inputs and outputs of each stage.

The first column, 'Stage,' represents the four stages of the ADEPT Method for thematic analysis. These phases outline the sequential progression of activities involved in conducting thematic analysis. The second column, 'Description,' provides a brief description of each phase, explaining its purpose and objectives. This description gives researchers an overview of what they aim to achieve in each phase and how it contributes to the overall process of thematic analysis.

The third column, 'Key Activities,' outlines the specific tasks or actions that researchers undertake during each phase. These activities represent the practical steps researchers need to follow to move forward in the thematic analysis process. It provides guidance on what needs to be done at each phase to ensure a comprehensive and systematic analysis.

The fourth column, 'Inputs,' highlights the data or information required as input for each phase. It specifies the type of data or output from the previous phase that serves as the starting point for the subsequent phase. This column clarifies the flow of information and ensures that researchers have the necessary resources to proceed to the next phase.

The fifth column, 'Outputs,' describes the desired outcomes or results of each phase. It represents the deliverables or achievements obtained at the completion of each phase, which become the foundation or input for the subsequent phase. The outputs column helps researchers evaluate their progress and ensures that they have successfully accomplished the objectives of each stage before moving forward.

Let us use this quiz exercise to test your knowledge of thematic analysis.

What is thematic analysis?

a.   A statistical method for quantitative data analysis
b.   A qualitative research method for analysing themes and patterns in textual data
c.   A technique for conducting surveys and questionnaires
d.   A method for data visualisation and mapping.

How many phases are involved in the ADEPT Method?

a.   Two phases
b.   Three phases
c.   Four phases
d.   Five phases

Which phase of the ADEPT Method involves immersing oneself in the qualitative data and gaining a deep understanding of its content?

a.   Analysis
b.   Data Exploration
c.   Pattern Identification
d.   Theme Development

What is the purpose of the coding phase in thematic analysis?

a.   To organise and categorise data based on themes or patterns
b.   To develop comprehensive themes
c.   To conduct data exploration
d.   To identify variations and nuances in the data

In the ADEPT Method, what is the purpose of theme mapping and reporting?

a.   To analyse and interpret the themes in relation to the research question
b.   To create a visual representation of the relationships between themes
c.   To refine and modify the identified themes
d.   To present the findings in a clear and organised manner

What is the significance of iterative refinement in thematic analysis?

a.   It ensures the accuracy and alignment of identified themes with the data complexity
b.   It helps in data exploration and pattern identification
c.   It creates a visual representation of the themes
d.   It facilitates the interpretation of themes

Which phase of the ADEPT Method involves the analysis of relationships, connections, and variations between the data segments?

a.   Analysis
b.   Data Exploration

(Continued)

c.   Pattern Identification
d.   Theme Development

What is the purpose of the ADEPT Method in thematic analysis?

a.   To generate insights and contribute to theoretical advancement
b.   To simplify the data analysis process
c.   To quantify qualitative data
d.   To standardise the research methods across disciplines

Answers:

b.   A qualitative research method for analysing themes and patterns in textual data

d.   Five phases

a.   Analysis

a.   To organise and categorise data based on themes or patterns

b.   To create a visual representation of the relationships between themes

a.   It ensures the accuracy and alignment of identified themes with the data complexity

c.   Pattern Identification

a.   To generate insights and contribute to theoretical advancement

10.6 Data analysis strategy: Narrative analysis

Narrative analysis is a valuable approach to data analysis that focuses on understanding and interpreting the subjective interpretations and experiences of participants. It is commonly employed in qualitative research, particularly in social sciences, psychology, anthropology and related fields where subjective experiences and interpretations are of interest.

At its core, narrative analysis involves capturing and making sense of the stories or narratives shared by individuals. It involves embracing the sequence of activities or events that hold meaning and significance to the narrator, such that researchers gain insights into the essence of an experience. In general, interviews are a commonly used method to capture participants' narratives effectively. This approach encourages participants to provide key narratives related to specific phenomena, enabling researchers to gather rich and detailed data.

But it is worth noting that narrative analysis is just one approach among various qualitative data analysis methods. However, its strength lies in its systematic approach to interpreting and understanding the narratives expressed by participants. This makes it useful for the researcher to uncover patterns, themes and deeper insights from the narratives, enhancing the overall qualitative research process.

Another perspective on narrative analysis is that it allows researchers to examine the narrator's or informant's story, thereby revealing how the narrative fits together seamlessly and persuades the listener of its authenticity. This approach opens up opportunities to extract knowledge, which can then be effectively communicated through documentation while maintaining its holistic nature through interpretation.

From our vantage point, the primary objective of narrative analysis is to capture the social context in which the informant or research participant operates. This aims to clearly identify or highlight the nature of actions that took place, their consequences, and subsequent events. However, it is crucial to analyse this information in its original form to preserve the significance of the context in which the events occurred. This easily sets the narrative analysis apart from other data analysis methods. Unlike other data analysis methods that may focus on numerical or objective data, narrative analysis probes into the qualitative aspects of data, exploring the richness and depth of human experiences.

To guide the process of narrative analysis, we adopt the acronym SWHCSO, which stands for:

- Subject/Story
- What is the story about?
- Happened (What happened, to whom, whereabouts, and why?)
- Consequences
- Significance
- Outcome.

What sets the SWHCSO strategy apart from other narrative analysis approaches is its logical sequence that serves as a helpful reminder and can be easily applied in a simple manner. The acronym itself, consisting of Subject/Story, What is the story about? Happened (What happened, to whom, whereabouts, and why?), Consequences, Significance, and Outcome, acts as a guide for researchers throughout the analysis process. This logical sequence ensures that researchers systematically address crucial aspects of the narrative analysis. It starts by identifying the subject or topic of the narrative, allowing researchers to focus their analysis. The next step involves understanding the overarching theme or central idea of the narrative, providing a clear direction for further exploration.

Moving forward, the researcher turns to focus attention on the specifics of what happened, to whom, where, and why, unravelling the events and circumstances within the narrative. This step ensures that no important details are overlooked and that the context surrounding the events is thoroughly understood. The consequences of the events described in the narrative are then examined, shedding light on the outcomes and impacts that resulted from the experiences shared. This step contributes to a comprehensive understanding of the broader implications and effects of the narrative.

The researcher then focuses their attention on the significance of the events, analysing the deeper meanings, symbolism and implications embedded within the narrative. This step encourages researchers to consider the broader social, cultural and historical contexts that shape the narrative and its interpretation.

Finally, the outcome of the narrative is explored, providing closure to the analysis. This step helps the researcher understand how the events unfolded and the ultimate resolution or outcome that emerged from the narrative.

The logical sequence of SWHCSO acts as a reminder for researchers to consider these essential elements throughout the narrative analysis process. Its simplicity and clarity make it easy to apply, ensuring that researchers cover all the crucial aspects of capturing and interpreting narratives in a comprehensive and systematic manner. This sets the SWHCSO strategy apart from other approaches that may lack such a straightforward and structured framework.

The diagram illustrates the sequential steps of narrative analysis using SWHCSO approach.

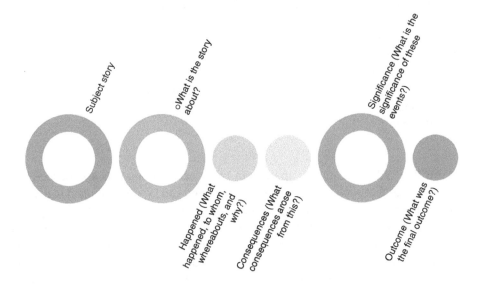

10.7 Case study exercise: Exploring narratives in qualitative research

Learning outcomes

- Apply narrative analysis principles and techniques to analyse qualitative data.
- Understand the steps involved in narrative analysis, including subject identification, central theme exploration, event examination, consequence analysis, significance interpretation and outcome assessment.

- Interpret narratives in the context of broader research questions or theoretical frameworks.

Reflect on the strengths and limitations of narrative analysis in qualitative research

Objective

The objective of this case study exercise is to provide students with an opportunity to apply narrative analysis principles and techniques to a real-life scenario.

Case Scenario

You are a researcher conducting a study on the experiences of individuals who have overcome significant challenges in their lives. You decide to employ narrative analysis to gain a deeper understanding of their journeys and the meaning they ascribe to their experiences.

Instructions

- Familiarise yourself with the principles and steps of narrative analysis discussed in class and in the course materials.
- Review an interview transcript of a participant who has overcome a significant challenge. The transcript should contain a detailed narrative of their experience.
- Apply the SWHCSO framework (Subject/Story, What is the story about? What happened, to whom, whereabouts, and why?), Consequences, Significance, and Outcome) to analyse the narrative in a systematic manner.
- Using the SWHCSO framework, identify and analyse the key elements of the participant's narrative, including the subject, central theme, events, consequences, significance and ultimate outcome.
- Reflect on the social context in which the participant's experience unfolded and consider how it influenced their narrative.
- Interpret the narrative, drawing connections between the participant's experiences and the broader research question or theoretical framework.

Provide a written analysis that summarises your findings, insights and interpretations based on the narrative analysis. Include a discussion of the strengths and limitations of the narrative analysis approach in this case.

10.8 Data analysis strategy: Discourse analysis

Discourse analysis is a research approach used to examine and interpret language, communication and social interactions within a specific context. It aims to understand how language constructs and shapes social reality, power dynamics and the production of meaning. It can be presented as an approach employed to investigate the use of language in social and cultural contexts. It is commonly used in fields such as linguistics, sociology, anthropology, psychology and communication studies.

One way to understand discourse analysis is that it explores the ways in which language is used to convey and negotiate meaning, and how it influences social practices and relationships. To this extent, it goes beyond analysing individual words and sentences, focusing on larger units of communication, such as conversations, interviews, written texts, media discourses and institutional documents.

What is often forgotten is that the primary goal of discourse analysis is to uncover and examine the underlying structures, ideologies and power relations within discourses. It explores how language is used to shape identities, construct social realities, and maintain or challenge existing social norms and power structures.

Yes, discourse analysis involves several key principles and techniques. It emphasises the context in which language is produced and interpreted, considering factors such as cultural norms, historical background and social settings. In fact, researchers are prone to analyse various aspects of discourse, including the choice of words, grammar, tone, metaphors, silences and non-verbal cues, to understand the deeper meanings and ideologies embedded within the communication.

As a related but important note, one of the main concepts in discourse analysis is the idea of 'discursive formations,' which refers to the social and linguistic practices that shape and are shaped by language use. This helps examine how language both reflects and constructs social reality. Discourse analysis offers a range of approaches and methodologies, with critical discourse analysis being one prominent example. Critical discourse analysis operates on the assumption that individuals' constructions of language not only make sense but also have the potential to reproduce or challenge the ideological belief systems that underlie society as a whole. This approach uncovers the ways in which language contributes to the perpetuation or transformation of power dynamics and social structures.

10.9 Data analysis strategy: Grounded analysis

Grounded analysis is an approach in qualitative research that involves a systematic and open approach that seeks to examine data to derive meaningful insights and interpretations. While it is closely related to the notion of grounded theory as they share similarities which underpin their principles, it differs in subtle ways. One explanation is that grounded theory is primarily used for developing theories or conceptual frameworks that emerge from data analysis. It follows an iterative and systematic process of data collection and analysis, where researchers continuously compare data, identify patterns and generate theories based on the data itself. The focus is on generating theory grounded in the data rather than testing pre-existing theories. In other words, grounded theory allows for the discovery of new insights and theoretical explanations through inductive reasoning. Another way of thinking about grounded theory is to remember that it was developed by Glaser and Strauss in the 1960s and used for developing theories or conceptual frameworks that emerge from data analysis. Of course, grounded theory follows an iterative and systematic process of data collection and analysis, where researchers continuously compare data, identify patterns and generate theories based on the data itself. Typically, the focus is on generating theory grounded in the data rather than testing pre-existing theories. Among other considerations, grounded theory allows for the discovery of new insights and theoretical explanations through inductive reasoning.

On the other hand, grounded analysis is a broader term that encompasses various methods and approaches that are grounded in empirical data. Grounded analysis is not limited to theory development, but rather includes a range of qualitative research techniques used to analyse and interpret data. It involves an in-depth examination of the data, identifying themes, patterns and meanings that emerge from the analysis. Grounded analysis is an approach in qualitative research that involves a systematic and rigorous examination of data to derive meaningful insights and interpretations. It is a flexible and iterative process that allows researchers to explore and understand the complexities of a research topic based on the data collected.

The key principle of grounded analysis is that the analysis should be grounded in the data itself, meaning that interpretations and conclusions should emerge from the data rather than being imposed based on preconceived theories or assumptions. This approach emphasises the importance of staying close to the data and allowing it to shape the analysis and findings.

The process or principles of grounded analysis typically involves several steps. We consider that there are seven main steps to achieving such an analysis:

Data Collection: This involves the collection of data through various methods such as interviews, observations, documents or audiovisual recordings. The data can be collected through purposeful sampling, seeking participants or sources that provide diverse perspectives and rich information.

Data Familiarisation: This involves immersing oneself in the data by reading or listening to it repeatedly. This process helps in becoming familiar with the content, identifying patterns, and gaining a holistic understanding of the data.

Open Coding: This involves engaging in open coding and includes breaking down the data into smaller segments and assigning descriptive labels or codes to capture the main ideas or concepts represented in the data. This step allows for the identification of patterns, themes or categories that emerge from the data.

Axial Coding: This involves the exploration of the relationships and connections between the codes generated in the previous step. Here the goal is to analyse how different codes are related to each other, their interrelationships, and how they contribute to the overall understanding of the research topic.

Selective Coding: Here, the researcher focuses on developing a more comprehensive and coherent interpretation by selecting core codes that represent the central aspects of the data. They refine and elaborate on these codes to build a cohesive narrative that captures the essence of the data.

Data Interpretation: The researcher interprets the findings by weaving together the codes, themes and categories identified in the previous steps. This involves contextualising the data within relevant theoretical frameworks, literature and research objectives. The interpretations should be well-supported by evidence from the data.

Triangulation: Here the research often engages in triangulation, which involves comparing and contrasting different sources of data or using multiple analytical techniques to enhance the validity and reliability of the analysis. Triangulation helps ensure that the findings are robust and grounded in different perspectives.

10.10 Summary

- This chapter has explored various approaches to qualitative data analysis. As we have discovered, these methods provide valuable tools for analysing empirical data by following predetermined procedures. We note that employing these procedures will greatly assist students in their data analysis journey.
- The chapter captures that grounded analysis allows researchers to discover new insights, patterns and theoretical explanations that may not have been anticipated at the outset of the study. It encourages an inductive approach to knowledge generation, allowing the data to guide the analysis and theory development.
- The chapter explores the features and characteristics of qualitative data analysis, highlighting its association with concepts derived from rich interpretations. It also explores effective strategies for preparing and managing qualitative data, emphasising the importance of tailoring the approach to the researcher's objectives.
- The three-step translation criterion process is introduced as a valuable tool for ensuring the validity and reliability of the transition process.
- Additionally, the chapter explores the concept of coding, which involves summarising or labelling text with concise words or phrases that capture its key ideas or themes.

- We also discussed thematic analysis, with a focus on the ADEPT Method, consisting of Analysis, Data Exploration, Pattern Identification, and Theme Development.
- Also, we presented the narrative analysis as an approach that seeks to understand and interpret participants' subjective interpretations and experiences.
- Our focus on discourse analysis as a research approach captures that it examines language, communication and social interactions within a specific context.
- Lastly, grounded analysis is introduced as a broad term encompassing various methods and approaches grounded in empirical data, not limited to theory development, but extending to qualitative research techniques for analysing and interpreting data.

Further reading

Bryman, A. (2016) *Social Research Methods*. 5th ed. London: Oxford University Press.

Bryman, A. and Bell, E. (2015) *Business Research Methods*. 4th ed. Oxford: Oxford University Press.

Creswell, J.W. (2014) *Research Design: Qualitative, Quantitative and Mixed Methods Approaches*. Los Angeles: Sage.

Norman K. Denzin and Yvonna S. Lincoln (2020). *The SAGE Handbook of Qualitative Research*. Sage.

Merriam, S.B. and Tisdell, E.J. (2015). *Qualitative Research: A Guide to Design and Implementation*. Sage.

Saunders, M., Lewis, P. and Thornhill, A. (2016) *Research Methods for Business Students*. 7th ed. Harlow, Essex: Pearson.

11

Evaluation of Qualitative Research

Learning outcomes

By the end of this chapter, you should be able to:

- assess the quality of qualitative research
- elucidate the traditional evaluation criteria for research
- explain the criteria widely used to appraise the trustworthiness of qualitative research.

11.1 Introduction

Research methods should not only be viewed in terms of the aims and contexts of the research; priority should also be given to the quality of the study (Bush, 2002). Research, whether qualitative or quantitative, requires rigour to ensure that findings are trusted and believed (Merriam, 1995). By so doing, the confidence of the academic community can be satisfied regarding the credibility of the findings. This chapter will provide more insight into the traditional evaluation criteria for research such as reliability, validity and generalisability.

Qualitative research produces findings that are not based on deductive reasoning and, as discussed in earlier chapters, tend to follow a subjective lens. One of the major challenges confronting qualitative researchers is how to ensure the quality and trustworthiness of their study. The traditional approach to evaluating quantitative research does not hold for qualitative studies because of the different philosophical assumptions. As a result, alternative criteria such as trustworthiness, credibility, dependability, conformability, transferability, reflexivity and authenticity have been proposed by scholars. Within this chapter, we would be examining such alternative criteria in detail. We argue that the type of evaluation criteria adopted is determined by the research methodology and philosophical stance. Hence there is a need to assess the quality of qualitative studies from a unique lens.

11.2 Traditional evaluation criteria for research

The traditional criteria used for evaluating research are reliability, validity and generalisability.

Reliability

This refers to the reproducibility and repeatability of the results. It means how consistently a method measures something and whether the result can be reproduced when the study is conducted under similar conditions. An example is using your scale to measure your weight. A reliable scale would provide the same weight under the same conditions. Within Business and Management research, measures such as organisational performance, effectiveness and so on are usually examined to see if they are consistent. However, reliability is more aligned to quantitative research because of its focus on statistics. There are three types of reliability; test-retest reliability which assesses the consistency of a measure across time; inter-rater reliability which assesses the consistency of a measure across raters and internal reliability which assesses the consistency of a measurement itself.

Validity

This refers to the accuracy of a result. It is the extent to which the results are an accurate representation of the phenomenon. It relates to the integrity, genuineness and honesty of the research data. An example is the scale providing the accurate weight of the person. A measurement can be reliable and not valid. For example, if the scale is providing the same weight of 65kg and the person is 60kg, the result is reliable but not valid.

Similar to reliability, validity is a concept more aligned to quantitative research and there are three types of validity namely, construct validity, content validity and criterion validity.

- **Construct Validity:** This is also known as measurement validity. It is usually concerned about how the measure adheres to the existing theory and knowledge of the concept. It has to do with whether the measure that is obtained reflects the concept that it should be representing. For example, if a person has a high score in a survey for emotional intelligence, is the person truly emotionally intelligent?

- **Content Validity:** This is the extent to which the measurement covers all the content that it should with respect to the concept. For example, an English test that has no writing component may be said to lack content validity because it does not cover all aspects of comprehending English.
- **Criterion Validity:** This is the extent to which the result of a measure is related to other results that measure the same variable. Correlations can be conducted to determine the extent to which different instruments measure the same variable. A survey that examines customer buying preferences can be said to have a high criterion validity if the result accurately reflects their choices in the store.

Generalisability

This is also referred to as external validity. It is the degree to which the results of a study can be applied beyond the research context. Results are generalisable when they can be applied to a broader context and beyond the setting where the research was originally conducted. To achieve this, it is important that the sample employed reflects the characteristics of the entire population to be studied since not every member of the population can be selected. When the sample is representative of the population then the findings obtained can be said to be generalisable (see Chapter 7 for sampling in qualitative research).

11.3 Criteria for evaluating qualitative research

Qualitative research is a form of research which is employed when findings are not based on statistical procedure and numerical means as is seen with quantitative studies. The bulk of the analysis is subjective, offering different meanings for different people (Mandal, 2018). It is difficult to come up with a universal conclusion. As a result, one of the biggest challenges that faces qualitative researchers is ensuring the quality and trustworthiness of their research.

The major criticism that has been levelled against qualitative approach is the lack of scientific rigour and credibility compared to the traditional quantitative methods which are widely viewed as objective, impartial and value neutral. However, such a notion has been criticised by a number of scholars (for example Altheide and Johnson, 2013; Coffey, 1999). Furthermore, there has also been a wide disagreement about the efficacy and appropriateness of the traditional criteria discussed above (i.e. reliability, validity and generalisability) in evaluating qualitative inquiry (Popay et al., 1998; Morse, 1999). For example, Bochner (2000) and Altheide and Johnson (2013) stress that traditional empiricist criteria are not suitable or relevant in ethnographic studies.

As a result, many qualitative scholars have proposed alternative frameworks and criteria for assessing qualitative research (see Lincoln, 1995; Coffey, 1999; Tracy, 2010). Box 11.1. shows the distinction between some of the qualitative and quantitative criteria.

Box 11.1   Distinction between quantitative and qualitative criteria

Qualitative Criteria	Quantitative Criteria
Trustworthiness	Rigour
Credibility	Internal Validity
Dependability	Reliability
Confirmability	Objectivity
Transferability	Generalisability

Based on our research, we have identified six criteria that are widely used to appraise the trustworthiness of qualitative research namely, credibility, dependability, confirmability, transferability, reflexivity and authenticity. In the next sections, we will be exploring these criteria in detail.

11.4 Credibility

Credibility involves demonstrating that a true picture of the phenomenon under investigation is represented (Shenton, 2004). This is similar to the concept of internal validity (see section 11.2). According to Krefting (1991, p. 215), 'it asks whether the researcher has established confidence in the truth of the findings for the subjects or informants and the contexts in which the study was undertaken.' It means that the research findings are plausible and trustworthy. Lincoln and Guba (1985) refer to it as the 'truth value,' and it is perhaps the most important criterion for assessing a qualitative study (Krefting, 1991).

In ensuring credibility, we advise that you ask the following questions:

- How plausible are your findings?
- What is the evidence to back up your findings?
- Does the study truly reflect the context it intends to investigate?

Credibility of research is enhanced when well-established methods are adopted. Such methods chosen must be well explicated and justified. For example, if you adopted semi-structured interviews then it is pertinent that you provide a clear explanation of the reason for your choice. Why did you employ semi-structured interviews rather than other data collection methods such as participant observation, focus groups and so on? The data collection methods and the volume of data should be justified and appropriate to the chosen methodology (Stenfors et al., 2020).

There are several strategies for fostering credibility. One key strategy for ensuring credibility is the selection criteria used to recruit study participants. The sample should produce the type of knowledge necessary to understand the structure and processes within which the individuals or situations are located (Popay et al., 1998). As a result, it is advised that initial sampling decisions should be purposive, in that selection of participants is made on the basis of their ability to provide relevant data on the area under investigation. This is not to say that other sampling strategies such as convenience, **theoretical sampling** and so on are not appropriate for qualitative research. Ultimately, the choice of your sampling strategy is dependent on the research design and questions.

Another key strategy of gaining credibility in research is via triangulation. Triangulation involves the use of multiple investigators, multiple data sources or multiple methods to confirm emerging findings (Merriam, 1995). As Shenton (2004, p. 66) states, in triangulation, 'individual viewpoints and experiences can be verified against others and ultimately a rich picture of the attitudes, needs or behaviour of those under scrutiny may be constructed based on the contribution of a range of people.' Contrary evidence, often known as deviant cases, must be taken into consideration in the analysis to ensure that researcher bias does not affect or alter their perception of the data and any insights offered (Anderson, 2010). For example, in the study of entrepreneurial leadership, prior studies have taken a singular perspective and obtained data only from entrepreneurs. To triangulate data, Harrison et al. (2018), in addition to obtaining the perspective of the entrepreneurs, interviewed their employees to capture their perspectives. Triangulation goes beyond multiple sources of data collection and involves investigator triangulation which requires that more than one investigator collect and analyse the data, such that the findings emerge through consensus between or among them. There is also theory triangulation whereby emergent findings are examined in relation to existing theories.

Lincoln and Guba (1985) recognise member checking as an important provision in bolstering credibility. It involves continually testing the researcher's data, interpretations and conclusions with the participants (Krefting, 1991). Some scholars refer to it as respondent or participant validation (Bryman and Bell, 2011; Horsburgh, 2003). As Sandelowski (cited in Krefting, 1991, p. 216) stated, 'A qualitative study is credible when it presents such accurate descriptions or interpretations of human experience that people who also share that experience would immediately recognise the descriptions.' An example of member checking to ascertain credibility is when interview transcripts are given to the participants to ensure the accuracy of the data. However, though member checking seems to be an established strategy of ensuring credibility, it could be problematic because the participants and the researcher may have different agendas and perspectives.

Peer debriefing is a recognised strategy of establishing credibility in qualitative research (Creswell, 2009; Lincoln and Guba, 1985; Merriam, 1995; Shenton, 2004). It involves obtaining an external perspective to enhance the accuracy of the account (Creswell, 2009). For undergraduate/postgraduate students this can be achieved by having debriefing sessions regularly with their supervisors to obtain their expert perspective. Discussions could be focused around the methodological choices adopted, which is key to ensuring credibility. For doctoral students, they could attend research conferences involving senior researchers and colleagues where general feedback about their research can be obtained. Fresh perspectives obtained from such individuals can be valuable in shaping the research design and objectives.

A study's credibility may also be affected by bias from the respondents, especially when they elicit responses that they think sound favourable to the researcher, or intentionally withhold sensitive information (Krefting, 1991). This is particularly common when using interviews as the mode of qualitative data collection. One way to address the issue of bias during interviews is through prolonged engagement with each interviewee. Probing methods and iterative questioning during the interview can be used to elicit detailed data, and questions re-phrased to elicit frank responses from participants.

11.5 Dependability

Dependability is similar to reliability in quantitative research (see section 11.2). It refers to the assurance that the research process is logical, traceable and documented (Wigren, 2007). It is the extent to which the research could be replicated in a comparable setting. It is as an auditing approach or trail in which the research process is detailed and explicit.

To ensure dependability, it is expected that a complete record of all phases of the research process is kept. For example, data such as the interview transcripts, fieldwork notes, personal journal, notes, as well as process notes concerning the methodological stance used in the research should be kept. Not only should they be kept but they should be explained, and the gathering of data made transparent. There should be a description of the social context, for example, background information about the overall structures, settings and frameworks within which participants were situated (Horsburgh, 2003). This is important so that sufficient information is made available for another researcher to follow the same procedural steps, albeit possibly reaching different conclusions (Stenfors et al., 2020).

Most importantly, the process of data collection and data analysis should be described elaborately for another researcher to follow the same steps. This includes a description of its analytic strategy and an analytic framework. Peers would act as auditors during the research to ensure that all procedures have been followed. For many studies, it provides a rationale for coding decisions and a coding scheme with clearly defined steps. An example of a study considering the dependability of its findings is presented in Case 11.1

Case 11.1   Enhancing dependability in an entrepreneurial leadership research

Harrison et al. (2018) conducted a qualitative study about entrepreneurial leadership within a developing economy. Beyond looking at the credibility of the study, dependability was also sought especially at the analysis phase.

A code/re-code method was carried out on data during the analytical phase of the study. The coding and re-coding was carried out every two weeks during the descriptive coding phase to ensure that the results obtained were consistent. In this regard, member checking was valuable in bolstering dependability. The interview transcripts were given to the respondents to ensure that the recorded information was accurate.

Peers were used as auditors to ensure that all procedures stated for the research were followed. They checked and confirmed that the process had been logically followed. Despite the large volume of data, colleagues were patient in assessing the research procedure. The aim was not to ensure replicability (since variability is expected in qualitative research), but to provide a rich description of entrepreneurial leadership. The emphasis of this research was on the uniqueness of the human situation, so variation in terms of respondents' experiences was expected.

Finally, in ensuring dependability, we advise that you ask the following questions:

- Are the processes of data collection and analysis transparent?
- Has a detailed account of how the findings were produced been included?

11.6 Confirmability

According to Bryman and Bell (2011, p. 398), 'Confirmability is concerned with ensuring that, while recognising that complete objectivity is impossible in business research, the researcher can be shown to have acted in good faith; in other words, it should be apparent that he or she has not overtly allowed personal values or theoretical inclinations manifestly to sway the conduct of the research and findings deriving from it.' Steps should be taken to ensure that the findings of the research are grounded in the experiences and ideas of the participants, rather than in those of the researcher (Shenton, 2004). In the write-up of the findings, confirmability is enhanced by the inclusion of quotes or similar research data that depict the experiences of the participants.

The use of an audit trail is a key strategy in ensuring confirmability (Lincoln and Guba, 1985; Seale, 1999; Shenton, 2004). The descriptions of the method used for obtaining data and of the step-by-step decisions made during the research are instrumental in ensuring confirmability. Similar to enhancing dependability, there is a need for transparency in the data that was collected and in the criteria that were used in selecting the participants for the study. Results obtained from the study, and the recommendations drawn from both data and literature should be clearly stated (Shenton, 2004). Peers could serve as auditors scrutinising the research process from the beginning, and critically review records retained for the study (such as process and personal notes).

Miles and Huberman (1994) state that a basic issue for confirmability is the extent to which researchers acknowledge their own bias. In every qualitative study, it is important that the method of choice, the rationale behind the use of a qualitative approach rather than other approaches and the limitation of the chosen design is acknowledged. This is essential in enhancing the confirmability of the research. Reflexivity is another key strategy for bolstering confirmability. The researcher must acknowledge their role in influencing data during the research. Reflexivity is discussed in detail in section 11.8.

11.7 Transferability

Transferability emphasises the extent to which the studied situation matches other situations in which one is interested (Schofield, 2002). Here, you are interested in how clear the basis is for drawing wider inference (Lewis et al., 2003) from your study. Can the findings of your study be transferred to another group, context or setting? Lincoln and Guba (1985) refer to this as 'fittingness.'

The focus of qualitative research is not to generalise its findings which is the norm of quantitative studies but to provide rich insights within a particular context or setting. Qualitative researchers refrain from asserting the generalisability of their findings to a broader population (Fossey et al., 1998). Instead, their primary focus lies in the applicability of their findings within a comparable context. Nonetheless, the transferability of these findings from one setting to another hinges on the resemblance of the contextual factors. As a result, it is important that all background information about the study, respondents, research context and specific setting are provided. By providing the relevant information the onus rests on the individual who wants to transfer the findings to another study. The only responsibility of the researcher of the study is to provide sufficient descriptive data that would be of value when making judgements about such transferability (Bryman and Bell, 2011). This is not to say that the researcher should not think about the wider implications of their findings but modifies the expectation from being the intent of the study.

To enable future investigators to adequately assess the transferability of findings from a study, the following information should be provided:

- the type of respondents and how they were selected
- the number of participants involved in the fieldwork
- the data collection method used
- the time allotted for the data collection
- the period during which the data was collected.

11.8 Reflexivity

Reflexivity is about recognising your role in the study. As a qualitative researcher, you are part of the study and your prior experiences and beliefs may affect the research process. The subjective nature of qualitative research makes it inevitable that one's identity, context and status could affect the research process and outcome. Reflexivity refers to the assessment of the influence of the researcher's background, experience, perception and intentions upon a study (Krefting, 1991). It refers to the acknowledgement by researchers that it is impossible for their actions not to affect the outcome of the research (Horsburgh, 2003). That means neutrality is impossible.

Roulston (2010) defined reflexivity in research as the researcher's 'ability to be able to self-consciously refer him or herself in relation to the production of knowledge about research topics' (p. 116). It is the active recognition by the researcher that their actions and decisions will inevitably impact upon the context of the process being investigated. We define reflexivity as the process of continuously examining your own experiences, judgements, beliefs and practices to ensure the trustworthiness of the research. During reflexivity, your own assumptions must be questioned as you play an integral role in the research process. There is a shift from the respondents to the researcher and a general acceptance that the researcher can actively influence the outcome of the process. For example, a researcher who is a pharmacist could be conducting a study which involves fellow pharmacists about the challenges they faced during the Covid-19 pandemic. It is almost inevitable that the researcher who is a pharmacist has an existing belief system, opinion and bias which if not acknowledged could potentially impact the outcome of study especially if the researcher was working during the pandemic as a pharmacist. Therefore, reflexivity is paramount in qualitative research.

One of the core arguments for reflexivity in qualitative research is that although the outcome is dependent on the information provided by the respondents, the process is led by the researcher. The researcher is involved in the data collection, analysis and reporting which are core to the eventual outcome of the study. As a result, it is important that the researcher's potential bias is acknowledged and does not influence the outcome of the study. The experience, values, status and opinion a researcher brings to the research should not always be viewed negatively and most times could be positive. It could be a guide and an opportunity to derive more knowledge. For example, with the previous instance about the pharmacist conducting a study. The researcher as a pharmacist conducting interviews with other pharmacists has a better understanding of the terrain and this would be valuable in eliciting more information that should shape the study. It could also have a lasting impact on the researcher and not the study. For example, during the pandemic, many pharmacists had emotional experiences because of the high mortality rate. The traumatic narratives provided during the interviews may have a long-lasting effect and impact on the researcher after the study has been concluded (see retrospective reflexivity)

Reflexivity has been categorised in several ways. Some scholars have classified it into prospective and retrospective reflexivity, where prospective reflexivity refers to the effects of the researcher on the study and retrospective refers to the effect of the study on the researcher (Attia and Edge, 2017). Some have categorised it into personal reflexivity, functional reflexivity and reflexive thematic analysis. Personal reflexivity is the process of reflecting on your own values, life experiences and beliefs to iden-tify your impact on the study which is similar to prospective reflexivity. Functional reflexivity goes beyond values, experiences and beliefs but focuses on the process of conducting research. It reflects on how key decisions are made while conducting the study and the rationale for making them. Finally, reflexive thematic analysis employs the researcher's personal experience and values to make sense of data during the analysis.

Since reflexivity is important in ensuring the trustworthiness of your study, one way to do is by keeping a reflexive journal.

Reflexive journal

It is good practice to keep a reflexive or field journal while conducting qualitative research. This journal can be used to interpret and describe your behaviour within the research context. We propose that the reflexive journal should contain the following information.

- your background, previous and current experience
- your relationship with the participants of the study (i.e., How do I know these participants?)

- your perceptions and opinions (What are my perceptions and opinions and how can I affect the outcome of the study?)
- your daily schedule and rationale behind the decisions made during the research such as data collection and analysis
- personal thoughts and ideas about the research process.

The information and questions should be answered regularly throughout the process. However, although we propose the use of a reflexive journal there are other ways reflexivity can be conducted. Reflexivity can be done through open dialogue with other colleagues, internal reflection and other creative approaches. Regardless of the method employed, it is important that the researcher acknowledges the role of their personal experience, status, rank, beliefs and values in shaping the research process.

11.9 Authenticity

Authenticity is defined as the extent to which researchers capture the multiple perspectives and values of participants in their study. It refers to fairness in the presentation of the views of the participants involved in the research. Their voices and views must be recognisable within the data.

Bryman and Bell (2011) proposed five types of authenticity namely,

- Ontological authenticity: This form of authenticity stresses that research should help participants arrive at a better understanding of their social context.
- Educative authenticity: Within educative authenticity, the research should help participants to appreciate better the perspective of other members of their social context.
- Catalytic authenticity: Catalytic authenticity stresses that the research should act as an impetus for members to engage in action to change their situation.
- Tactical authenticity: The research should empower members to take steps necessary for action.
- Fairness: Research should provide a fair representation of the different viewpoints of members of the social context.

Generally, authenticity as a criterion for evaluating qualitative research focuses on ensuring that participants' viewpoints are fair and visible in the description and interpretation that the researcher provides. Fossey et al. (2002) state that a thick description should be provided which helps us to understand people's actions and experiences in the context that informs them. Since qualitative research provides a subjective experience of the world, the use of quotations of participants put together with the researcher's description and interpretation helps in fostering the authenticity of the findings.

One of the ways of ensuring authenticity is by providing evidence that participants were involved in the process and gave their feedback about its findings. This could be in the form of participant validation/respondent validation/member checking as discussed earlier (see section 11.4 on credibility). For example, after the interview transcript has been produced, the researcher could make it available to the respondents to ascertain whether it is the true reflection of their voice and whether the account provided is authentic. Reflexive reporting is another medium of fostering authenticity (see section 11.8 on reflexivity). It helps distinguish participant voices from that of the researcher and to ensure that the researcher's bias does not affect its authenticity.

11.10 Other quality criteria for qualitative research

Though we have discussed in detail six criteria that we believe are critical in evaluating qualitative studies, there have been several criteria and schemes provided by researchers. Lincoln and Guba (1985) who are key proponents of the alternative criteria for qualitative studies put forward two primary criteria namely, trustworthiness and authenticity. Trustworthiness refers to the rigour in a qualitative inquiry. They propose that to ensure rigour, four criteria have to be examined namely, credibility, transferability, dependability and confirmability which has already been discussed earlier in the chapter. Authenticity is also suggested to be important along with the four criteria for establishing trustworthiness.

Yardley (2000) proposed four criteria for evaluating the quality of qualitative research which include:

- Commitment and rigour: it involves engagement with the subject topic and having the appropriate skill set.
- Transparency and coherence: the research design needs to be transparent and clearly presented. The argument has to be clearly articulated.
- Impact and importance: The qualitative study should be impactful and make a contribution to theory and practice.
- Sensitivity to context: sensitivity should go beyond the context in which the research was conducted but also to the theoretical positions and ethical issues.

An extensive list has also been provided by Fossey et al. (2002) by drawing on two philosophical paradigms namely interpretive and critical research that underpin qualitative research methodologies. They put forward that the criteria for evaluating the quality of qualitative research include methodological rigour and interpretive rigour. The criteria for methodological rigour include congruence, responsiveness to social context, appropriateness, adequacy and transparency. Interpretive rigour include authenticity, coherence, reciprocity, typicality and permeability of the researchers' intentions, engagement and interpretations. They, however, state that it should be borne in mind that not all criteria proposed are equally important or applicable in every qualitative setting given the differing philosophical stance.

Overall, the application of the traditional criteria of reliability, validity and generalisability is inappropriate for qualitative research as the focus and philosophical positioning are different. Though several arguments still exist about the criteria for establishing the quality of qualitative research, there is a consensus that the discussion of such criteria enhances the rigour which is a norm for quantitative research. There remains not a one size fits all approach to evaluating qualitative research, but the criteria discussed serve as a good guide for fostering its quality.

Case Study   Evaluating the quality of qualitative research

Title: Investigating the impact of Nigerian SMEs in West African Markets: A qualitative inquiry.

This case study revolves around the evaluation of a qualitative research study that explores the impact of Nigerian Small and Medium-sized Enterprises (SMEs) operating in West African markets. The researcher aims to assess the quality of the thesis by adopting a set of criteriology, including credibility, dependability, confirmability and transferability. The study addresses the concerns raised about the value of qualitative research and emphasises the importance of establishing quality. The researcher, following the advice of experts like Yin (2018) and Lincoln and Guba (1985), embarks on an in-depth investigation of Nigerian SMEs operating in West African markets. The study utilises a qualitative approach, employing multiple data collection methods, such as semi-structured interviews, documentation review and direct observation. The researcher aims to present a credible and insightful exploration of the experiences of the participants while ensuring the reliability and validity of the findings.

Evaluation of the quality

Credibility and dependability

Divide the class into small groups and provide each group with a qualitative research study or case study. Instruct each group to assess the credibility and dependability constructs of the study based on the methods used, the data collection process, and the credibility of the findings. The groups should discuss the strengths and weaknesses of the study and provide suggestions for improvements.

(Continued)

Confirmability and transferability

The researcher acknowledges certain limitations in generalising findings beyond the context of Nigerian SMEs in West African markets. The study's major contribution lies in investigating this specific context, and the researcher cautions against making broad generalisations to other developing countries. As a class, discuss the challenges of confirmability and transferability in qualitative research. Have students brainstorm strategies to enhance the transferability of findings while recognising the unique contextual factors that may influence the study's applicability to other settings. Also, the researcher establishes credibility through in-depth engagement with participants, direct observation and peer debriefing with the supervisory team. To ensure dependability, conduct an inter-rater review of the transcribed data, validating the identified themes. Confirmability is achieved through reflexive journalling, **bracketing** biases, and involving key participants in data presentation and discussion.

Class Exercise

In groups, students should discuss the importance of credibility, dependability and confirmability in qualitative research. Have them come up with real-world examples of how researchers can ensure these criteria are met and share their findings with the class.

Takeaways

Through the case study, students can learn about the critical aspects of evaluating qualitative research and the importance of establishing trustworthiness.

Source: Omeihe, K.O. (2023). *Trust and Market Institutions in Africa: Exploring the Role of Trust-Building in African Entrepreneurship*. (Palgrave Studies of Entrepreneurship in Africa). Cham, Switzerland: Palgrave Macmillan.

11.11 Summary

- Research methods should not only be viewed in terms of the aims and contexts of the research; priority should also be given to the quality of the study (Bush, 2002). Research, whether qualitative or quantitative, requires rigour to ensure that findings are trusted and believed.
- The traditional criteria used for evaluating research are reliability, validity and generalisability.
- Reliability refers to the reproducibility and repeatability of the results. It means how consistently a method measures something and the result can be reproduced when the study is conducted under similar conditions.

- Validity refers to the accuracy of a result. It is the extent to which the results are an accurate representation of the phenomenon.
- Generalisability is also referred to as external validity. It is the degree to which the results of a study can be applied beyond the research context.
- The major criticism that has been levelled against the qualitative approach is the lack of scientific rigour and credibility compared to the traditional quantitative methods which are widely viewed as objective, impartial and value neutral.
- There are alternative criteria that are widely used to appraise the trustworthiness of qualitative research namely, credibility, dependability, confirmability, transferability, reflexivity and authenticity.
- Credibility involves demonstrating that a true picture of the phenomenon under investigation is represented.
- Dependability is similar to reliability in quantitative research. It refers to the assurance that the research process is logical, traceable and documented.
- Confirmability is concerned with ensuring that, while recognising that complete objectivity is impossible in business and management research, the researcher can be shown to have acted in good faith; in other words, it should be apparent that he or she has not overtly allowed personal values or theoretical inclinations to sway the conduct of the research.
- Transferability emphasises the extent to which the studied situation matches other situations in which one is interested.
- Reflexivity refers to the assessment of the influence of the researcher's background, experience, perception and intentions upon a study. It refers to the acknowledgement by researchers that it is impossible for their actions not to affect the outcome of the research.
- Authenticity is defined as the extent to which researchers capture the multiple perspectives and values of participants in their study. It refers to fairness in the presentation of the views across the participants involved in the research. Their voices and views have to be recognisable within the data.

Self-check questions

1. What does triangulation mean?
2. What is member checking?
3. What is peer debriefing?
4. What are the types of validity?
5. What are the questions you need to consider when establishing credibility?

(Continued)

6.   What are the questions you need to consider when establishing dependability?

7.   What information should be provided in a reflexive journal?

8.   What are the five criteria for authenticity proposed by Bryman and Bell?

Questions for review and discussion

1.   Discuss the strategies you would adopt to ensure that your qualitative research is credible.

2.   Create a reflexive journal and reflect on the information that you should provide to ensure reflexivity.

3.   Think about a research topic that you would like to undertake and how you would evaluate the quality based on six criteria namely; credibility, dependability, confirmability, transferability, reflexivity and authenticity.

Self-check answers

1.   Triangulation involves the use of multiple investigators, multiple data sources or multiple methods to confirm emerging findings (Merriam, 1995). As Shenton (2004, p. 66) states, in triangulation, 'individual viewpoints and experiences can be verified against others and ultimately a rich picture of the attitudes, needs or behaviour of those under scrutiny may be constructed based on the contribution of a range of people.' Contrary evidence, often known as deviant cases, must be taken into consideration in the analysis to ensure that researcher bias does not affect or alter their perception of the data and any insights offered (Anderson, 2010).

2.   Member checking involves continually testing the researcher's data, interpretations and conclusions with the participants (Krefting, 1991). Some scholars refer to it as respondent or participant validation (Bryman and Bell, 2011; Horsburgh, 2003).

3.   Peer debriefing involves obtaining an external perspective to enhance the accuracy of the account (Creswell, 2009). For undergraduate/postgraduate students this can be achieved by having debriefing sessions regularly with their supervisors to obtain their expert perspective. Discussions could be focused on the methodological choices adopted which is key to ensuring credibility. For doctoral students, they could attend research conferences involving senior researchers and colleagues where general

feedback about their research can be obtained. Fresh perspectives obtained from such individuals can be valuable in shaping the research design and objectives.

4. There are three types of validity namely, construct validity, content validity and criterion validity. Construct validity is usually concerned about how the measure adheres to the existing theory and knowledge of the concept. It has to do with whether the measure that is obtained reflects the concept that it should be representing. Content validity is the extent to which the measurement covers all the content that it should with respect to the concept. Criterion validity is the extent to which the result of a measure is related to other results that measure the same variable. Correlations can be conducted to determine the extent to which different instruments measure the same variable.

5. In ensuring credibility, we advise that you ask the following questions:

    o   How plausible are your findings?
    o   What is the evidence to back up your findings?
    o   Does the study truly reflect the context it intends to investigate?

6. In ensuring dependability, we advise that you ask the following questions:

    o   Are the process of data collection and analysis transparent?
    o   Has a detailed account of how the findings were produced been included?

7. The reflexive journal should contain the following information.

    o   Your background, previous and current experience
    o   Your relationship with the participants of the study (i.e. How do I know these participants?)
    o   Your perceptions and opinions (What are my perceptions and opinions and how can I affect the outcome of the study?)
    o   Your daily schedule and rationale behind the decisions made during the research such as data collection and analysis
    o   Personal thoughts and ideas about the research process

8. Bryman and Bell (2011) proposed five types of authenticity namely,

    o   Ontological authenticity: This form of authenticity stresses that research should help participants arrive at a better understanding of their social context.
    o   Educative authenticity: Within educative authenticity, the research should help participants to appreciate better the perspective of other members of their social context.
    o   Catalytic authenticity: Catalytic authenticity stresses that the research should act as an impetus for members to engage in action to change their situation.

(Continued)

o   Tactical authenticity: The research should empower members to take steps necessary for action.

o   Fairness: Research should provide a fair representation of the different viewpoints of members of the social context.

Further reading

Fossey, E., Harvey, C., Mcdermott, F. and Davidson, L. (2002) Understanding and evaluating qualitative research. *Australian and New Zealand Journal of Psychiatry*, Vol. 36, pp. 717–32.

Krefting, L. (1991) Rigor in qualitative research: The assessment of trustworthiness. *The American Journal of Occupational Therapy*. Vol. 45, pp. 214–22.

Lincoln, Y. S. and Guba, E. (1985) *Naturalistic enquiry.* Beverly Hills, CA: Sage.

Shenton, A.K. (2004) Strategies for ensuring trustworthiness in qualitative research projects. *Education for Information*, Vol. 22, pp. 63–75.

12

Writing Good Qualitative Research Proposals and the Dissertation Process

---

Learning outcomes

By the end of this chapter, you should be able to:

- write up your research for a dissertation project
- identify what you require for a quality research proposal
- adopt an effective writing style for your project report
- conceptualise the process of undertaking a dissertation
- elucidate the process of academic referencing and citing properly.

12.1 Introduction

The previous chapters provided a detailed description of qualitative research examining its philosophical positions, design, modes of data collection, sampling, ethical considerations, evaluation and so on but it is necessary that we explore the process of writing. How can a research project be written effectively? What are the strategies that you can adopt in writing a research proposal? The writing-up phase could be problematic and many students struggle with this part of the project. In this chapter, we examine the strategies that are employed in writing up a research project.

A research proposal is a brief and clear summary of your proposed research. It sets out the central issues or questions that you intend to address. However, based on our experience over the years, students find it difficult to provide a quality research proposal. This is important to show the current state of knowledge and the significance of your research project. Within this chapter, in addition to providing you with practical advice for drafting a research proposal, we provide exemplars that can be adopted in designing quality research proposals.

Writing a dissertation is a skill and an effective writing style has to be adopted. Such a writing style needs to be convincing and clear. Within this chapter, we will examine the characteristics of a good qualitative dissertation and its structure and spotlight the writing approach that can convince and persuade your readers.

Finally, academic references are vital in every research project. It is important that you acknowledge the sources where the information has been derived. It helps to make it clear to your reader how you have used the work of others to shape your study. Failure to reference and cite other people's work may lead to issues of plagiarism. This chapter examines the different types of academic referencing and how you cite effectively within your dissertation.

12.2 Writing your dissertation

Many students believe that writing is the last part of the process. Although it is the last chapter of the book, it should not be the last task that you embark on. It is easy to neglect the writing phase of your book to concentrate on the research but the essence of the study in the first place is to convey your findings to an audience, hence it is important that it is written. We encourage you to see writing as a continual process during the study.

Right from the literature review, it is helpful that you start writing as it informs your thinking about how the literature will be sourced. This is also applicable to all the sections within your dissertation. As a result, we advise that you adopt the following strategies.

Start early and create time for writing

We advise that you start early. You should not consider writing up your dissertation as something you do when you have collected and analysed your data. It is not something that you allocate little time for. Many students make the mistake of underestimating the time required to write up the research. They spend so much time on the fieldwork and run out of time to write up the dissertation, especially with the tight deadline for submission. No matter how groundbreaking your research is, if it is not written properly then your reader would not be able to appreciate and comprehend it. Some people tend to allocate some hours every day to write, while some give themselves word count targets for each day. There is no one-size-fits-all approach. The approach you adopt should suit your situation and be realistic for you.

Find the pattern and place that suits you

Saunders et al. (2023) proposed that you should write when your mind is fresh. We agree that you write at the time of the day when you have the highest productivity since writing is a creative process. Mental alertness is important and you should know when you are able to work better. Some students write better at the early hours of the day, so they wake up early and plan their tasks to accommodate them. While others write better at night. The onus is on you to find the pattern that suits you. Writing has to be done in a comfortable environment. Many of us have comfortable places where we write. Some people are more comfortable writing in their offices, some in their homes, libraries and others even go for writing retreats to write. Regardless of the location, you need to ensure that the environment is comfortable with the least distraction.

Creating a writing plan with clear milestones

As we highlighted earlier, it is important to have clear milestones to be achieved during the writing process. Sometimes writing could be an arduous task, hence clear milestones and targets are required so that you can celebrate short term wins. Having targets such as the set number of words or even the number of hours allocated each day will make you more disciplined and more likely to get the writing finished on time.

In addition to having clear milestones, you also need to have a writing plan. Mind mapping is very important and you can put the ideas you need and would guide your writing in form of maps. More information about mind mapping is provided in Section 12.5.

Persuade your reader

Bryman and Bell (2011) stress that writing up your research is not simply reporting but providing a persuasive account of your study. You have to persuade your reader that your research outcome is plausible and significant. For a dissertation, the novelty of your work is paramount, so you would need to let the reader know what makes your work original, how you went about conducting the fieldwork and how you obtained your findings.

Feedback

We can get so engrossed in the writing process and believe that our work is perfect. This applies to almost everyone, hence it is important that we get feedback from others about our work. The feedback can come from your peers in the form of a critical friend. The critical friend must understand your work and be ready to provide constructive feedback about the writing task. Supervisors are another means of obtaining feedback. Your institution would likely have allocated you a dissertation supervisor. The role of your dissertation supervisor is to guide you through the process and also provide feedback on your research. However, it is important that you provide sufficient time for him or her to read your work so that feedback can be obtained on time.

12.3 Developing an effective writing style

The comprehension of the dissertation is based on the effectiveness of your writing style. Your writing style is important in ensuring that your reader understands the arduous task that you have undergone during your research. Poor writing does not do justice to any research work, hence we propose that you consider the following strategies in developing an effective writing style.

Make it clear and simple

Saunders et al. (2023) advise that clarity and simplicity are core to developing an effective writing style. You do not need to write long sentences to convey your point of view. Try and make your sentences express an idea and not be too lengthy. Many students feel the need to impress by overuse of jargon within the report. We believe that clarity is important and if your write-up is filled with jargon it will affect the reader's comprehension of your work.

Check your grammar, spelling and tenses

Grammar errors affect the credibility of our writing (Saunders et al., 2012). It is important that you go through your work to ensure that it is free from grammar errors. That is why you must start writing early to ensure that sufficient time is available to go through your work. Spelling errors are also common in writing up research projects and this could distract the reader from the project. For example, manger instead of manager. Such errors can be eliminated by proof reading and the assistance of a critical friend. In addition, word processing software packages such as Microsoft Word and Google Doc help in checking errors so could be a useful tool in addressing them.

Finally, you must ensure that the tense you adopt is consistent and suitable. In dissertations, the traditional convention adopted is the use of a third person and passive voice. However, sometimes this is not always the case in all sections, especially when you are providing a reflexive account. It is also important to ensure that the account provided is free of sexist, racist and discriminatory language.

12.4 Structuring your project report

The word count of a dissertation may vary depending on your level. For many undergraduate and postgraduate students, the word count is usually about 10,000 to 15,000 words. For doctoral students, it could be as high as 60,000 to 80,000 words. Regardless of the word count, every dissertation must have a clear structure. It should be divided into a series of chapters. We propose this structure as a guide for your dissertation.

Title page

Every dissertation needs a title page. The title page should provide the name of the researcher, their affiliation and the title of the project. The content of the title page may vary across institutions, so we advise that you know what is required by your institution in drafting your title page.

Dedication

Many students dedicate their work to someone. It could be a parent, spouse, relative, friend and so on.

Acknowledgement

This is used to acknowledge people who have been involved and valuable in your research project. It could be your supervisors, friends and even participants of the study. It shows your appreciation for their commitment and support.

Table of Contents

It is important to have a table of contents which shows the constituent chapters and content of the dissertation. Many word processing packages can be used to automatically generate a table of content.

List of tables and figures

We propose that a list of tables and figures is provided. This would help the reader to comprehend your table and figures especially if there are many in your dissertation.

Abstract

This is a snapshot of your dissertation. It is a very important part of your work as it provides a summary of the entire dissertation. For many examiners, this is the first part that they would read before assessing your dissertation. For your readers, it provides a clear account of what is to come within your dissertation. Depending on the institution guidelines, the abstract could be structured with sections or unstructured. Regardless of the format, we stress that every abstract should provide the purpose of the study, its design, methodology and approach, findings, limitation, implications and novelty of the work.

Writing a good abstract is not easy but its efficacy is its ability to provide the key points of the study with brevity. The word count may vary based on institution or journal requirements. However, the common word count for many universities is usually about 250 to 300 words. Though the abstract comes at the start of the dissertation, we advise that you write it after you have finished the study. This is because you can provide a better synopsis of your work after it has been conducted. Box 12.1. provides an example of a structured abstract.

Box 12.1   A structured abstract on entrepreneurial leadership research in a developing economy

Abstract

Purpose – The purpose of this paper is to examine entrepreneurial leadership and to determine the entrepreneurial leadership skills which are important for success in a developing economy environment. Specifically, the focus of this research was on entrepreneurial leadership within the retail pharmacy sector in Nigeria.

Design/methodology/approach – This study was guided by an interpretivist-constructionist perspective. By adopting a qualitative approach, the lived experiences of the retail pharmacy entrepreneurs could be understood. In total, 51 semi-structured interviews were the mode of data collection, and data were triangulated via three sources: entrepreneurs, employees, and literature.

Findings – From the study results, a vivid picture of entrepreneurial leadership was formed, which in turn provides the basis for an empirical skill-based model of this phenomenon in a developing economy. This study identifies four distinct entrepreneurial leadership skill categories. These include technical/business skills, interpersonal skills, conceptual skills and entrepreneurial skills. The findings of this study also show the factors and conditions necessary for entrepreneurial leadership in a developing economy.

Originality/value – The findings of this study have implications in theory and practice. Its results provide an empirical, skill-based framework on entrepreneurial leadership in a developing economy, a subject area for which there exists a lack of background literature. In practice, the findings of this study serve as a useful reference for practitioners and policy makers of the skills and other factors required for people to succeed as entrepreneurial leaders.

Source: Harrison, C., Burnard, K and Paul, S. (2018). Entrepreneurial leadership in a developing economy: a skill-based analysis. *Journal of Small Business and Enterprise Development,* 25(3), 521–48 https://doi.org/10.1108/JSBED-05-2017-0160

Introduction

The introduction should give the reader a clear idea of what the research is about. It should provide a general background of the study. It is also ideal that statements of your research aim, objectives and questions are provided in this section.

Some students may choose to explain the context of the sector, organisation, country or setting you are investigating within this chapter or you could have a separate chapter for the context. For a doctoral thesis, the introduction could also highlight the originality and contribution to knowledge. The structure of the dissertation and overview of the chapters should be provided. The introduction should not be too lengthy but a valuable starting point for every dissertation.

Literature review

This is a valuable chapter in your dissertation. This is where you draw on prior studies that have examined your area of interest. It should have the relevant theoretical foundation that shapes your reasoning (see Chapter 3 on the process of conducting a literature review). It is expected that your research questions and objectives will be informed by your literature review depending on the nature of your study. You may also have more than one literature review chapter depending on the extent of the literature that you want to review and how important it is to your work. For example, a researcher examining entrepreneurial leadership may decide to have a chapter on entrepreneurship and another on leadership to have a better understanding of the paradigm since it emerged from both fields.

Methodology

Similar to the literature review, this is a core part of every dissertation. It should cover all the methodological choices made in the study. This includes the research approach, paradigm, philosophical stance, method, design, data collection process, sampling, data analysis, evaluation of the research and ethical considerations. It is important that when discussing your methodological choices you justify why they have been made. This is important to ensure the credibility of your findings.

Results

In qualitative research, we prefer to call it findings. In this chapter, you will present the findings of your research. You would report the facts that you have discovered in your study. This is where you would use the quotes from the interviews, narrative accounts of your observation and so on depending on the mode of data collection employed. The voice of your respondents has to be reflected in your results.

It is important that your findings are not based on your opinion but should reflect the voice of the participants. It is also crucial that your findings are presented clearly. There are several ways to do this. One common way is to structure your findings in line with the research objectives. Another way is to report your findings based on themes. The method of analysis you adopt most of the time could shape how you present this chapter.

Finally, the results chapter may be more than one, so you need to ask yourself if you need more than one chapter for your dissertation. This is usually common in mixed methods research where quantitative and qualitative techniques are adopted and the researcher presents their findings separately for more clarity.

Discussion

The discussion chapter is another core chapter of your dissertation. Within this chapter, it is expected that you reflect on how your findings relate to literature and prior scholarly work in the area. Do your findings support the work of others or do they provide contrary views? The discussion chapter provides the opportunity to justify the novelty and contribution of your work. In this chapter, you can discuss the empirical construct that may have emerged from your study. We advise that the discussion chapter is distinct from the results chapter. However, in some institutions and subject areas, both are merged. You need to consider the expectations of your organisation and subject topic while writing this chapter.

Conclusion

The conclusion is a very important part of the dissertation. Many students do not pay attention to this section, and this should not be the case. The conclusion is meant to bring the dissertation to a logical close and tie all the elements and constituent chapters together. But it should do more than just summarise the study, your conclusion should provide the implications of the research and its contribution to theory and practice. It should reflect on the limitations of your study and provide recommendations for future research.

References

It is expected that every dissertation should have a reference list. There are different types of referencing systems e.g. Harvard, American Psychological Association (APA) etc. We suggest that you consult your subject librarian and institution to ascertain the ideal type of referencing to be adopted for your dissertation. Waiting till the end to start compiling your references could be tedious, we advise that you add it as you go along. The use of reference management software such as EndNote, Mendeley and Zotero could be a useful resource in managing this process.

Appendices

Appendices are useful in the dissertation. It shows the reader that the research process has been conducted rigorously. You may consider putting your interview guide, observation schedule, participant information sheet, consent form, coding form and so on in this section.

12.5 Writing a qualitative research proposal

Writing a qualitative research proposal is a crucial step in the research journey as it acts as a roadmap for conducting a study. In this section, we will discuss the meaning and significance of a research proposal, emphasise its importance and rationale, and offer valuable guidelines and tips to students and researchers embarking on this academic endeavour. While it is widely acknowledged that the assumptions underlying a research proposal closely align with the final dissertation process, as the proposal precedes the actual dissertation, it is vital for individuals to be well-prepared by understanding the fundamentals and rationale of the proposal. Recognising the need to explore further into this aspect, we firmly believe in the necessity of providing insightful information. The first approach for us is to define the research proposal.

A research proposal can be defined as a comprehensive document that outlines the plan and framework for a research study. It serves as a detailed blueprint or roadmap for conducting research, providing a clear description of the research objectives, methodology, timeline, and resources required. The fact is that it typically includes an introduction to the research problem or topic, a review of relevant literature, a statement of research objectives or questions, a description of the research methodology, an outline of the anticipated outcomes or contributions, and a discussion of the feasibility and significance of the proposed study.

One common mistake students often make is failing to grasp the importance of clearly outlining the key elements and methodologies of a study in a research proposal. In our classes and conversations, we emphasise that a research proposal serves as a detailed plan for investigating a research question or problem, guiding researchers through the entire process of data collection, analysis and interpretation. Researchers can establish credibility and ensure the validity of their study through a well-structured proposal.

In essence, a research proposal functions as a persuasive document, aiming to convince the intended readership (such as examiners, funding agencies, academic supervisors, or research committees) of the value, feasibility and ethical considerations of the proposed research. Therefore, a well-written research proposal is crucial for securing support, funding and approval to proceed with the research project.

12.6 Guidelines and tips for writing a research proposal

Clearly Define Research Questions and Objectives: The foundation of any study lies in a well-defined research question. It serves as a guiding force throughout the research process. A good approach, in this case, is to take the time to clearly articulate your objectives and research questions, ensuring they meet the criteria of being specific, measurable, achievable, relevant and time-bound (SMART). This level of clarity not only helps one to stay focused but also influences subsequent methodological decisions. By having a precise research question, you can navigate through the research requirements with purpose and direction.

Review Relevant Literature: Given the considerations, the logical next step is to thoroughly examine the existing body of literature. This step is essential for gaining a comprehensive understanding of the subject matter. A valuable approach is to conduct a meticulous review of relevant theories, concepts and studies pertaining to your research topic. It is important to recognise that the literature review serves multiple purposes. First, it showcases your familiarity with the subject matter and demonstrates your ability to position your study within the broader academic discourse. Second, it allows you to identify gaps in knowledge that your research aims to address. By acquiring knowledge from these insights, you can make a valuable contribution to the existing knowledge base while establishing a strong foundation for your own study.

Describe the Methodological Approach: Of course, it is important to provide a detailed account of the qualitative research methods and strategies you intend to employ. One good way to navigate this is to explain how these methods align with your research questions and justify their appropriateness for your study. In this vein, it is important to discuss various aspects such as sampling techniques, data collection methods (e.g., interviews, observations), and data analysis procedures (e.g., thematic analysis, grounded theory). This should embrace a thoughtful consideration of the tools and techniques necessary to gather and interpret data effectively. Overall, this should ultimately enhance the credibility and validity of your research.

Address Ethical Considerations: Ethical considerations play a paramount role in any research involving human participants, yet they are often taken for granted. It is of utmost importance to thoroughly discuss the potential ethical issues associated with your study and outline the measures you will implement to safeguard the rights and confidentiality of participants. This step involves providing a clear and detailed plan for obtaining informed consent, ensuring voluntary participation, and maintaining anonymity and confidentiality of data. It is essential that every well-crafted research proposal demonstrates a strong commitment to upholding ethical standards and prioritising the welfare of the participants involved in the research. Simply put, every good proposal must demonstrate the commitment to upholding ethical standards and protecting the welfare of participants involved in the research.

Consider Feasibility and Resources: An essential aspect of a strong research proposal is a thorough evaluation of its feasibility. This evaluation entails considering several factors, including time constraints, access to participants, funding requirements and logistical considerations. A well-crafted research proposal should provide a justification for why the proposed research is feasible and realistic within the given constraints. Moreover, it is important to acknowledge any limitations and challenges that may arise and propose effective strategies to mitigate them. This provides the chance to successfully carry out your research project with the available resources.

Develop a Realistic Timeline: Setting realistic deadlines is crucial, considering the complexity and time requirements of each task. To ensure the smooth progress and timely completion of your research project, it is essential to create a comprehensive timeline that outlines different stages, including data collection, analysis and reporting. During the timeline construction, it is important to consider potential dependencies between tasks and allocate sufficient time for unforeseen circumstances. A well-developed timeline serves multiple purposes. First, it provides a clear structure and roadmap, aiding in organisational efforts. This allows for effective prioritisation of time and resources. Second, the timeline serves as a tool to track project progress. Regular reviews and updates enable monitoring of schedule adherence and facilitate necessary adjustments. Additionally, it is advisable to incorporate a buffer period to accommodate unexpected challenges or delays that may arise during the research process.

The research proposal

To effectively articulate the essential elements of a research proposal, it is important to acknowledge that the following points are not an exhaustive compilation. Rather, they serve as invaluable recommendations to facilitate the construction of a well-structured and comprehensive proposal. Recognising the research proposal as a fundamental framework for the primary dissertation or research endeavour, it becomes paramount to meticulously cultivate a captivating narrative that appeals to the project supervisor, examiner, grant agency and other pertinent stakeholders.

When embarking on the development of a research proposal, it is crucial to incorporate key features that encompass the expected components of a meticulously designed proposal. Although this list is not exhaustive, it presents valuable guidelines to establish a strong foundation for the proposal's structure similar to those outlined above. The research proposal functions as a blueprint for the main dissertation or research project, demanding meticulous attention to detail to ensure its efficacy for the intended audience. The ultimate objective is to construct a compelling narrative that resonates with the project supervisor, examiner, grant agency, and any other relevant stakeholders involved.

To describe the essential elements expected in a research proposal, it is important to include the following features:

- Introduction
- Background
- Research aim
- Research Objectives (and Questions)
- Literature review
- Proposed methodology
- Planned contribution.
- Research timeline
- References
- Appendices

Abstract

The abstract serves as a concise summary of the research proposal, encompassing the research problem, objectives, methodology and expected outcomes. It begins by emphasising the significance of the study and introducing the specific research problem and central research question. The purpose of the study and its theoretical foundations are outlined, along with key research questions. Furthermore, a brief overview of the research methodology, methods and data analysis procedures is provided. The abstract concludes by summarising the fundamental research findings. In essence, the abstract acts as a summary of the entire project or dissertation. It is placed at the beginning but completed at the end, as it can only be accurately summarised once the proposal itself has been finalised.

Introduction

The introductory section of the proposal serves to effectively introduce the research topic, establish its context, and emphasise the significance of the study. To achieve this, the introduction should begin by presenting the study, followed by providing clear definitions of key concepts, and subsequently providing a concise overview of the core topic. Additionally, it should outline the contents of the proposal. A useful approach is to describe the subject matter of the study, the rationale behind conducting the study (identifying any existing gaps), and the potential implications arising from the research. This introductory section should not exceed one page in length.

Background

This section provides a comprehensive review of existing knowledge and research related to the topic, laying the foundation for the proposed study. It summarises relevant literature, highlighting the current problem's significance and identifying the gap the study aims to address. Additionally, it emphasises the study's importance beyond filling a literature gap. To engage the reader, the introduction can begin with a compelling statement and be supported by pertinent statistics cited from reputable sources. The research problem should be clearly stated, building upon or challenging recent research within the past three to seven years. It is vital to address a significant gap in the current research literature, including both the general problem statement and the specific problem statement.

Research aim

The research aim should clearly articulate the overarching goal of the research, establishing a concise and specific statement that connects the problem being addressed with the focus of the study. It expresses the intention and desired outcome of the research project in a single sentence, enabling clear identification of its achievement. Keep to 20 words.

Literature review

In this section, a thorough and critical assessment of relevant scholarly literature should be conducted to identify gaps and ongoing debates in the field, which the proposed research aims to address. The review encompasses a comprehensive analysis of the current literature, encompassing studies that align with the study topic and chosen methodology. The various approaches adopted by researchers in the discipline to tackle the problem should be explored, with a careful examination of the strengths and weaknesses inherent in each approach.

Proposed methodology

This section details the research design, including data collection methods, sample selection and analytical techniques. It introduces and explains the concept of philosophy, and its types, and identifies the philosophy that aligns with the study, justifying its selection. The section also introduces the search approach, encompassing deductive, inductive and abductive reasoning. Tables or diagrams should be used to support and illustrate the discussions.

See Figure 12.1

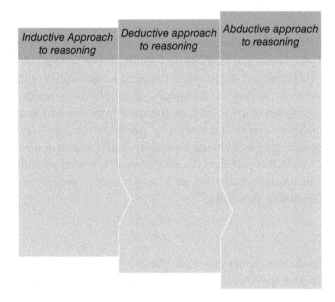

Figure 12.1

When discussing the research method, it is important to follow a similar approach. Begin by introducing the method, clearly identifying and justifying the choices made. Support these choices with relevant academic references to provide a strong foundation for the selected research method.

The same principle applies to the choice of sampling, and a detailed explanation of how data will be collected should be provided. This should be supported by citing relevant articles and sources that advocate for the chosen methodology. Additional relevant information can be found in the appendix.

The data analysis plan includes identifying the software to be used for analyses and explaining the relevant data analysis procedures for the study. The chosen method of analysis should be briefly stated and discussed. The plan should provide a detailed description of the analysis, including its various components and steps. Additionally, it is crucial to outline how the results will be interpreted within the study's context.

Example: Thematic analysis phases

Stage	Description	Key activities	Inputs	Outputs

When crafting a research proposal, it is crucial to address additional considerations. These include explaining the intended research validity, balancing relevance and rigour, and providing a brief overview of ethical procedures for participant access and data treatment. This entails addressing concerns regarding recruitment materials, data anonymity, confidentiality and protection measures. Additionally, it is recommended to emphasise the planned contributions or implications section, which underscores the study's significance, and impact on theory, practice and policy. Lastly, the conclusion should effectively convey a powerful takeaway message, summarising the core of the research for readers.

The structure and layout of the proposed study deserve careful attention. To enhance understanding, a diagram closely accompanies this section, illustrating the study's structure and flow.

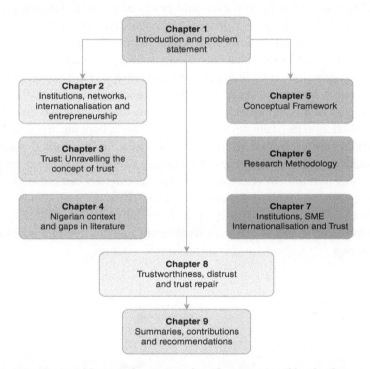

Figure 12.2   Structure and layout of a proposed study on trust and institutions

Source: Omeihe, K. (2019). *Trust, SME internationalisation and Networks: A study of three main Nigerian cultural blocs*. University of the West of Scotland.

12.6 Mind mapping

Mind mapping is a powerful technique that can greatly enhance the research process. It is a visual and creative tool used to organise and generate ideas, concepts and connections related to a research topic. It offers a holistic approach to brainstorming and outlining research projects. It involves the use of diagrams or charts through which one can capture and visualise complex relationships between various components of their study.

To illustrate this point, the first step is to ensure that the central idea or research question is placed at the centre of the mind map. This serves as the focal point. From there, a network of branches radiates outwards, representing different aspects or subtopics. These branches can be further expanded into sub-branches, creating a hierarchical structure that captures the depth and breadth of the research. As a matter of fact, the real power of mind mapping lies in its flexibility and non-linear nature. This is because it enables the rearrangement and reorganisation of elements within the map, facilitating the exploration of new ideas and potential research directions. It allows it to promote a free-flowing thought process and encourages creativity.

Of course, mind mapping allows researchers to visually identify relationships and connections between different elements. This visual representation helps in identifying knowledge gaps, potential linkages, and areas that require further investigation. And in this vein, it serves as a visual guide throughout the research process, aiding in the development of a comprehensive and well-structured study. We do like to point out that in addition to its brainstorming and organisation benefits, mind mapping also enhances information retention. In this case, the visual nature of mind maps engages both the analytical and creative sides of the brain, making information more memorable and easier to recall. To create a mind map, researchers can use dedicated mind mapping software or simply draw one on paper. There are various techniques and styles that can be employed, depending on personal preference and the complexity of the research project. Below are some illustrations that demonstrate how mind maps can be designed.

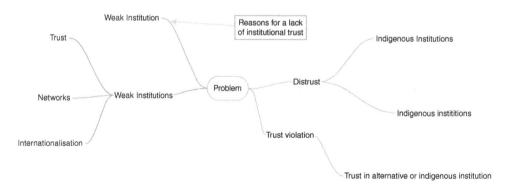

Figure 12.3   **Sample One**

12.7 Summary

In this chapter, we have accomplished the following key objectives:

- In examining the characteristics and structure of a good qualitative dissertation:
  - ○ We examined the essential qualities that define a strong qualitative dissertation.
  - ○ We explored the recommended structure and organisation for presenting research findings effectively.
  - ○ We highlighted the importance of engaging writing approaches that can convince and persuade readers, such as clear and concise language, logical flow, and compelling arguments.

- In examining strategies for writing a dissertation:
  - ○ We emphasised the significance of starting early and dedicating ample time for the writing process, allowing for thorough research and thoughtful analysis.
  - ○ We discussed the importance of finding the pattern and environment that best suits individual writing preferences, whether it's a quiet study space or a bustling coffee shop.
  - ○ We emphasised the value of creating a writing plan with clear milestones, enabling systematic progress and effective time management.
  - ○ We highlighted the need to seek and incorporate feedback from advisors and peers to enhance the quality of the dissertation.

- In developing an effective writing style and structuring project reports:
  - ○ We explored the importance of cultivating an effective writing style, which involves clarity, coherence and appropriate language choices to engage readers and convey research findings effectively.
  - ○ We underscored the significance of structuring project reports in a logical and organised manner to facilitate comprehension and ensure a seamless flow of information.

- In writing research proposals:
  - ○ We defined a research proposal as a comprehensive document outlining the plan and framework for a research study.
  - ○ We discussed the essential components of a well-crafted research proposal, including the research objectives, methodology, timeline and expected outcomes.
  - ○ We provided guidelines on how to write a compelling research proposal that demonstrates the significance, feasibility and originality of the proposed study.

- In utilising mind maps as a creative process:
  - ○ We explored the concept of mind maps as a creative tool for organising and visualising ideas and concepts related to research.
  - ○ We highlighted the benefits of mind mapping in promoting creativity, identifying relationships between different elements, and enhancing information retention.

- o We discussed how mind maps can serve as a visual guide throughout the research process, aiding in the development of a comprehensive and well-structured study.

12.8 Case study task: crafting a research proposal

Introduction

In this case study task, you will have the opportunity to apply your knowledge and skills in crafting a research proposal. The objective of this task is to provide a realistic scenario where you can demonstrate your understanding of the essential components and considerations involved in developing a research proposal. Through this exercise, you will strengthen your proposal writing abilities and enhance your ability to effectively communicate the significance and feasibility of your research project.

Case study scenario

You are a graduate student in the field of social sciences, specialising in education. You have a keen interest in exploring the impact of technology integration on student engagement and academic performance in elementary schools. As part of your academic programme, you are required to develop a research proposal for this study. The proposal will serve as a basis for seeking approval from your research committee and potential funding agencies.

Task description

Your task is to develop a research proposal for the study on the impact of technology integration on student engagement and academic performance in elementary schools. Your proposal should address the following key components:

- Abstract: Clearly provide a concise overview of the research study, highlighting its key components and significance.
- Research Introduction: Introduce the research topic, establish its context, and emphasise the significance of the study.
- Research Background: Provide a comprehensive review of existing knowledge and research related to the topic, laying the foundation for the proposed study.
- Research Aim and Objectives: Clearly define the research aim, objectives and research questions that will guide your study.
- Literature Review: Conduct a comprehensive literature review to establish the existing knowledge and research gaps related to technology integration, student engagement and academic performance in elementary schools.

- Methodology: Describe the research design, sampling strategy, data collection methods and data analysis techniques you will employ. Justify your choices based on the research objectives and the nature of your study.
- Ethical Considerations: Identify and address any ethical concerns that may arise during your research, such as obtaining informed consent from participants and ensuring data privacy and confidentiality.
- Timeline and Budget: Develop a realistic timeline outlining the various stages of your research project, including data collection, analysis and report writing. Additionally, estimate the budget required for conducting the study, considering factors such as research materials, participant incentives and data analysis software.
- Expected Outcomes and Significance: Clearly articulate the expected outcomes of your research and explain the potential significance of your findings in the context of educational practices and policies.

Task deliverables

Prepare a well-structured research proposal document that includes all the components mentioned above. Your proposal should be concise, persuasive and written in a clear and coherent manner. Ensure that your proposal demonstrates a strong theoretical foundation, a sound research methodology, and a compelling rationale for conducting the study.

Takeaway

This exercise will allow you to apply your knowledge, critical thinking skills and creativity to formulate a well-rounded and convincing proposal. Remember to pay attention to the details, adhere to ethical guidelines, and consider the practical aspects of conducting research.

Good luck!

Self-check questions

1. What is a research proposal?
2. List the strategies you should consider while writing a dissertation.
3. What are the key considerations in developing an effective writing style?
4. How do you structure your project report or dissertation?
5. What is the importance of having a reference list in your research project?
6. Feedback is important while writing your research proposal and dissertation. Who should you seek feedback from?
7. Why do you need a literature review section in your dissertation and proposal?
8. What is an abstract?

(Continued)

Questions for review and discussion

1. Discuss the strategies you would adopt in writing a qualitative research proposal.
2. Discuss with your peers why it is important to develop an effective writing style and share your writing with them to obtain their feedback.
3. Think about a research topic that you would like to undertake and draft a plan on how you would structure the dissertation.

Self-check answers

1. A research proposal is a brief and clear summary of your proposed research. It sets out the central issues or questions that you intend to address. This is important to show the current state of knowledge and the significance of your research project.
2. In writing your dissertation you need to start early and create time for writing, find the pattern and place that suits you, create a writing plan with clear milestones, provide a persuasive account of your study to the reader and elicit feedback from your peers and supervisors.
3. An effective writing style has to be clear and simple. Long sentences are not required to convey your point of view. Excess use of jargons would affect the reader's comprehension of the work. The grammar, spelling and tenses should be appropriate. It is also important to ensure that the account provided is free of sexist, racist and discriminatory language.
4. The value of the research process is via its dissemination. A typical dissertation or project report should have an introduction, literature review, methodology, results, discussion, conclusion, references and appendices.
5. Academic references are vital in every research project. It is important that you acknowledge the sources where the information has been derived. It helps to make it clear to your reader how you have used the work of others to shape your study. Failure to reference and cite other people's work may lead to issues of plagiarism.
6. Feedback can come from your peers in the form of a critical friend. The critical friend has to understand your work and be ready to provide constructive feedback about the writing task. Supervisors are another means of obtaining feedback. Your institution would likely have allocated you a dissertation supervisor. The role of your dissertation supervisor is to guide you through the process and also provide feedback on your research. However, it is important that you provide sufficient time for him or her to read your work so that feedback can be obtained on time.

7. The literature review is a valuable chapter in your dissertation. This is where you draw on prior studies that have examined your area of interest. It should have the relevant theoretical foundation that shapes your reasoning. It is expected that your research questions and objectives will be informed by your literature review depending on the nature of your study.

8. This is a snapshot of your dissertation. It provides a summary of the entire dissertation. Every abstract should provide the purpose of the study, its design, methodology and approach, findings, limitation, implications and novelty of the work.

Further reading

Bryman, A. and Bell, E. (2011) *Business Research Methods*. 3rd ed. Oxford, England: Oxford University Press

Harrison, C., Burnard, K. and Paul, S. (2018) Entrepreneurial leadership in a developing economy: a skill-based analysis. *Journal of Small Business and Enterprise Development*, 25(3), 521–48 https://doi.org/10.1108/JSBED-05-2017-0160

Omeihe, K. (2019) *Trust, SME internationalisation and Networks: A study of three main Nigerian cultural blocs*. University of the West of Scotland.

Saunders, M., Lewis, P. and Thornhill, A. (2012) *Research Methods for Business Students*. 6th ed. Edinburgh Gate, Harlow, Essex, England: Pearson Education Limited.

Glossary

Action Research   A research approach involving collaboration between researchers and practitioners to address practical problems.

Anonymity   Protecting participants' identities by not disclosing personal information in research findings.

Archival Research   The examination of historical documents and records for research purposes.

Authenticity   Ensuring that the research findings reflect the genuine perspectives and experiences of the participants.

Bracketing   The process of setting aside preconceived beliefs and biases during data analysis in phenomenological research.

Case Study   A research method that investigates a single individual, group, or phenomenon in depth.

Coding   The process of categorising and organising qualitative data into meaningful themes.

Confidentality   Safeguarding participants' data and ensuring it remains private and secure.

Confirmability   Ensuring that research findings are based on data rather than biased interpretations of the researcher.

Convenience Sampling   A non-probability sampling method where the researcher selects the most accessible participants.

Correlation   A statistical relationship between two or more variables, indicating how they are related.

Credibility   The extent to which the findings accurately represent participants' experiences and the study context.

Critical Incident Technique   A data collection method focusing on significant events that influence outcomes.

Data Analysis   The process of organising, interpreting, and making sense of qualitative data collected during research.

Debriefing   Providing participants with additional information and addressing any concerns after their involvement in the research.

Delphi Method   A structured communication technique used to gather and build consensus among experts.

Dependability   The consistency and stability of qualitative research findings over time and across different researchers.

Diary Methods   Data collection through participants keeping diaries or journals about their experiences.

Dissertation Process   The steps involved in writing and completing a dissertation or research project.

Ethical Approval   The process of obtaining formal clearance from an ethical review board before conducting research involving human participants.

Ethnography   An in-depth study of a culture or social group conducted through participant observation and immersion.

Evaluation of Qualitative Research   Assessing the quality and credibility of qualitative research studies.

Focus Groups   A data collection method involving group discussions to explore specific topics.

Gaining Research Access   The process of obtaining permission and entry into research sites and obtaining cooperation from participants.

Grounded Analysis   An approach to data analysis that allows themes and theories to emerge from the data itself, rather than imposing pre-existing frameworks.

Grounded Theory   An inductive research method aiming to develop theories based on observations and data.

In-depth Interviews   A method of gathering data through open-ended, in-depth conversations with participants.

Index   An alphabetical list of keywords and terms used in the book, providing a reference for locating specific topics.

Informed Consent   Participants' voluntary agreement to participate in a research study after being informed about the study's purpose, procedures, and potential risks.

Informed Consent Form   A document provided to participants explaining the study's purpose, procedures and risks, which they must sign before participation.

Interviews   A method of gathering data through direct questioning and conversation with participants.

Literature Review   A critical examination of existing research and scholarly literature relevant to the research topic.

Mind Mapping   A visual tool for organising ideas and concepts to aid in the research and writing process.

Mixed-Methods Research   An approach that combines both quantitative and qualitative research methods within a single study.

Narrative Analysis   Analysing the structure and content of narratives and storytelling in qualitative data.

Open Coding   The initial stage of coding, where data is broken down and examined for patterns.

Participant Observation   A data collection method where the researcher actively engages and observes participants in their natural settings.

Purposive Sampling   A sampling method where participants are selected intentionally based on specific characteristics.

Qualitative Data   Non-numerical data, such as words, images, or observations, are often analysed thematically.

Qualitative Data Collection   Methods for gathering data in qualitative research, such as observation, interviews and focus groups.

Qualitative Research   Research that focuses on understanding and interpreting phenomena in their natural settings, aiming to gain insights into the meaning and context of human experiences.

Quantitative Data   Numerical data that can be analysed using statistical methods.

References   A list of sources cited in the text, providing the readers with a way to access the original research and literature.

Reflexivity   The researcher's self-awareness and acknowledgement of their biases and influence on the research process.

Reflexive Journal   A researcher's written record of thoughts, feelings and reflections throughout the research process.

Research Approaches   Specific methods and techniques used to collect and analyse data within a chosen research paradigm.

Research Design   The plan or structure of a research study, outlining the methods and procedures to be used.

Research Ethics Committee   A group responsible for reviewing and approving the ethical aspects of research studies involving human participants.

Research Methodology   The systematic approach and techniques used to conduct research and gather data.

Research Paradigms   Fundamental assumptions and beliefs underlying research philosophies.

Research Philosophies   Different theoretical frameworks and perspectives guiding the researcher's approach to data collection and analysis.

Research Population   The entire group of individuals or items that the researcher is interested in studying.

Research Proposal   A written plan outlining the research project's objectives, methodology, and potential outcomes.

Research Triangulation   Combining multiple methods or data sources to corroborate findings and enhance research validity.

Research Validity   The extent to which a study accurately measures what it intends to measure.

Research Validity Threats   Factors that can compromise the validity of a research study, such as bias, confounding variables or low sample size.

Richness   The depth and complexity of data obtained in qualitative research.

Rigour   The degree of accuracy and precision in qualitative research design, data collection, and analysis.

Sampling   The process of selecting a subset of individuals or items from a larger population for research purposes.

Sampling Frame   A list or representation of the research population used for sampling.

Snowball Sampling   A technique where participants refer others who meet the study's criteria to participate.

Structured Observation   An observational method with predetermined criteria for recording behaviours or events.

Surveys   A data collection method using questionnaires to gather information from a large number of participants.

Thematic Analysis   A data analysis strategy that identifies and explores themes and patterns within qualitative data.

Theoretical Sampling   A sampling approach in grounded theory, where data collection is guided by emerging theories.

Transcription   The process of converting recorded interviews or discussions into written text.

Transferability   The extent to which research findings can be applied to other settings or contexts.

Triangulation   The use of multiple data sources or methods to validate and enhance the credibility of research findings.

Trustworthiness   The degree to which qualitative research findings are considered reliable and believable.

Verbatim Transcription   A transcription method where interviews or discussions are transcribed word-for-word, preserving participants' exact language and expressions.

Visual Methods   Using images, photographs, or videos as a means of data collection or analysis.

References

Ågerfalk, P.J. (2014) Insufficient theoretical contribution: a conclusive rationale for rejection? *European Journal of Information Systems*, *23*, 593–599.

Altheide, D.L. and Johnson, J.M. (2013) Reflections on interpretive adequacy in qualitative research. In N.K. Denzin and Y.S. Lincoln (eds), *Collecting and Interpreting Qualitative Materials* (4th edn, pp. 381–411). Thousand Oaks, CA: Sage Publications.

Alvesson, M. and Kärreman, D. (2007) Constructing mystery: Empirical matters in theory development. *The Academy of Management Review*, 32(4), 1265–1281. https://doi.org/10.2307/20159366.

Amoako, I.O. and Lyon, F. (2014) We don't deal with courts: Cooperation and alternative institutions shaping exporting relationships of small and medium sized enterprises in Ghana. *International Small Business Journal*, *32*(2), pp. 117–139.

Anderson, A.R. and Starnawska, M. (2008) Research practices in entrepreneurship: Problems of definition, description and meaning. *The International Journal of Entrepreneurship and Innovation*, *9*, 221–230.

Anderson, C. (2010) Presenting and evaluating qualitative research. *American Journal of Pharmaceutical Education*, 74(8).

Argyris, C., Putnam, R., and McLain Smith, D. (1985) *Action Science, Concepts, methods, and skills for research and intervention*. San Francisco: Jossey-Bass.

Attia, M. and Edge, J. (2017) Be (com) ing a reflexive researcher: a developmental approach to research methodology. *Open Review of Educational Research*, *4*(1), 33–45.

Beckers, R., van der Voordt, T. and Dewulf, G. (2016) Why do they study there? Diary research into students' learning space choices in higher education. *Higher Education Research & Development*, *35*(1), 142–157, https://doi.org/10.1080/07294360.2015.1123230.

Bell, E., Bryman, A., and Harley, B. (2018) *Business Research Methods*. Oxford, England: Oxford University Press.

Bell, E., Bryman, A., and Harley, B. (2019) Business Research Methods (5th edn). – Oxford University Press

Bell, E., Bryman, A. and Harley, B. (2022) *Business research methods* (6th edn). Oxford University Press.

Belmont Report. (1979) *The Belmont Report: Ethical principles and guidelines for the protection of human subjects of research*. Retrieved January 12, 2023, from http://ohsr.od.nih.gov/guidelines/belmont.html

Bengson, J. and Moffett, Marc A. (2011) *Two Conceptions of Mind and Action: Knowledge How and the Philosophical Theory of Intelligence*. In John Bengson and Marc Moffett (eds.), *Knowing How: Essays on Knowledge, Mind, and Action*. Oxford University Press, pp. 3–55.

Bhaskar, R. (1989) *Reclaiming reality: a critical introduction to contemporary philosophy*. New York: Verso.

Bigante, E. (2010) The use of photo-elicitation in field research. *EchoGéo*, *11*, 1–20.

Blumberg, B., Cooper, D.S. and Schindler, P.S. (2011) *Business Research Methods*. (3rd edn). Maidenhead, Berkshire, England: McGraw-Hill Education.

Blumberg, B., Cooper, D.R. and Schindler, P.S. (2014) *Business Research Methods*. (4th edn). McGraw-Hill.

Bochner, A.P. (2000) Criteria against ourselves. *Qualitative inquiry*, *6*(2), 266–72.

Boyatzis, R. (1998). *Transforming qualitative information: Thematic analysis and code development*. Thousand Oaks, CA: Sage.

Brereton, P., Kitchenham, B.A., Budgen, D., Turner, M. and Khalil, M. (2007) Lessons from applying the systematic literature review process within the software engineering domain. *Journal of Systems and Software*, *80*(4), 571–583.

British Psychological Society (2021) *Code of Ethics and Conduct*. Available at: https://cms.bps.org.uk/sites/default/files/2022-06/BPS%20Code%20of%20Ethics%20and%20Conduct.pdf

Bryant, A. and Charmaz, K. (2007) *The SAGE Handbook of Grounded Theory*. Los Angeles: Sage.

Bryman, A. and Bell, E. (2011) *Business Research Methods*. (3rd edn). Oxford: Oxford University Press.

Bryman, A., and Bell, E. (2015) *Business Research Methods*. (4th edn). Oxford: Oxford University Press.

Bryman, A (2016) *Social Research Methods*. (5th edn). London: Oxford University Press

Bunge, M. (1993) *Realism and antirealism in social science. Theory and Decision*, *35*(3), 207–235.

Busenitz, L.W. and Barney, J.B. (1997) Differences between entrepreneurs and managers in large organisations: Biases and heuristics in strategic decision-making. *Journal of Business Venturing*, *12*, 9–30.

Burrell, G. and Morgan, G. (1979) *Sociological Paradigms and organisational analysis*. England: Ashgate.

Burrell, G. and Morgan, G. (2005) *Sociological Paradigms and Organisational Analysis: Elements of the sociology of corporate life*. (5th edn). Farnham, Hants: Ashgate Publishing.

Bush, T. (2002) Authenticity-reliability, validity, and triangulation. In M. Coleman and A. Briggs, (eds), *Research Methods in Educational Leadership and Management*. London: Sage, pp. 59–72.

CABS/BAM/HEA Ethics guide (2015) *Ethics Guide 2015: Advice and Guidance* https://charteredabs.org/wp-content/uploads/2015/06/Ethics-Guide-2015-Advice-and-Guidance.pdf

Carlsen, A. and Mantere, S. (2007). Pragmatism. In S.R. Clegg and J.R. Bailey (eds), *International Encyclopedia of Organization Studies*. Sage publications.

Chell, E. and Pittaway, L (1998) A Study of Entrepreneurship in the Restaurant and Café Industry: Exploratory Work Using the Critical Incident Technique as a Methodology, *International Journal of Hospitality Management*, *17*, pp. 23–32.

Clarke, M. and Chalmers, I. (2018) Reflections on the history of systematic reviews. *BMJ Evidence-Based Medicine*, *23*(4), 121–122.

Clark, C., Harrison, C. and Gibb, S. (2019) Developing a conceptual framework of entrepreneurial leadership: A systematic literature review and thematic analysis. *International Review of Entrepreneurship*, *17*(3), 347–84 https://www.senatehall.com/entrepreneurship?article=639

Coffey, A. (1999) The ethnographic self: Fieldwork and the representation of identity. *The Ethnographic Self*, 1–192.

Creswell, J.W. (2009) *Research Design. Qualitative, Quantitative, and Mixed Methods Approaches*. (3rd edn). London: Sage.

Creswell, J.W. (2014) *Research Design: Qualitative, Quantitative and Mixed Methods Approaches*. (4th edn). Thousand Oaks, CA: Sage.

Crotty, M. (1998) *The Foundations of Social Research: Meaning and Perspective in the Research Process*. London: SAGE Publications.

Cryer, P. (2006) *The Research Student's Guide to Success*. Berkshire, England: McGraw-Hill International.

De la Cuesta Benjumea, C. (2014) Access to information in qualitative research. A matter of care. *Investigacion y educacion en enfermeria*, *32*(3), 480–487.

Delgado, M. (2015) *Urban Youth and Photovoice: Visual Ethnography in Action*. New York: Oxford University Press.

Denyer, D. and Tranfield, D. (2009) Producing a systematic review. In D.A. Buchanan and A. Bryman (eds), *The SAGE Handbook of Organizational Research Methods*. London: Sage, pp. 671–689.

Denzin, N.K. and Lincoln, Y.S. (2003) *The landscape of qualitative research theories and issues*. Thousand Oaks, CA: Sage Publications Ltd.

Denzin, N.K. and Lincoln, Y.S. (2005) Introduction: The Discipline and Practice of Qualitative Research. In N.K. Denzin and Y.S. Lincoln (eds), *The Sage handbook of qualitative research* (pp. 1–32). Thousand Oaks, CA: Sage Publications Ltd.

Easterby-Smith, M., Thorpe, R. and Lowe, A. (2008) *Management Research* (3rd edn). London: Sage.

Easterby-Smith, M., Thorpe, R. and Jackson, P.R. (2015) *Management and Business Research* (5th edn). London: SAGE.

Easterby-Smith, M., Jaspersen, l.J., Thorpe R., Valizade, D. (2021) *Management and business research*. Sage, Cambridge.

Eden, C. and Huxham, C. (1996) Action Research for Management Research. *British Journal of Management*, 7: 75–86

Eriksson, P. and Kovalainen, A. (2011) *Qualitative Methods in Business Research*. London: Sage.

Fink, A. (2010) *Conducting Research Literature Reviews* (3rd edn). Los Angeles, CA: Sage.

Flanagan, J.C. (1954) The critical incident technique. *Psychological Bulletin*. *51*(4), pp. 327–358.

Flick, U. (2011) *An Introduction to Qualitative Research* (4th edn). London: Sage.

Flick, U. (2011). *Introducing Research Methodology: A Beginner's Guide to Doing a Research Project*. Los Angeles: Sage.

Flick, U. (2020). *Introducing Research Methodology: Thinking Your Way through Your Research Project.* 3rd edn. London: Sage.

Fossey, E., Harvey, C., McDermott, F. and Davidson, L. (2002) Understanding and evaluating qualitative research. *Australian and New Zealand Journal of Psychiatry, 36,* 717–732.

Galloway, L. and Kelly, S.W. (2009) Identifying entrepreneurial potential? An investigation of the identifiers and features of entrepreneurship. *International Review of Entrepreneurship, 7*(4), 1–24.

Gill, J. and Johnson, P. (1997) *Research Methods for Managers.* London: Paul Chapman Publishing Ltd.

Glaw, X., Inder, K., Kable, A. and Hazelton, M. (2017) Visual methodologies in qualitative research: Autophotography and photo elicitation applied to mental health research. *International Journal of Qualitative Methods, 16*(1).

Gray, D.E. (2009) *Doing Research in the Real World.* London: Sage.

Gray, D.H. (2020) *Doing Research in the Real World.* London: SAGE Publications.

Godfrey Smith, P. (2015) *Pragmatism: Philosophical Aspects.* In International Encyclopedia of the Social and Behavioral Sciences, edited by J. Wright, 2nd edition (2015), Vol 18. Oxford: Elsevier. pp. 803–807.

Guba, E.G. and Lincoln, Y.S, (1994) *Paradigmatic controversies, contradictions, and emerging confluences.* In: Denzin Lincoln (eds.) Handbook of Qualitative Research. New York: SAGE Publications. pp. 106.

Guest, G., Bunce, A. and Johnson, L. (2006) How many interviews are enough? An experiment with data saturation and variability. *Field Methods, 18*(1), pp. 59–82.

Guetzkow, J., Lamont, M. and Mallard, G. (2004) What is originality in the humanities and the social sciences? *American Sociological Review, 69*(2), 190–212.

Harrison, A. (2002) *Case Study Research.* In D. Partington, (ed.), *Essentisl Skills for Management Research.* London: Sage, pp. 158–180.

Harrison, C. (2018) *Leadership Theory and Research: A Critical Approach to New and Existing Paradigms,* Switzerland: Palgrave MacMillan. http://www.palgrave.com/gb/book/9783319686714#

Harrison, C., Burnard, K. and Paul, S. (2018) Entrepreneurial leadership in a developing economy: a skill-based analysis. *Journal of Small Business and Enterprise Development, 25*(3), 521–48 https://doi.org/10.1108/JSBED-05-2017-0160

Harrison, C., Paul, S. and Burnard, K. (2016) Entrepreneurial leadership: a systematic literature review. *International Review of Entrepreneurship, 14*(2), 235–264 https://www.senatehall.com/entrepreneurship?article=544

Hart, C. (2009) *Doing a Literature Review* (8th edn). London: Sage.

Heron, J. and Reason, P. (1997) A Participatory Inquiry Paradigm. Qualitative Inquiry, 3, 274–294.

Horsburgh, D. (2003) Evaluation of qualitative research. *Journal of Clinical Nursing, 12,* 307–312.

Hyde, K.F. (2000) Recognising deductive processes in qualitative research. *Qualitative Market Research: An International Journal, 3*(2), pp. 82–90.

James, W. (2000) *Pragmatism and Other Writings*, ed. Giles B. Gunn. New York: Penguin Books.

Johnstone, B.A. (2007) Ethnographic methods in entrepreneurship research, in H. Neergaard, and J.P. Ulhoi (eds), *Handbook of Qualitative Research Methods in Entrepreneurship*. Cheltenham: Edward Elgar Publishing Limited, pp. 97–121.

Ketokivi, M., and Mantere, S. (2010) Two strategies for inductive reasoning in organizational research. *The Academy of Management Review, 35*(2), pp. 315–333. JSTOR, http://www.jstor.org/stable/25682414. Accessed 16 Jan. 2024

King, N. and Horrocks, C. (2012) *Interviews in Qualitative Research*. London: Sage.

Krefting, L. (1991) Rigor in qualitative research: The assessment of trustworthiness. *The American Journal of Occupational Therapy, 45*, 214–222.

Kvale, S. (1996) *Interviews: An Introduction to Qualitative Research Interviewing*. London: Sage Publications.

Lewis, J., Ritchie, J., Ormston, R. and Morrell, G. (2003) Generalising from qualitative research. *Qualitative Research Practice: A guide for social science students and researchers, 2*, 347–362.

Lincoln, Y.S. and Guba, E. (1985) *Naturalistic Enquiry*. Beverly Hills, CA: Sage.

Lincoln, Y.S. (1995) Emerging criteria for quality in qualitative and interpretive research. *Qualitative Inquiry 1,* 275–289.

Lincoln, Y.S. and Guba, E.G. (2000) *Paradigmatic controversies, contradictions, and emerging confluences*. In N.K. Denzin and Y.S. Lincoln, *The Handbook of Qualitative Research* (2nd edn). Thousand Oaks, CA: Sage Publications, pp. 1065–1122

Lind, J. (1753) *A Treatise of the Scurvy in Three Parts*. Kincaid.

Mandal, P.C. (2018) Qualitative research: Criteria of evaluation. *Qualitative Research, 3*(2), 1–6.

Mantere, S. and Ketokivi, M. (2013) Reasoning in organization science. *The Academy of Management Review, 38*(1), 70–89. Http://www.jstor.org/stable/23416303

Massiah, P., Harrison, C., Odibo, E., McTavish, A. and Jones, M. (2017) Delphi methodology: from nuclear science to humanitarian disaster management. *British Academy of Management (BAM)*, Annual Conference, Warwick.

Marsh, David and Stoker, Gerry (eds) (2002) *Theories and methods in political science* (2nd edn). Basingstoke: Palgrave Macmillan.

McKenzie, B. (2007) Techniques for collecting verbal histories. In H. Neergaard and J.P. Ulhoi, (eds), *Handbook of Qualitative Research Methods in Entrepreneurship*. Cheltenham: Edward Elgar Publishing Limited, pp. 308–530.

Merriam, S.B. (1995) What can you tell from an N of 1? Issues of validity and reliability in qualitative research. *PAACE Journal of lifelong learning, 4*, 51–60.

Meyer, S.B. and Lunnay, B. (2013) The Application of Abductive and Retroductive Inference for the Design and Analysis of Theory-Driven Sociological Research. *Sociological Research Online, 18*(1), 86–96.

Miles, M.B. and Huberman, A.M. (1994) *Qualitative Data Analysis* (2nd edn). Thousand Oaks, CA: Sage.

Mintzberg, H. (1973) *The Nature of Managerial Work*. New York: Harper & Row

Mitchell, M.L and Jolley, J.M (2020) *Research design explained*. Wandsworth: Wadsworth Publishing Co.

Morse, J.M. (1999) Qualitative methods: The state of the art. *Qualitative Health Research, 9*(3), 393–406.

Myers, M.D. (2020) *Qualitative Research in Business and Management.* Thousand Oaks, CA: Sage Publications Limited.

Nasa, P., Jain, R. and Juneja, D. (2021) Delphi methodology in healthcare research: how to decide its appropriateness. *World Journal of Methodology, 11*(4), 116.

Omeihe, K. (2019) *Trust, SME internationalisation and Networks A study of three main Nigerian cultural blocs.* University of the West of Scotland. Available at: https://ethos.bl.uk/OrderDetails.do?uin=uk.bl.ethos.787868

Omeihe, K. (2020) The need for interview participant justification: reportability in qualitative research. In *BAM ISBE Virtual Doctoral Day,* British Academy of Management.

Omeihe, K.O. (2023) An overview of trust, institutions and African entrepreneurial networks. In *Trust and Market Institutions in Africa: Exploring the Role of Trust-Building in African Entrepreneurship* (1st edn, Vol. 1). (The Palgrave Studies of Entrepreneurship in Africa). Basingstoke: Palgrave Macmillan.

Omeihe, I., Harrison, C. and Omeihe, K. (2021) Authentic leadership: a systematic literature review. In *British Academy of Management 2021 Conference Proceedings* (pp. 1–29). British Academy of Management.

Omeihe, I., Harrison, C., Simba, A. and Omeihe, K.O. (2020) The role of the entrepreneurial leader: a study of Nigerian SMEs. *International Journal of Entrepreneurship and Small Business, 49*(2):187–215

Omeihe, K.O. (2023) *Trust and Market Institutions in Africa: Exploring the Role of Trust-Building in African Entrepreneurship.* (Palgrave Studies of Entrepreneurship in Africa). Cham, Switzerland: Palgrave Macmillan. Available at: https://link.springer.com/book/9783031062155.

Pansiri, J. (2005) Pragmatism: A methodological approach to researching strategic alliances in tourism, Tourism and Hospitality Planning & Development, 2:3, 191–206, https://doi.org/10.1080/14790530500399333

Petticrew, M. and Roberts, H. (2008) *Systematic Reviews in the Social Sciences: A Practical Guide.* Oxford: Blackwell.

Phillips, E.M. and Pugh, D.S. (1994) *How to Get a PhD.* (2nd edn). Buckingham: Open University Press.

Popay, J., Rogers, A. and Williams, G. (1998) Rationale and standards for the systematic review of qualitative literature in health services research. *Qualitative Health Research, 8*(3), 341–351.

Radcliffe, L.S. (2013) Qualitative diaries: Uncovering the complexities of work-life decision-making. *Qualitative Research in Organizations and Management: An International Journal, 8*(2), 163–180.

Reichertz, J. (2007) *Abduction: The logic of Discovery of Grounded Theory.* In A. Bryant and K. Charmaz (eds), *Handbook for Grounded Theory.* Los Angeles: Sage, pp. 214–222.

Rescher, N. (2003). *Epistemology: An Introduction to the Theory of Knowledge.* State University of New York Press

Resnick, D.B. (2015) *What is Ethics in Research and Why is it Important?* National Institutes of Health. Available at: https://www.niehs.nih.gov/research/resources/bioethics/whatis

Riese, J. (2019) What is 'access' in the context of qualitative research? *Qualitative Research*, *19*(6), 669–84.

Robson, C. (2002) *Real World Research*. (2nd edn). Oxford: Blackwell.

Roulston, K. (2010) Considering quality in qualitative interviewing. *Qualitative Research*, *10*(2), 199–228.

Salmons, J. (2022). *Doing qualitative research online*. SAGE Publications Ltd. Available at: https://doi.org/10.4135/9781473921955

Saunders, M., Lewis, P. and Thornhill, A. (2012) *Research Methods for Business Students*. (6th edn). Edinburgh Gate, Harlow, Essex, England: Pearson Education Limited.

Saunders, M., Lewis, P. and Thornhill, A. (2016) *Research Methods for Business Students*. Edinburgh Gate, Harlow, Essex, England: Pearson Education Limited.

Saunders, M., Lewis, P. and Thornhill, A. (2023) *Research Methods for Business Students* (9th edn). Edinburgh gate, Essex, England: Pearson Education Limited.

Sawyerr, E. and Harrison, C. (2019) Developing resilient supply chains: lessons from high-reliability organisations. *Supply Chain Management: An International Journal*, *25*(1), 77–100 https://doi.org/10.1108/SCM-09-2018-0329

Schofield, J.W. (2002) Increasing the generalisability of qualitative research. In A.M. Huberman and M.B. Miles (eds), *The Qualitative Researcher's Companion* (pp. 171–203). Thousand Oaks, CA and London: Sage Publications.

Schramm, W. (1971) *The Nature of Communication between Humans*. In W. Schramm and R.F. Roberts (eds), *The Process and Effects of Mass Communication* (pp. 3–516). Urbana, IL: University of Illinois Press.

Schwandt, T.A. (1999) On Understanding Understanding. *Qualitative Inquiry*, *5*(4), 451–464.

Seale, C. (1999) Quality in qualitative research. *Qualitative Inquiry*, *5*, 465–78.

Shane, S. and Venkataraman, S. (2000) The promise of entrepreneurship as a field of Research. *The Academy of Management Review*, *25*(1), pp. 217–226.

Shenton, A.K. (2004) Strategies for ensuring trustworthiness in qualitative research projects. *Education for Information*, *22*, 63–75.

Schensul, S.L., Schensul, J.J. and LeCompte, M.D. (1999) *Essential ethnographic methods: observations interviews and questionnaires*. Tucson: AltaMira Press.

Social Research Association. SRA (2021) *Research Ethical Guidelines*. Available at: https://the-sra.org.uk/common/Uploaded%20files/Resources/SRA%20Research%20Ethics%20guidance%202021.pdf

Somekh, B. and Lewin, C. (2005) *Research methods in the social sciences*. London: Sage.

Stake, R.E. (1994) *Case studies*. In N.K. Denzin and Y.S. Lincoln (eds), *Handbook of Qualitative Research* (pp. 236–247). Sage Publications, Inc.

Stenfors, T., Kajamaa, A. and Bennett, D. (2020) How to… assess the quality of qualitative research. *The Clinical Teacher*, *17*(6), 596–599.

Tracy, S.J. (2010) Qualitative quality: Eight 'big-tent' criteria for excellent qualitative research. *Qualitative Inquiry*, *16*(10), 837–851.

Tranfield, D., Denyer, D. and Smart, P. (2003) Towards a methodology for developing evidence–informed management knowledge by means of systematic review. *British Journal of Management*, *14*(3), 207–22.

Unterhitzenberger, C. and Lawrence, K. (2022) Diary method in project studies. *Project Leadership and Society*, *3*(5). Available at: https://www.google.com/url?sa=t&rct=j&q=&esrc=s&source=web&cd=&cad=rja&uact=8&ved=2ahUKEwiIwZ_3n5SEAxVKVkEAHRaNAm8QFnoECA4QAQ&url=https%3A%2F%2Fprints.whiterose.ac.uk%2F188582%2F&usg=AOvVaw3leMYeLno7jxRs9dejcSYu&opi=89978449

UWS, University Ethics Committee (2021) *Guidelines for Ethical Research*. Scotland: University of the West of Scotland Publications.

WHO (2020) *Shortage of Personal Protective Equipment Endangering Health Workers Worldwide*, Geneva, Switzerland, available at: https://www.who.int/news/item/03-03-2020-shortage-of-personal-protective-equipment-endangering-health-workers-worldwide.

Wigren, C. (2007) Assessing the quality of qualitative research in entrepreneurship. In H. Neergaard, and J.P. Ulhoi (eds), *Handbook of Qualitative Research Methods in Entrepreneurship*. Cheltenham: Edward Elgar Publishing Limited, pp. 383–405.

Woleński, J. (2004). *The History of Epistemology*. In M. Sintonen, J. Woleński and I. Niiniluoto (eds), *Handbook of Epistemology*. Kluwer Academic Publishers. pp. 3–54.

Wright, R.W., Brand, R.A., Dunn, W. and Spindler, K.P. (2007) How to write a systematic review. *Clinical Orthopaedics and Related Research (1976–2007)*, *455*, 23–29.

Xiao, Y. and Watson, M. (2019) Guidance on conducting a systematic literature review. *Journal of Planning Education and Research*, *39*(1), 93–112.

Yardley, L. (2000) Dilemmas in qualitative health research. *Psychology and Health*, *15*(2), 215–228.

Yin, R.K. (1994) *Case Study Research Design and Methods*. Thousand Oaks, CA: Sage Publications.

Yin, R.K. (2011) *Qualitative Research from Start to Finish*. London: Guilford Press.

Yin, R.K. (2014) *Case Study Research Design and Methods* (5th edn). Thousand Oaks, CA: Sage Publications.

Yin, R.K. (2018) *Case Study Research and Applications: Design and Methods* (6th edn). Thousand Oaks, CA: Sage.

Zagzebski, L. (2017) What is knowledge? *The Blackwell Guide to Epistemology*, 92–116.

Zikmund, W.G., Babin, B.J., Carr, J.C. and Griffin, M. (2013) *Business Research Methods*. Cengage learning.

Index

Page numbers in *italics* refer to figures; page numbers in **bold** refer to tables.